THE KING'S *Beast*

3

STORY & ART BY

Rei Toma

THE KING'S *Beast*
Characters and Story Thus Far

A female Ajin dressed like a man

Rangetsu
To avenge her younger brother Sogetsu's death, she hides her true identity as a woman and, by virtue of her military achievements, becomes Prince Tenyou's beast-servant.

Taihaku
Prince Tenyou's attendant.

A gentle prince

Fourth Prince Tenyou
He mourns the loss of Sogetsu and, along with Rangetsu, tries to clean up the intrigues in the imperial palace.

Beast-Servants
Ajin who serve the male members of the imperial family. It's said that the stronger the beast-servant, the more powerful the master. Many beast-servants possess superhuman abilities.

Prince Tenyou's Brothers and Their Beast-Servants

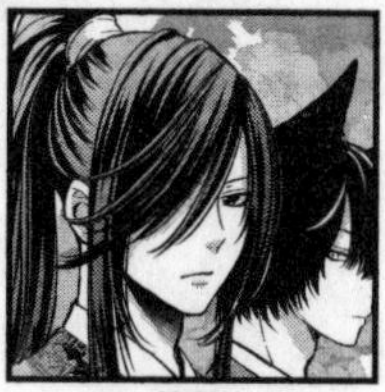

(??)
The third prince. Still shrouded in mystery.

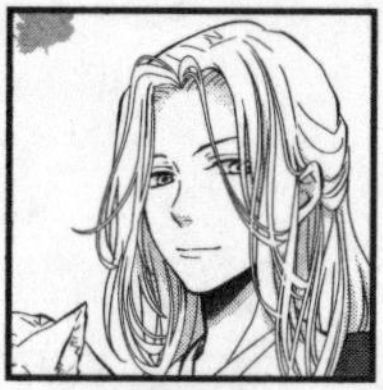

Reiun
The second prince. Intelligent and bored by his own idleness.

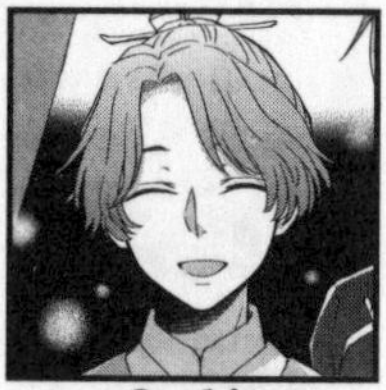

Oushin
The first prince. He is sickly and passive.

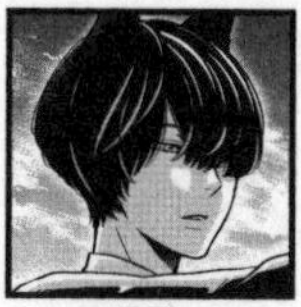

(??)
The third prince's beast-servant.

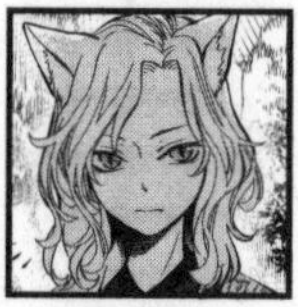

Youbi
Prince Reiun's beast-servant.

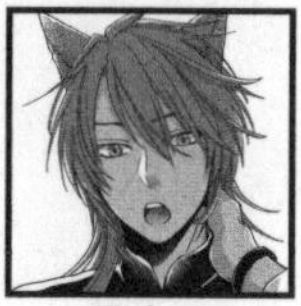

Teiga
Prince Oushin's beast-servant.

The Assassination of Sogetsu

Sogetsu, Rangetsu's twin, was brought to the imperial palace to serve Prince Tenyou as his beast-servant after it was discovered that he had special abilities. He was brutally killed soon after.

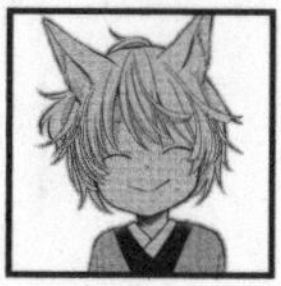

Sogetsu

Summary

In a world where humans rule the half-beast Ajin, Rangetsu disguises herself as a man and proves herself in battle to enter the imperial palace and become Fourth Prince Tenyou's beast-servant. She seeks revenge for the death of her brother Sogetsu.

Rangetsu feels hopeless when she discovers that her prime suspect, Prince Tenyou, is not the mastermind behind her brother's murder. But at the same time, she realizes that the prince is the only person who has mourned Sogetsu's death. He asks Rangetsu to value her own life, but Rangetsu tells Tenyou that she is willing to sacrifice it to avenge her brother's murder. Upon seeing Rangetsu's determination, Prince Tenyou earnestly vows to make the killer pay for the crime, and his sincerity is a beacon of hope for Rangetsu.

Meanwhile, Taihaku discovers that Rangetsu is really a woman. Although he is cautious about having a female Ajin in the palace, he recognizes her determination and accepts her as Prince Tenyou's beast-servant.

In the search for Sogetsu's killer, Rangetsu meets First Prince Oushin and his beast-servant Teiga. When Prince Oushin apathetically ignores false charges lodged against an Ajin, Rangetsu takes it upon herself to prove the Ajin's innocence. Could seeing the bond between a reckless Ajin beast-servant and the prince who supports him be enough to cause Prince Oushin to have a change of heart?!

THE
KING'S
Beast

3

CONTENTS

Chapter 8

005

Chapter 9

045

Chapter 10

087

Chapter 11

127

◆◆◆

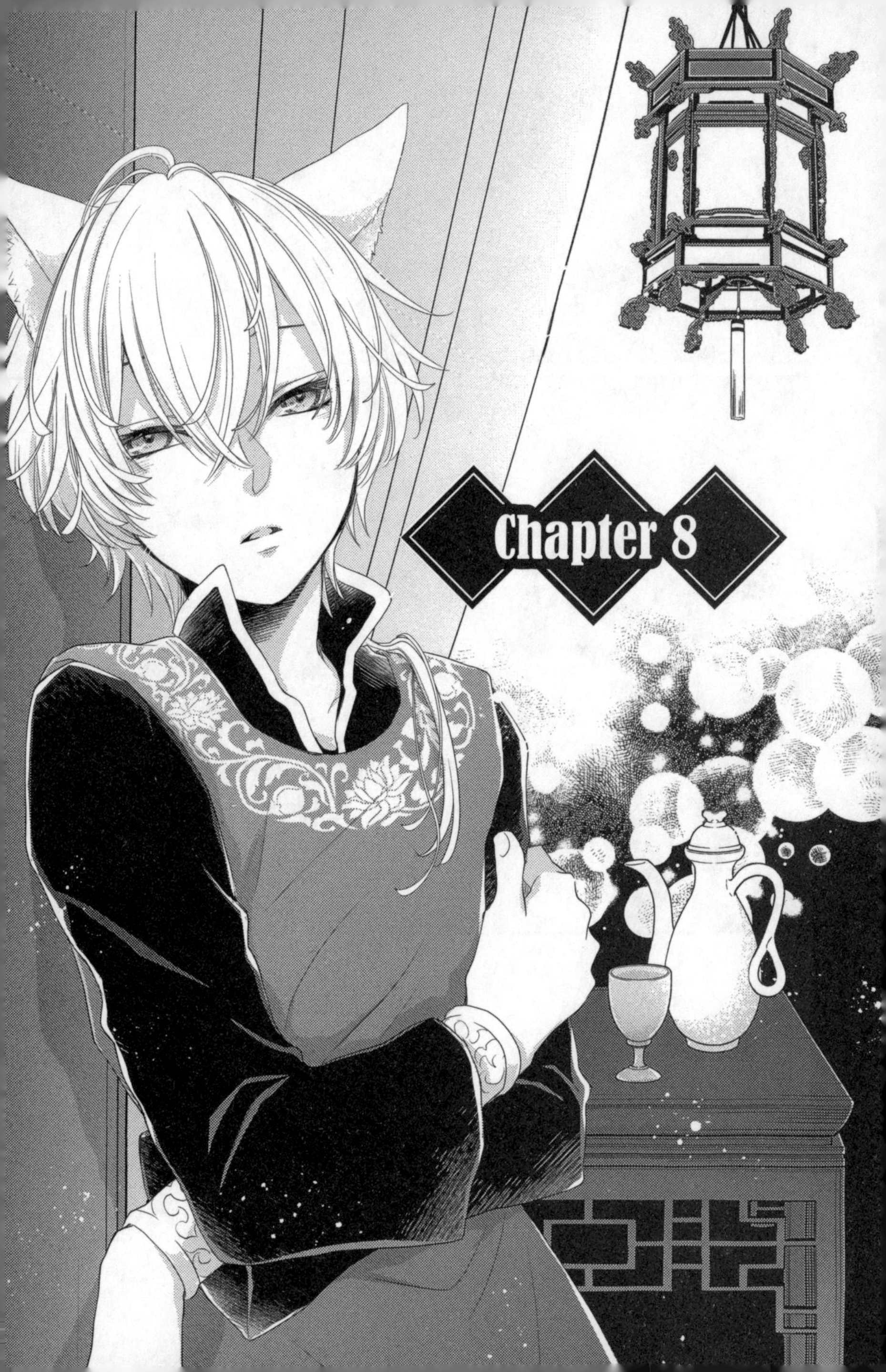
Chapter 8

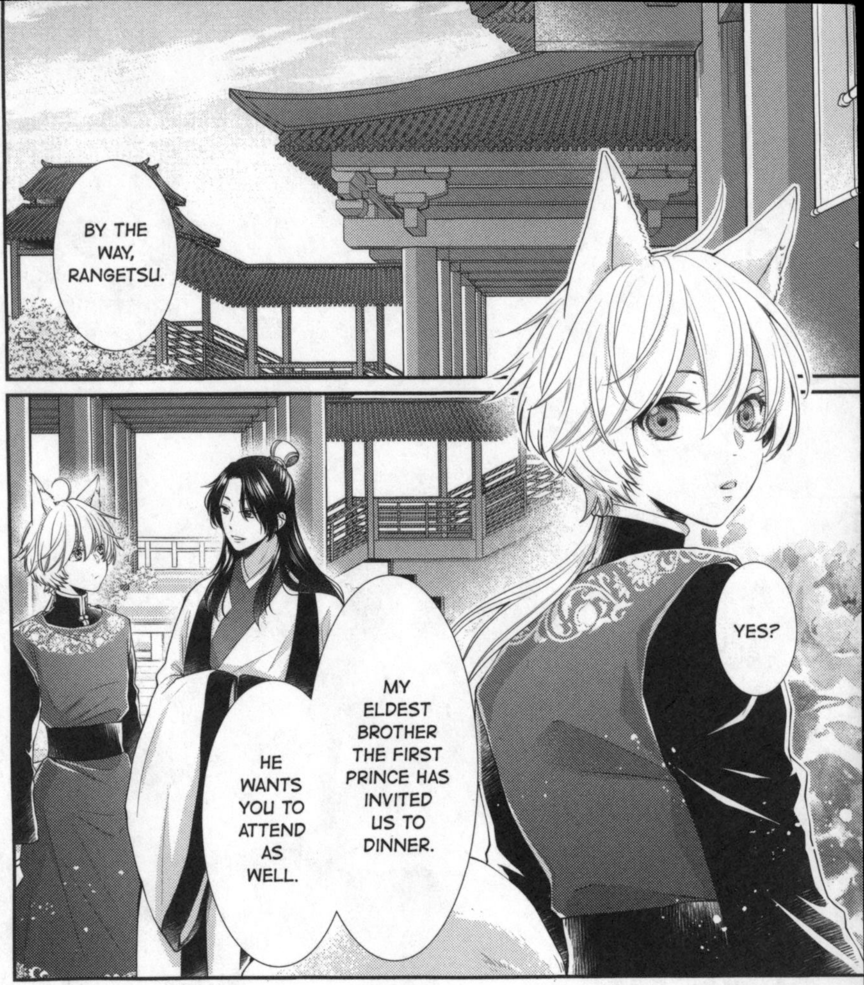
BY THE WAY, RANGETSU.
YES?
MY ELDEST BROTHER THE FIRST PRINCE HAS INVITED US TO DINNER.
HE WANTS YOU TO ATTEND AS WELL.

THE KING'S Beast

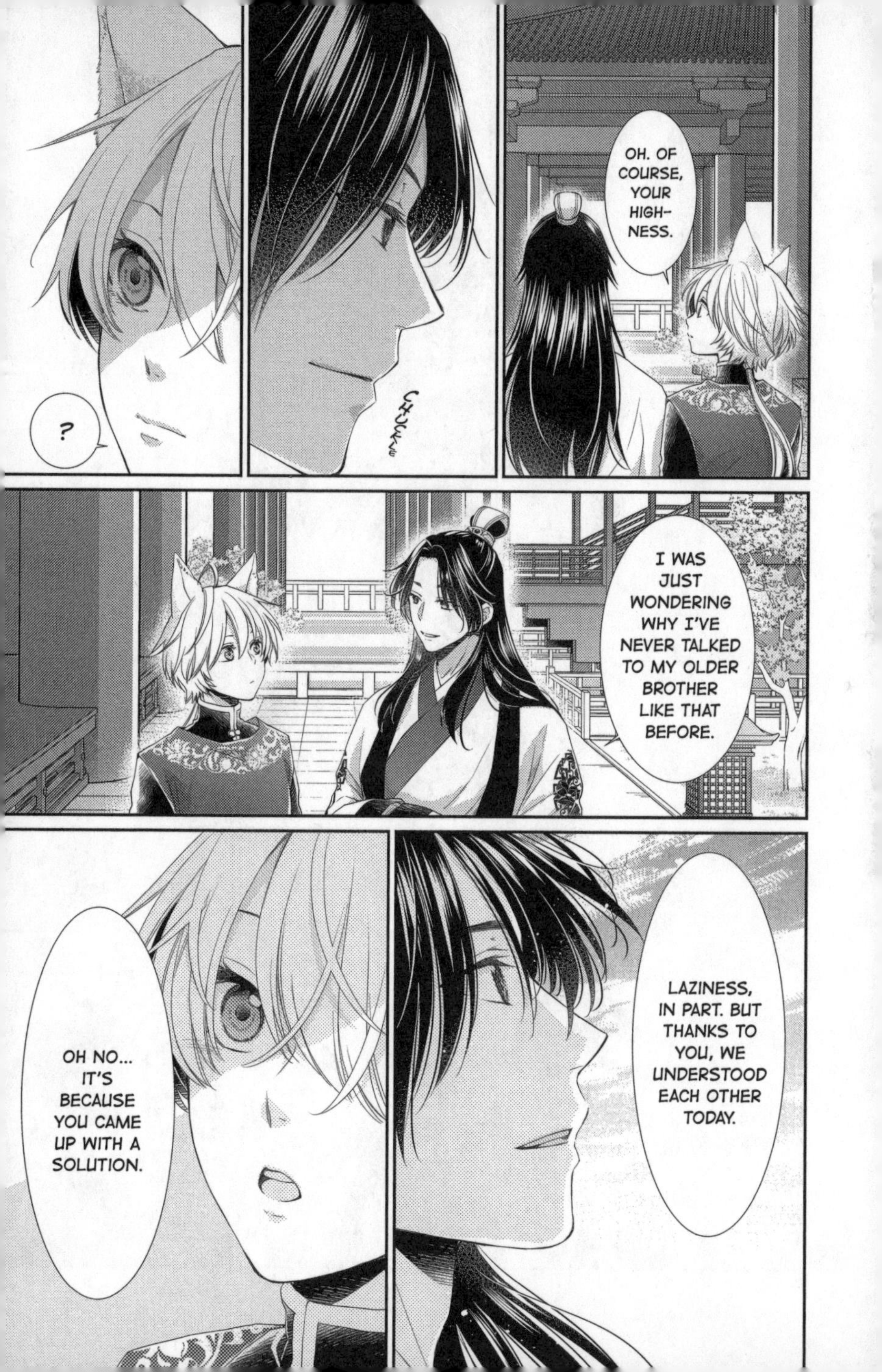
OH. OF COURSE, YOUR HIGH-NESS.
CHUCKLE
?
I WAS JUST WONDERING WHY I'VE NEVER TALKED TO MY OLDER BROTHER LIKE THAT BEFORE.
LAZINESS, IN PART. BUT THANKS TO YOU, WE UNDERSTOOD EACH OTHER TODAY.
OH NO... IT'S BECAUSE YOU CAME UP WITH A SOLUTION.

I SHOULD HAVE BEEN MORE SUPPORTIVE OF HIM IN THE PAST.

YOU'RE RIGHT. HIS CHARACTER IS QUITE TRANSPARENT.

HIS BEAST-SERVANT TEIGA'S AN IDIOT.

PRINCE OUSHIN DOESN'T SEEM LIKE THE SORT TO TAKE AIM AT YOU.

CUR

IRRESOLUTE

HA HA HA

Heh

8

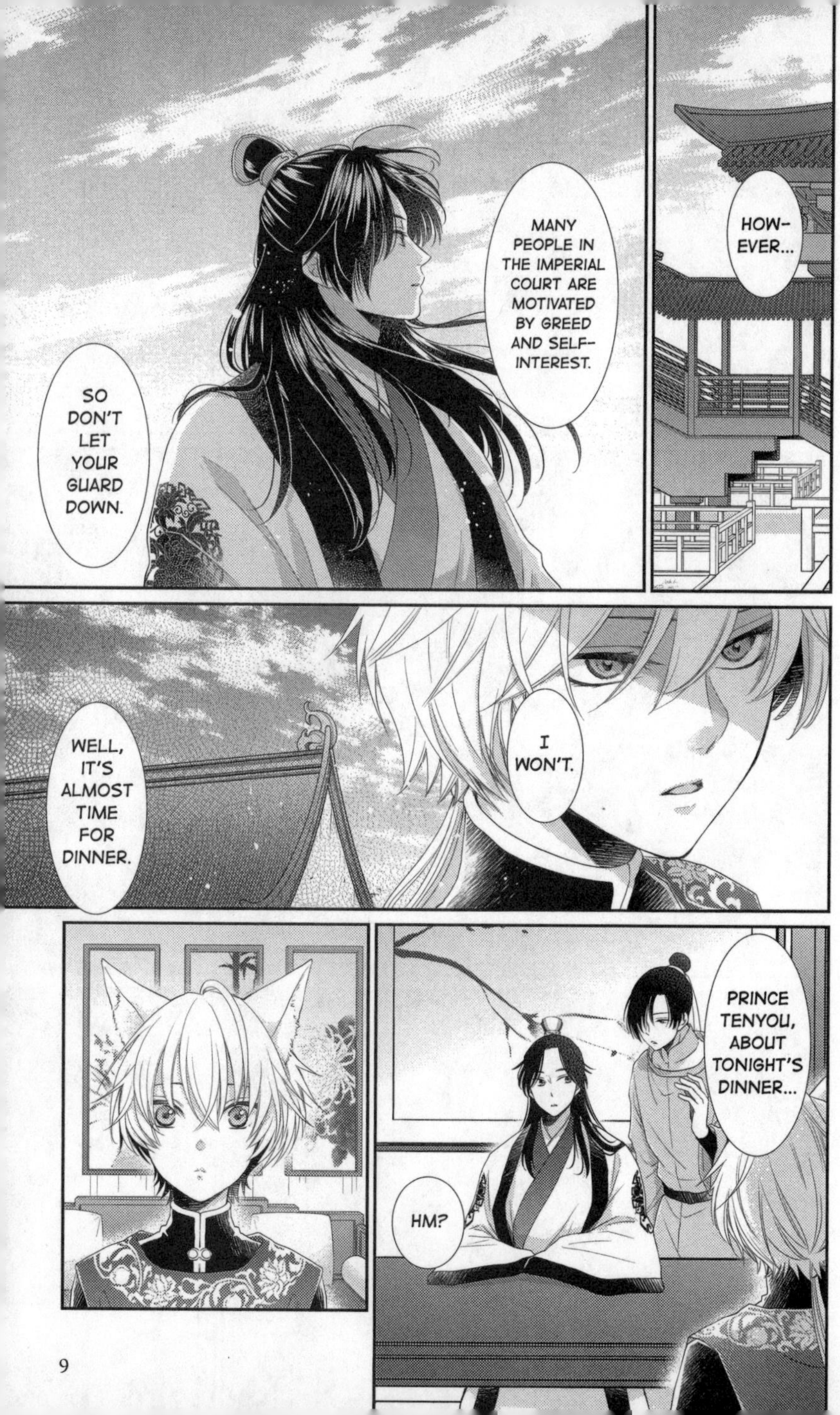
HOW-EVER...
MANY PEOPLE IN THE IMPERIAL COURT ARE MOTIVATED BY GREED AND SELF-INTEREST.
SO DON'T LET YOUR GUARD DOWN.
I WON'T.
WELL, IT'S ALMOST TIME FOR DINNER.
PRINCE TENYOU, ABOUT TONIGHT'S DINNER...
HM?

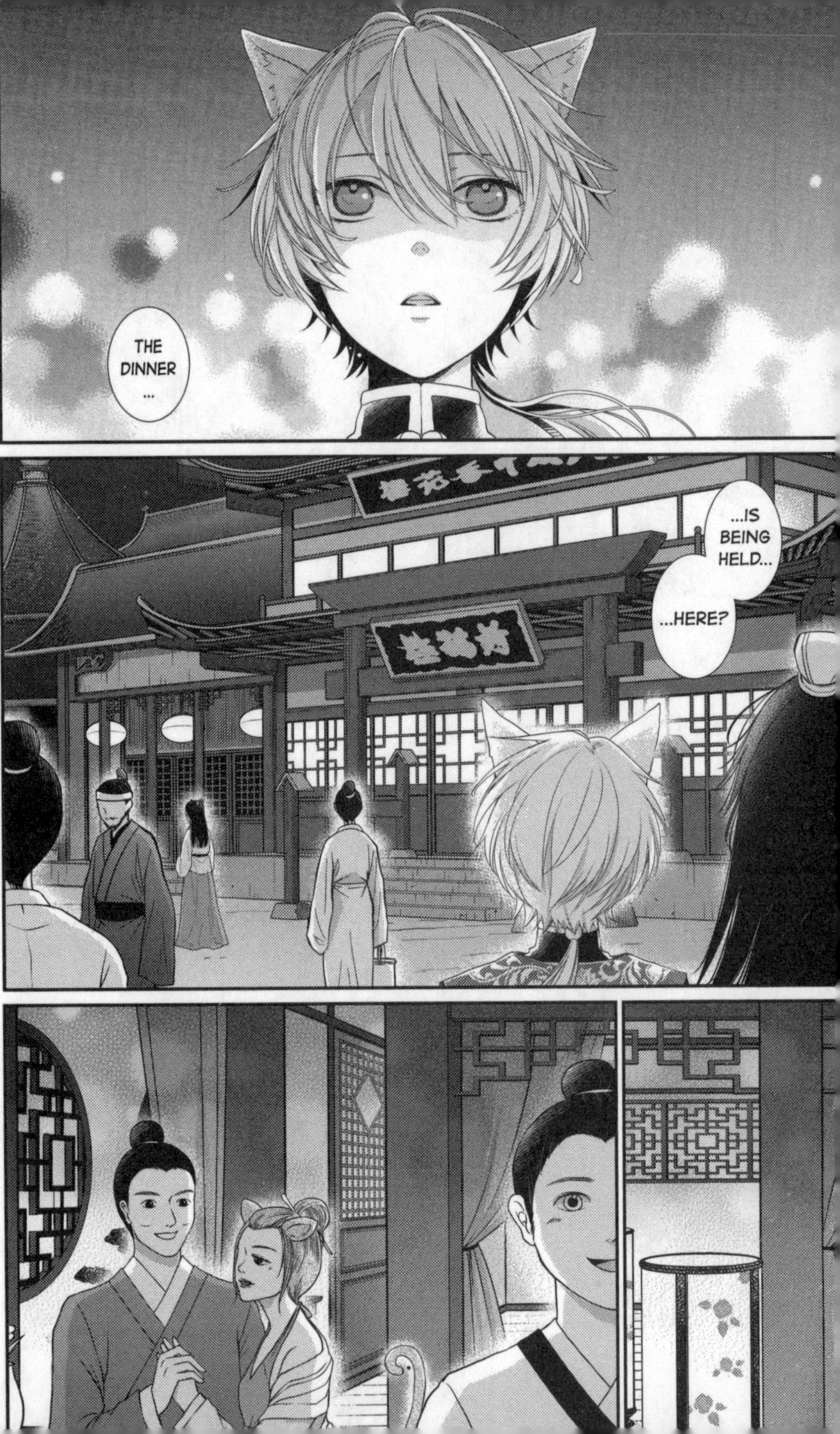
THE DINNER ...
...IS BEING HELD...
...HERE?

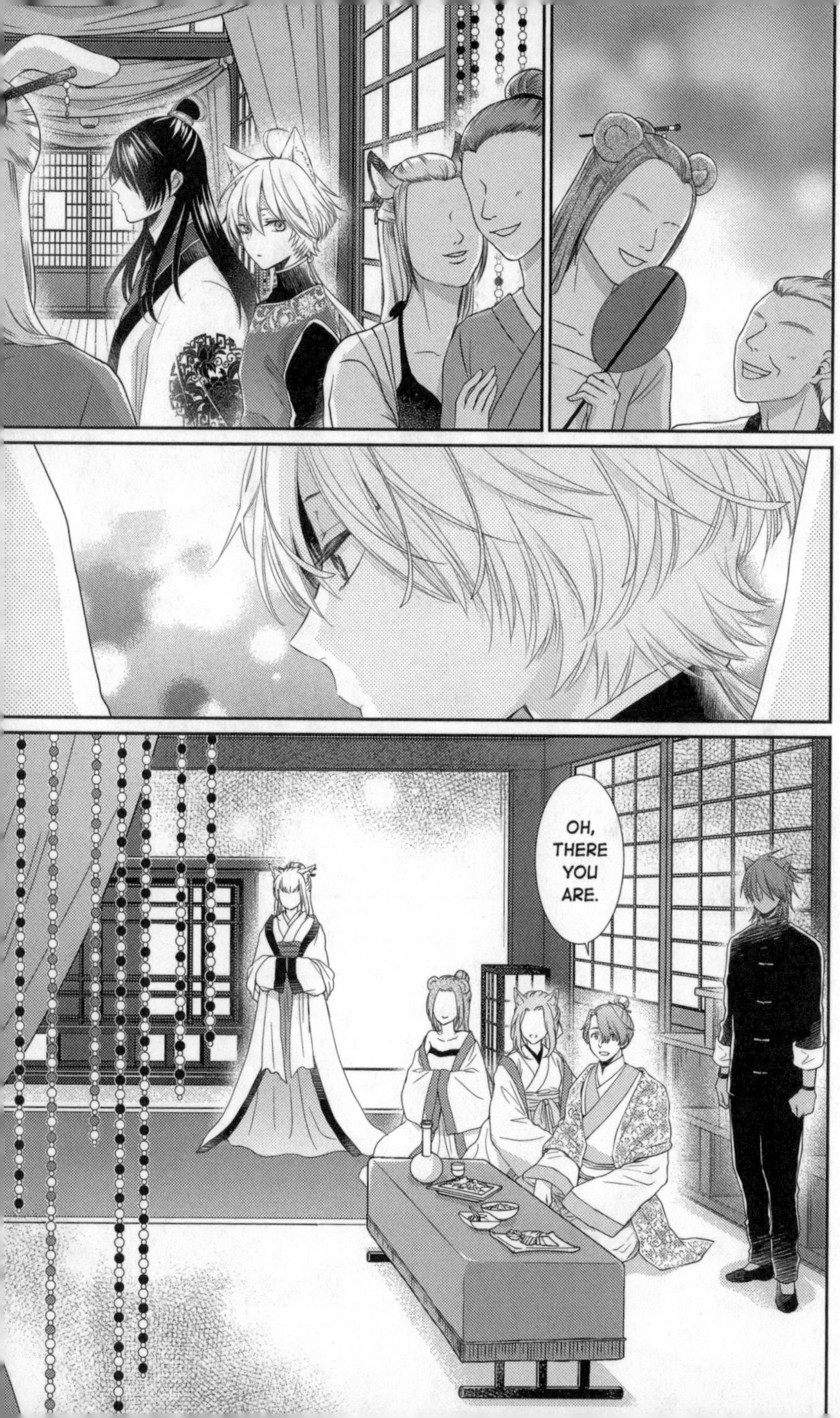
OH, THERE YOU ARE.

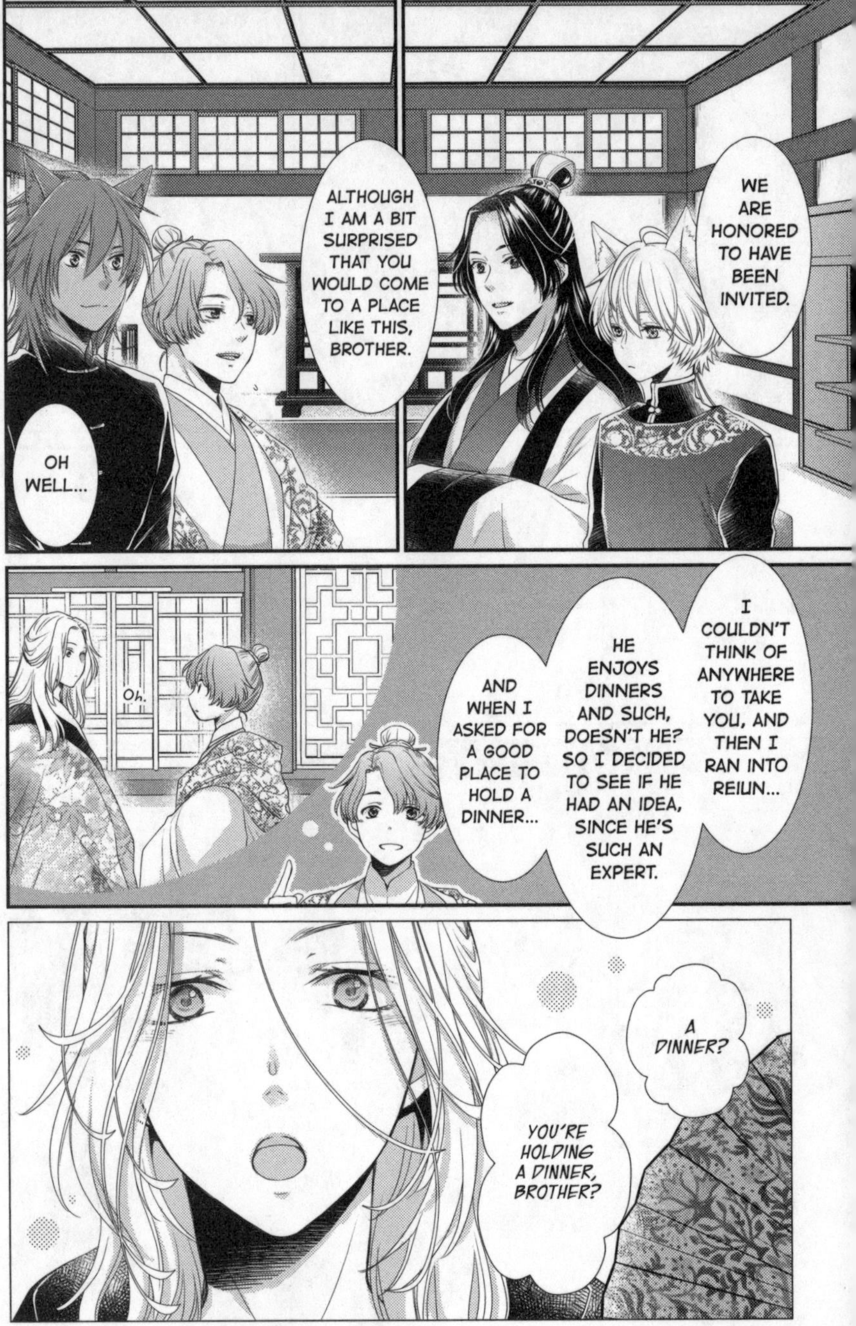
WE ARE HONORED TO HAVE BEEN INVITED.
ALTHOUGH I AM A BIT SURPRISED THAT YOU WOULD COME TO A PLACE LIKE THIS, BROTHER.
OH WELL...
I COULDN'T THINK OF ANYWHERE TO TAKE YOU, AND THEN I RAN INTO REIUN...
HE ENJOYS DINNERS AND SUCH, DOESN'T HE? SO I DECIDED TO SEE IF HE HAD AN IDEA, SINCE HE'S SUCH AN EXPERT.
AND WHEN I ASKED FOR A GOOD PLACE TO HOLD A DINNER...
Oh.
A DINNER?
YOU'RE HOLDING A DINNER, BROTHER?

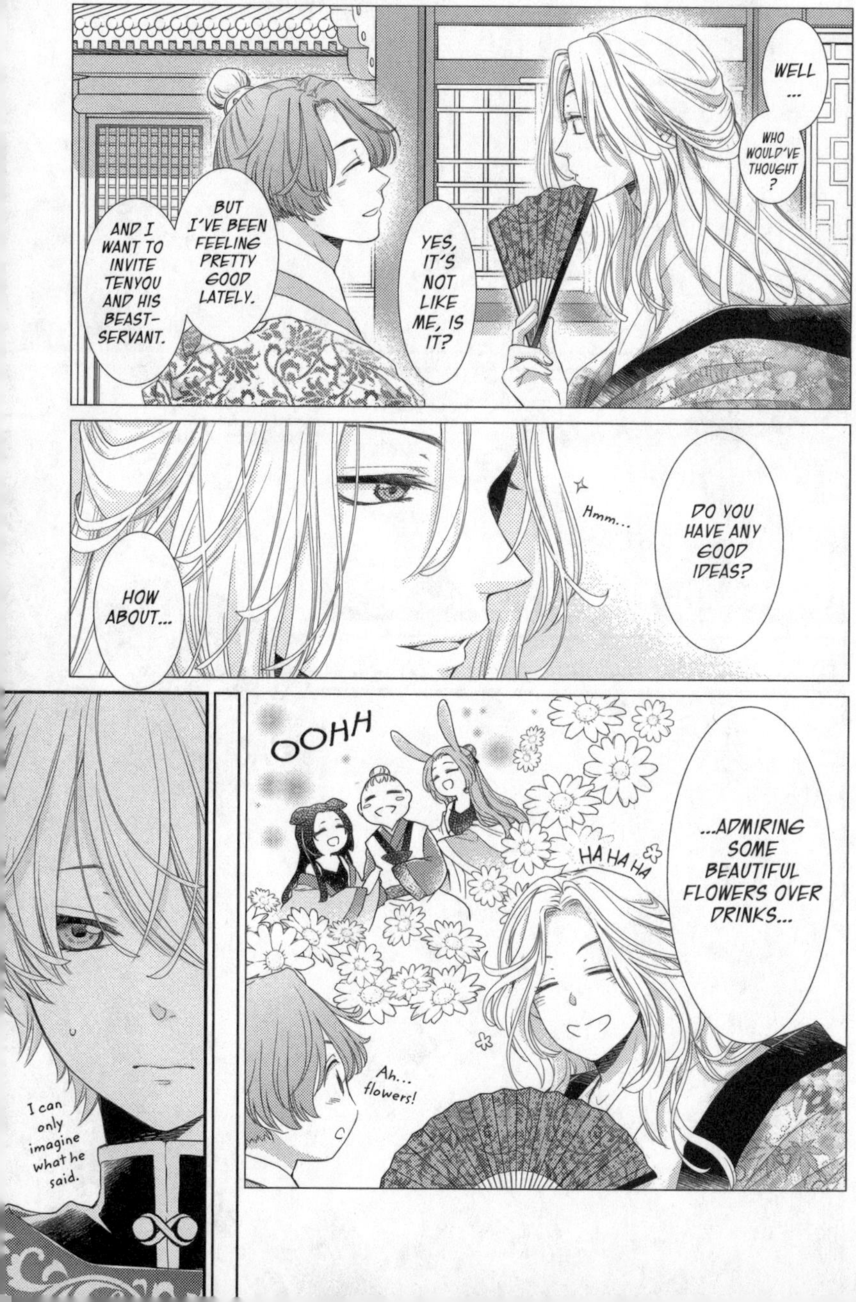
WELL ...
WHO WOULD'VE THOUGHT?
YES, IT'S NOT LIKE ME, IS IT?
BUT I'VE BEEN FEELING PRETTY GOOD LATELY.
AND I WANT TO INVITE TENYOU AND HIS BEAST-SERVANT.
DO YOU HAVE ANY GOOD IDEAS?
Hmm...
HOW ABOUT...
...ADMIRING SOME BEAUTIFUL FLOWERS OVER DRINKS...
HA HA HA
OOHH
Ah... flowers!
I can only imagine what he said.

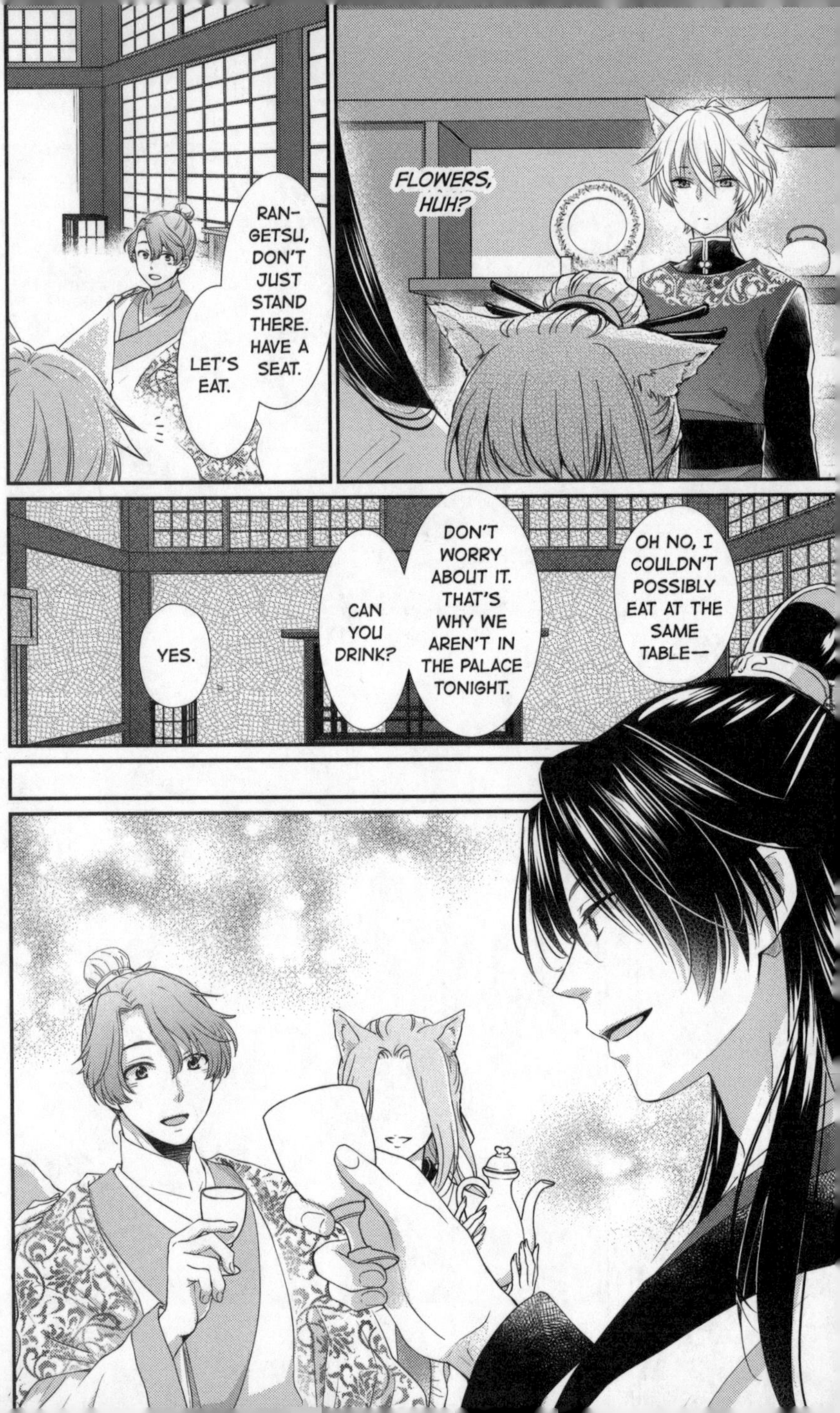
FLOWERS, HUH?
RAN-GETSU, DON'T JUST STAND THERE. HAVE A SEAT.
LET'S EAT.
OH NO, I COULDN'T POSSIBLY EAT AT THE SAME TABLE—
DON'T WORRY ABOUT IT. THAT'S WHY WE AREN'T IN THE PALACE TONIGHT.
CAN YOU DRINK?
YES.

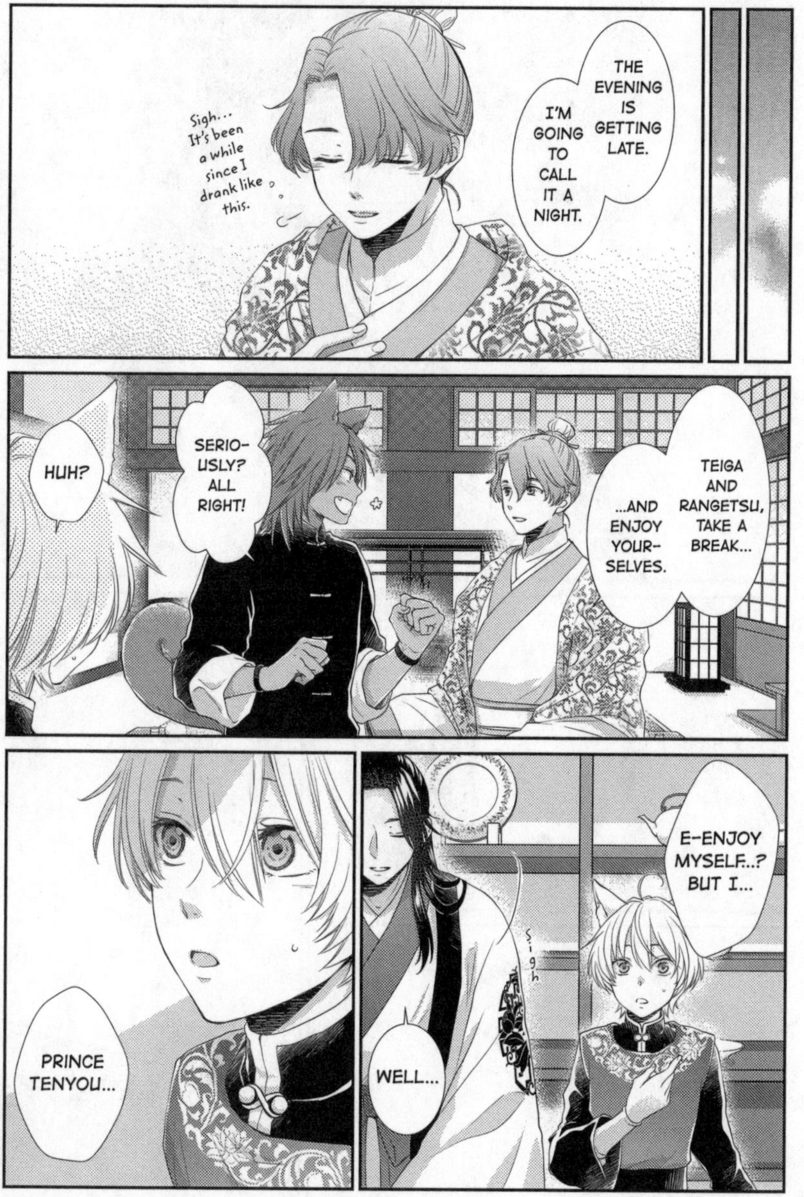
THE EVENING IS GETTING LATE.
I'M GOING TO CALL IT A NIGHT.
Sigh... It's been a while since I drank like this.
TEIGA AND RANGETSU, TAKE A BREAK...
...AND ENJOY YOURSELVES.
SERIOUSLY? ALL RIGHT!
HUH?
E-ENJOY MYSELF...? BUT I...
Sigh
WELL...
PRINCE TENYOU...

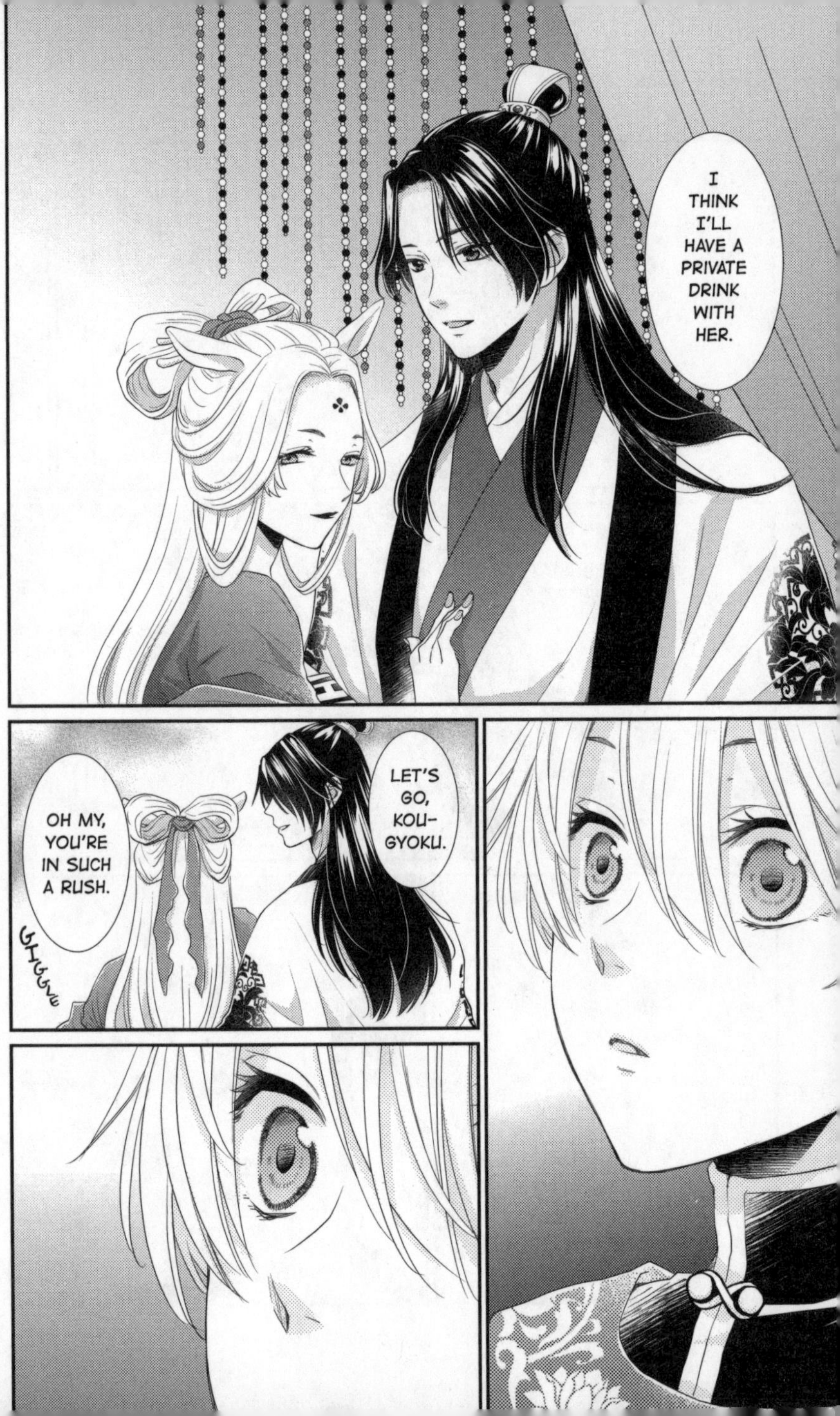
I THINK I'LL HAVE A PRIVATE DRINK WITH HER.
LET'S GO, KOU-GYOKU.
OH MY, YOU'RE IN SUCH A RUSH.
GIGGLE

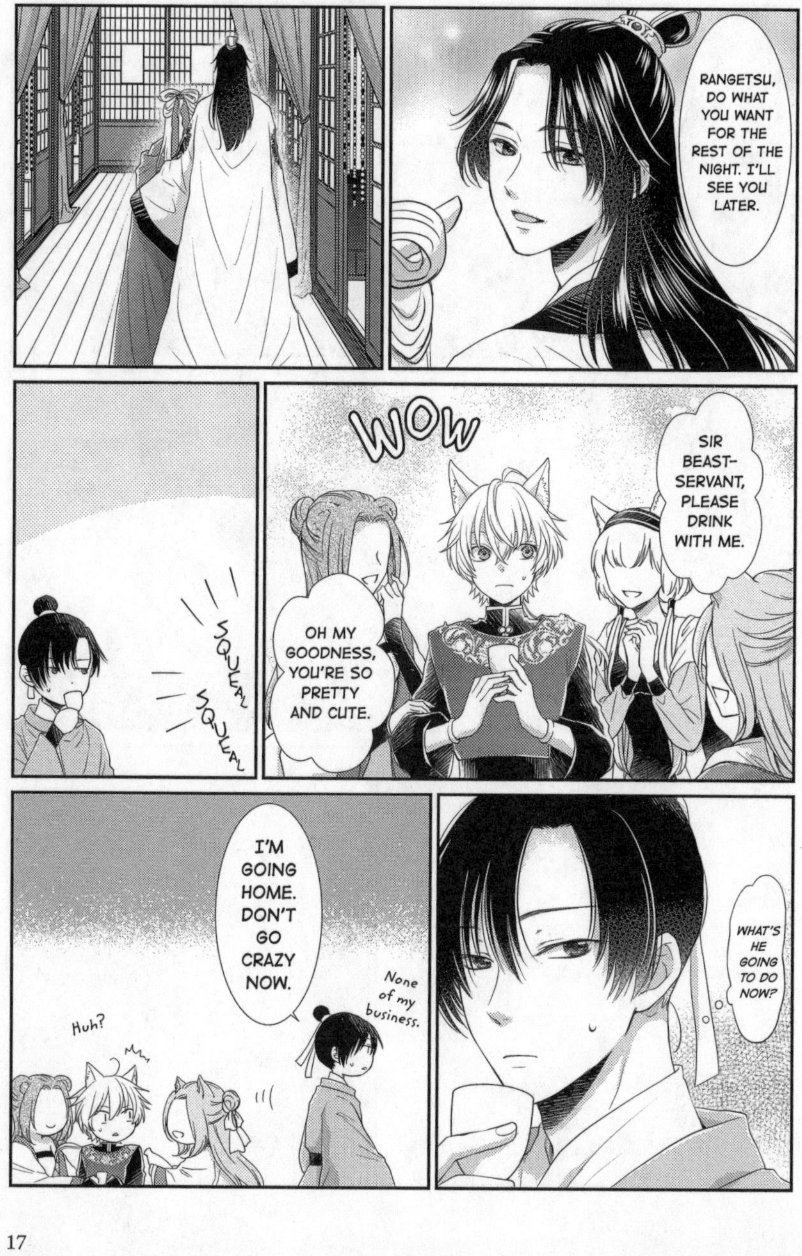
RANGETSU, DO WHAT YOU WANT FOR THE REST OF THE NIGHT. I'LL SEE YOU LATER.
WOW
SIR BEAST-SERVANT, PLEASE DRINK WITH ME.
OH MY GOODNESS, YOU'RE SO PRETTY AND CUTE.
SQUEAL
SQUEAL
WHAT'S HE GOING TO DO NOW?
I'M GOING HOME. DON'T GO CRAZY NOW.
None of my business.
Huh?

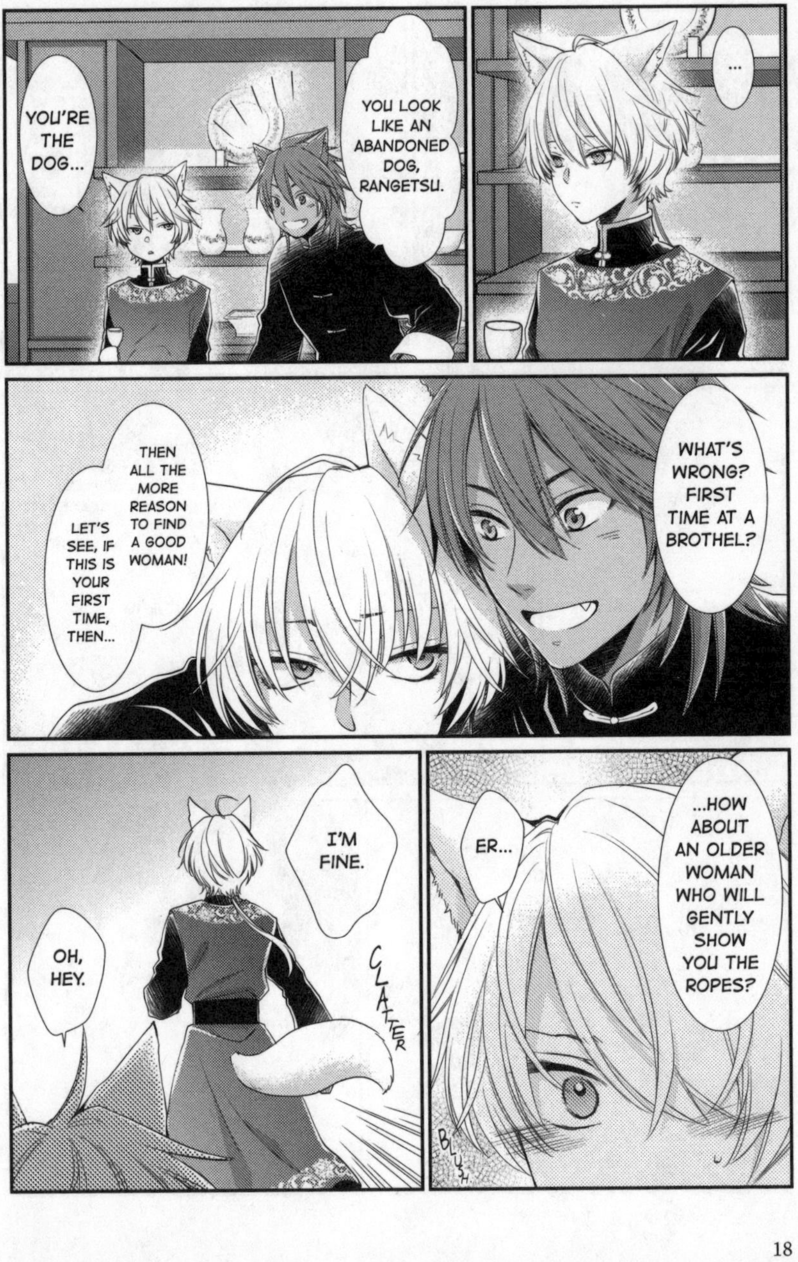
...
YOU LOOK LIKE AN ABANDONED DOG, RANGETSU.
YOU'RE THE DOG...
WHAT'S WRONG? FIRST TIME AT A BROTHEL?
THEN ALL THE MORE REASON TO FIND A GOOD WOMAN!
LET'S SEE, IF THIS IS YOUR FIRST TIME, THEN...
...HOW ABOUT AN OLDER WOMAN WHO WILL GENTLY SHOW YOU THE ROPES?
ER...
BLUSH
I'M FINE.
CLATTER
OH, HEY.

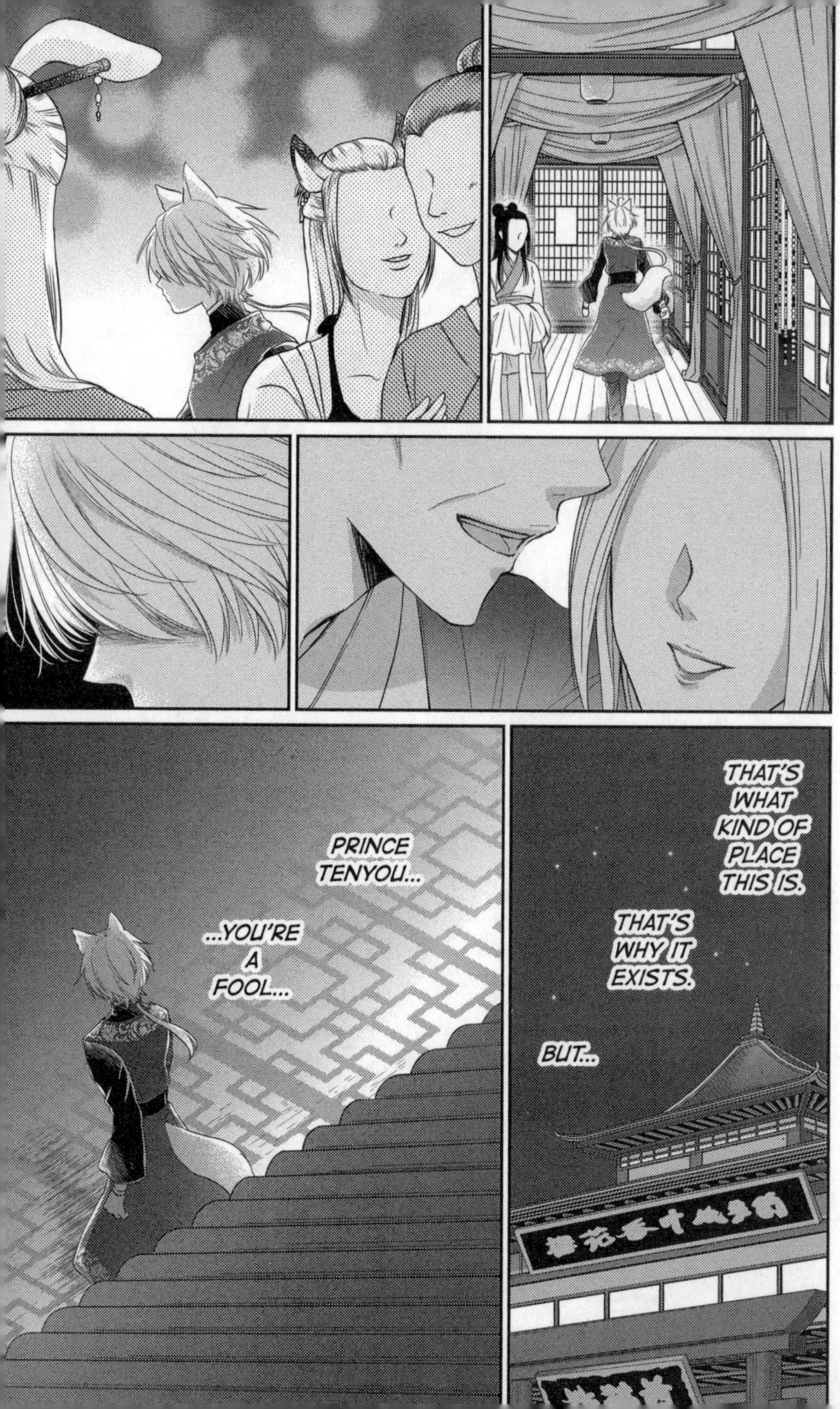
THAT'S WHAT KIND OF PLACE THIS IS.
THAT'S WHY IT EXISTS.
BUT...
PRINCE TENYOU...
...YOU'RE A FOOL...

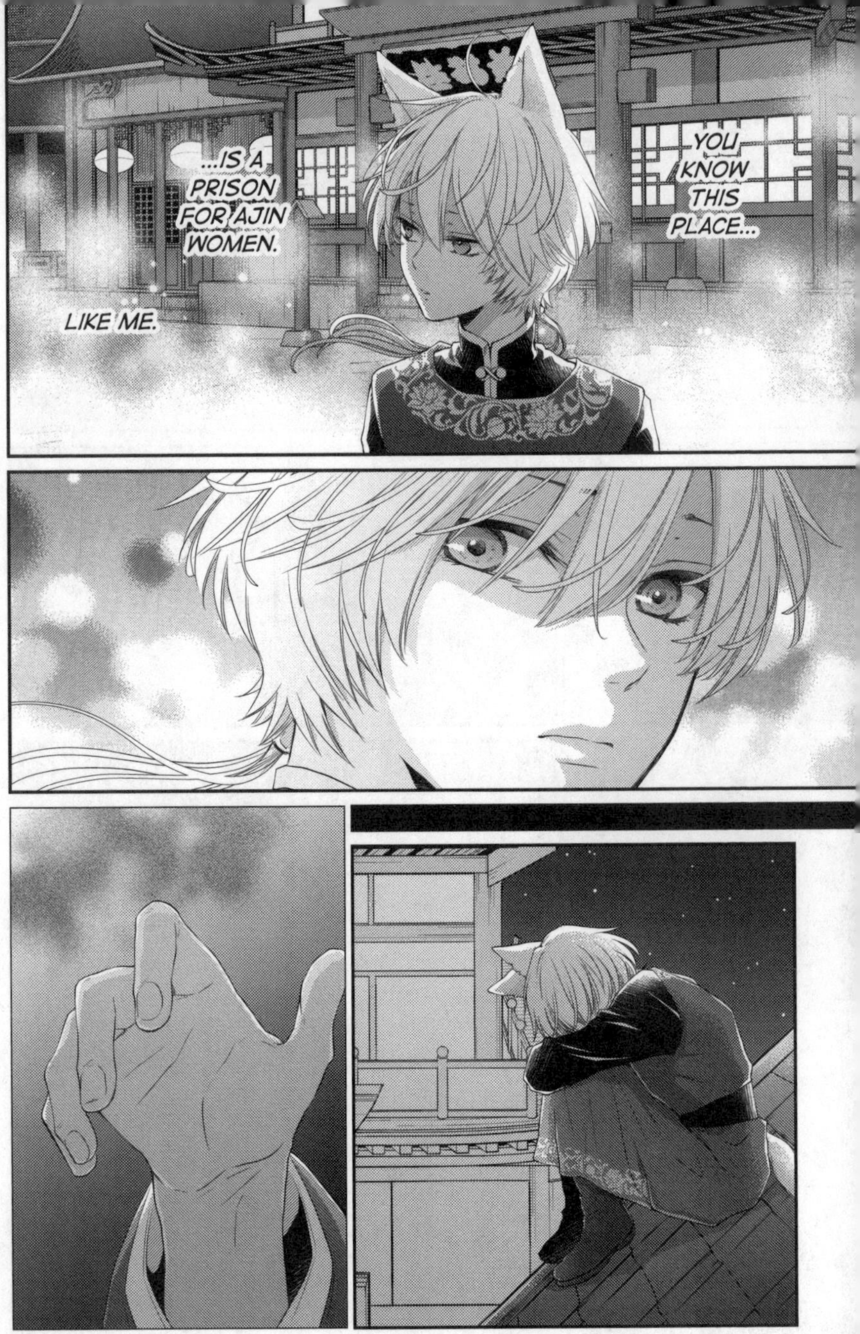
YOU KNOW THIS PLACE...
...IS A PRISON FOR AJIN WOMEN.
LIKE ME.

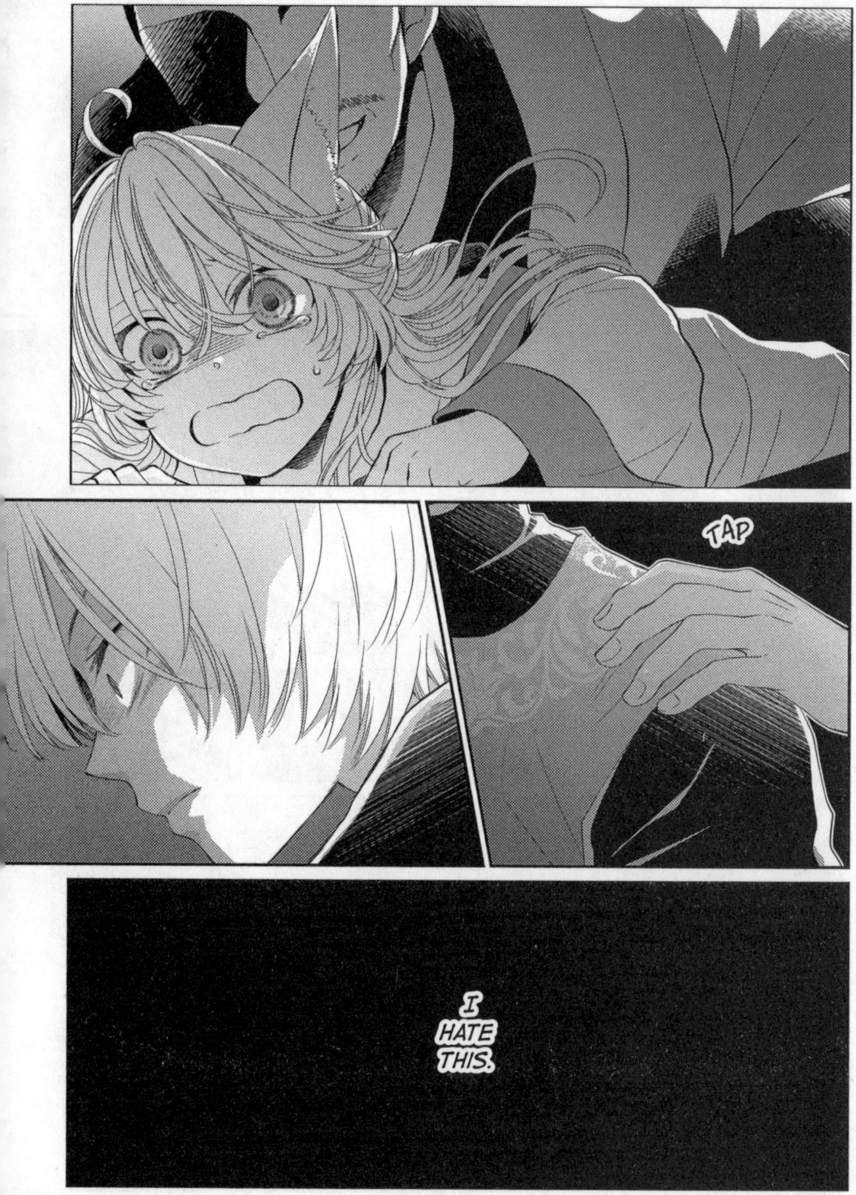
TAP
I HATE THIS.

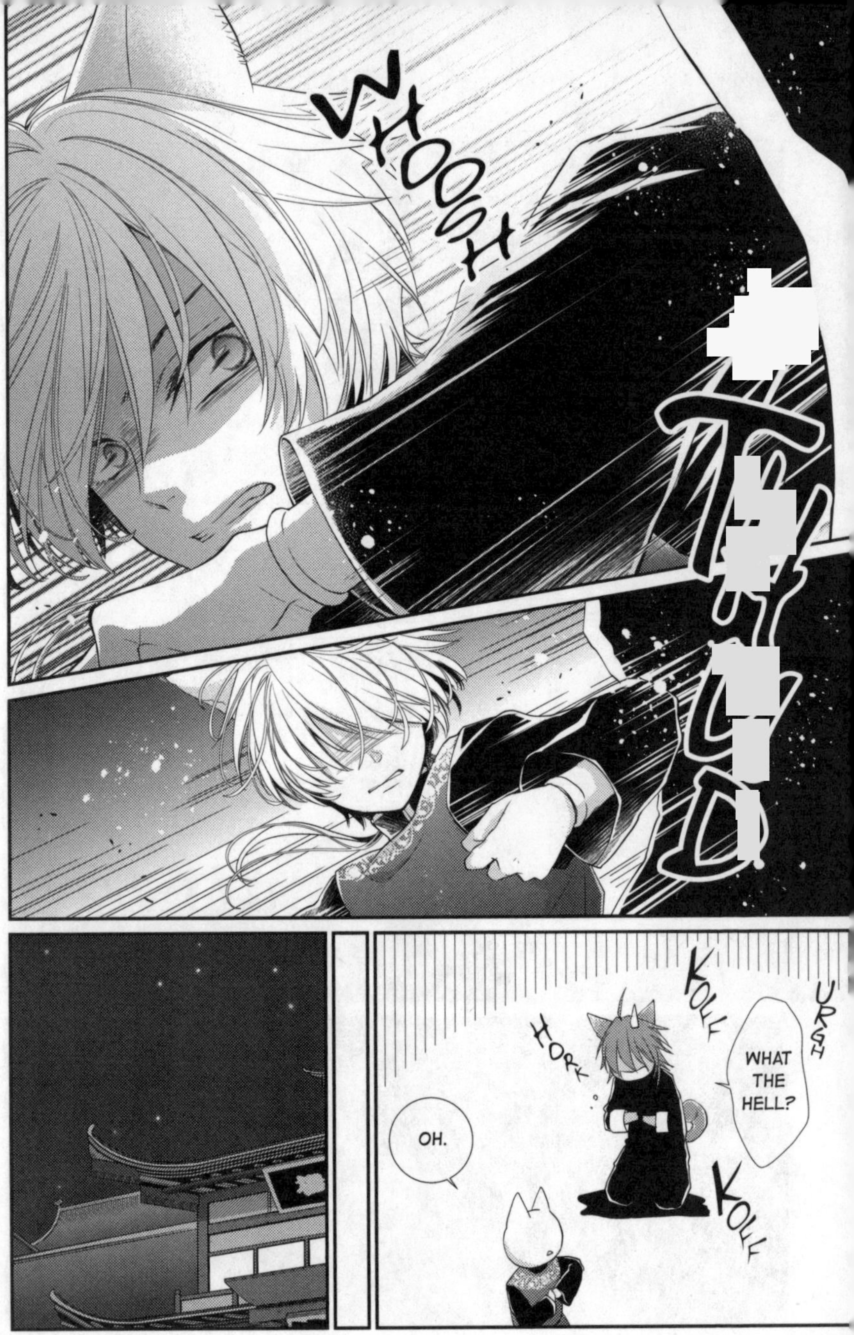
WHOOSH
THUD
URGH
WHAT THE HELL?
KOFF
HORK
KOFF
OH.

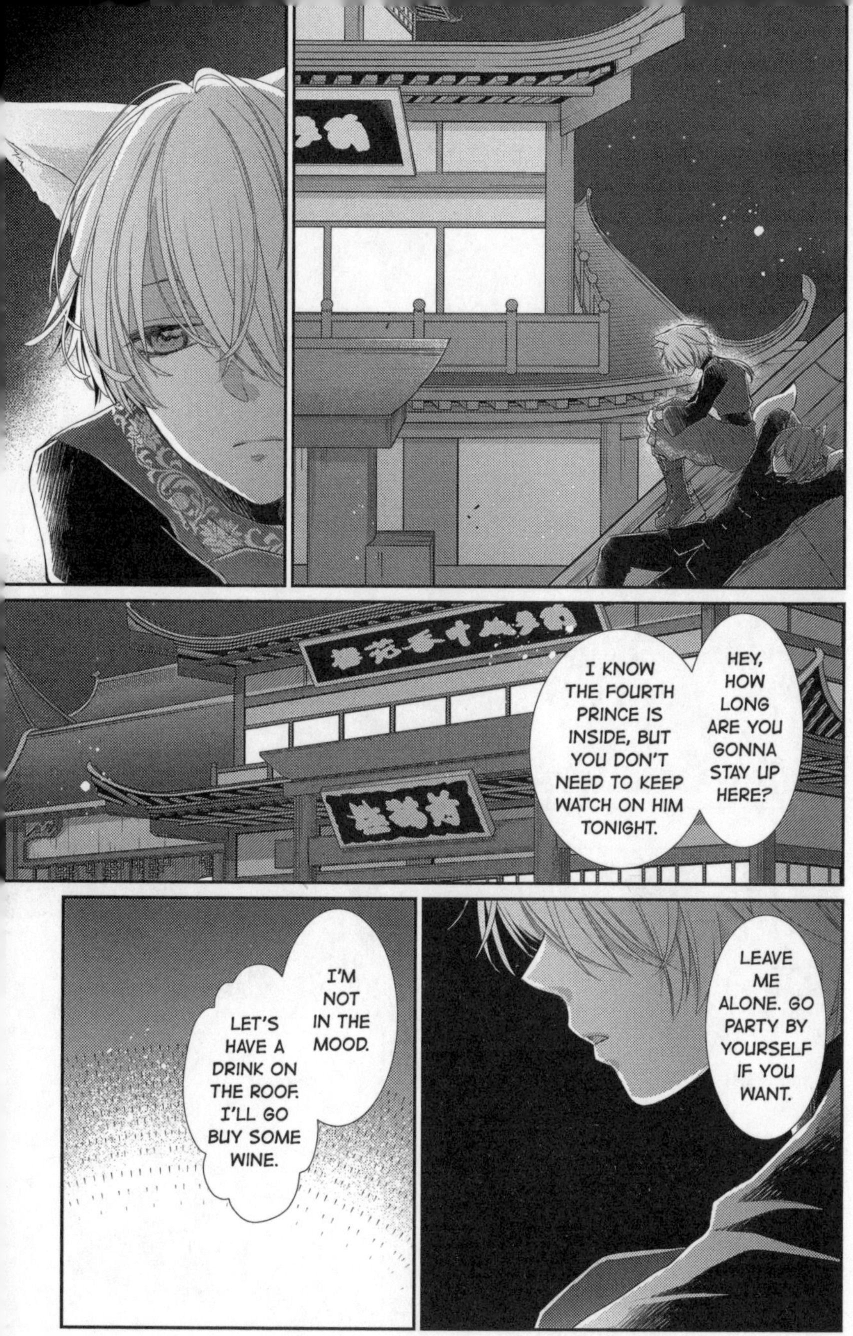
HEY, HOW LONG ARE YOU GONNA STAY UP HERE?
I KNOW THE FOURTH PRINCE IS INSIDE, BUT YOU DON'T NEED TO KEEP WATCH ON HIM TONIGHT.
LEAVE ME ALONE. GO PARTY BY YOURSELF IF YOU WANT.
I'M NOT IN THE MOOD.
LET'S HAVE A DRINK ON THE ROOF. I'LL GO BUY SOME WINE.

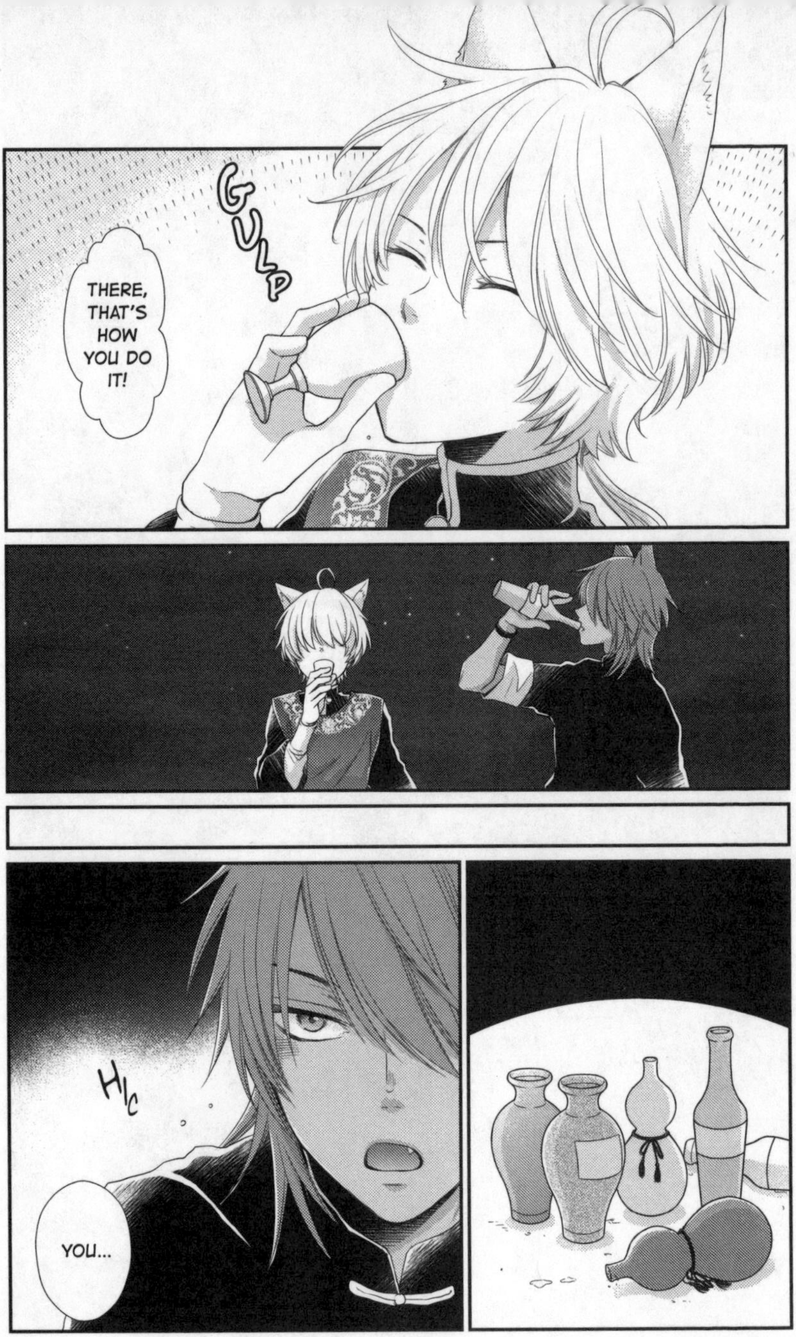
GULP
THERE, THAT'S HOW YOU DO IT!
YOU...
HIC

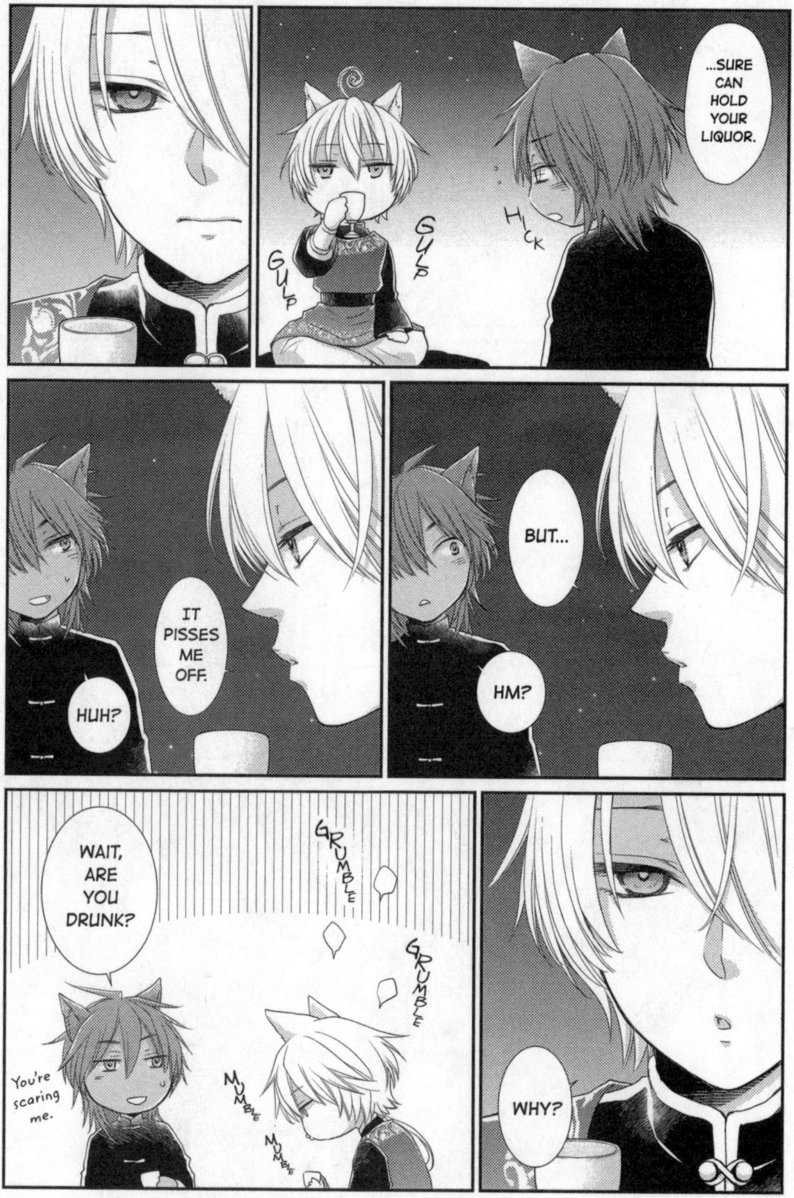
...SURE CAN HOLD YOUR LIQUOR.
HICK
GULP
GULP
BUT...
HM?
IT PISSES ME OFF.
HUH?
WHY?
GRUMBLE
WAIT, ARE YOU DRUNK?
GRUMBLE
MUMBLE
MUMBLE
You're scaring me.

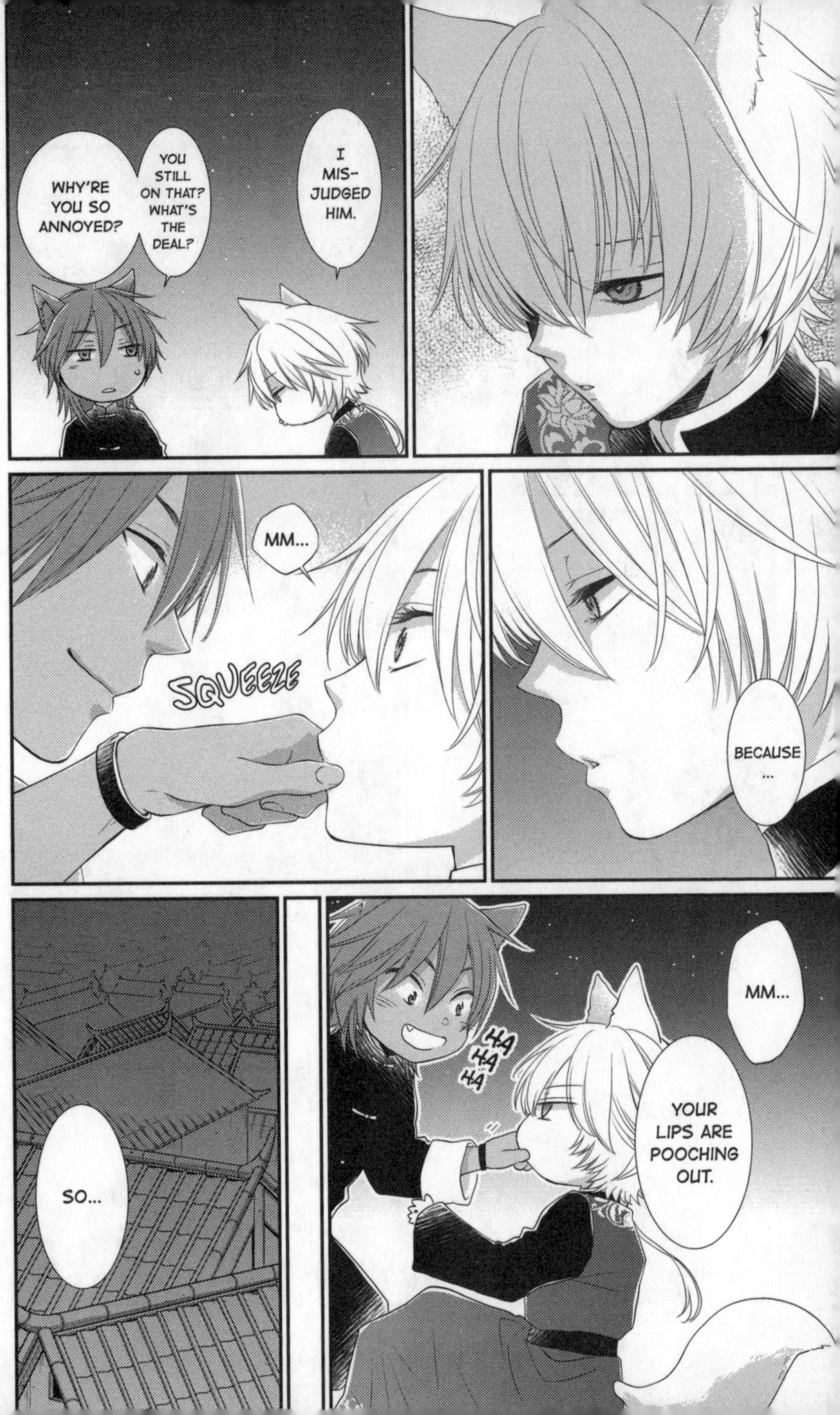
I MIS-JUDGED HIM.
YOU STILL ON THAT? WHAT'S THE DEAL?
WHY'RE YOU SO ANNOYED?
BECAUSE ...
MM...
SQUEEZE
MM...
YOUR LIPS ARE POOCHING OUT.
HA HA HA
SO...

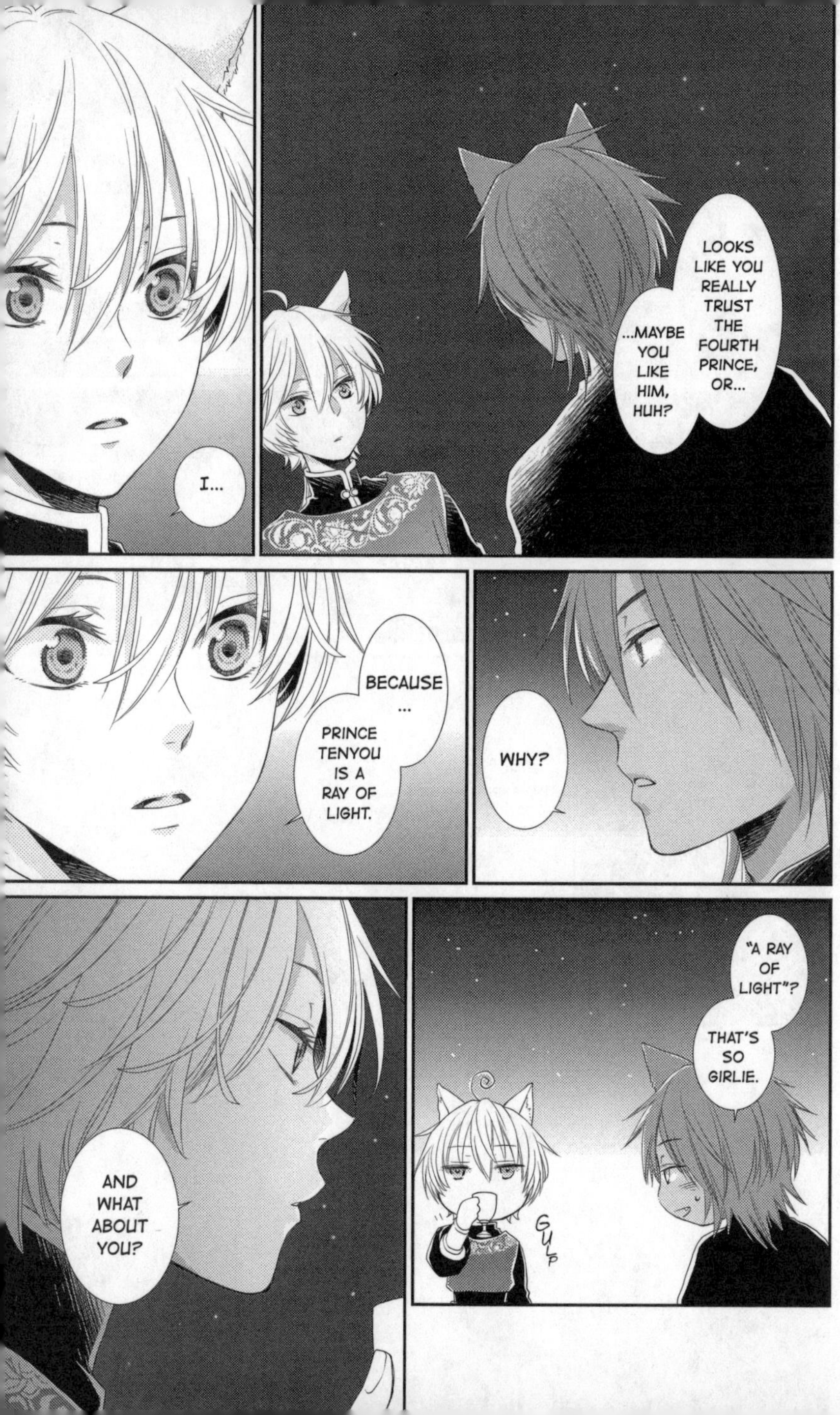
LOOKS LIKE YOU REALLY TRUST THE FOURTH PRINCE, OR...
...MAYBE YOU LIKE HIM, HUH?
I...
WHY?
BECAUSE ...
PRINCE TENYOU IS A RAY OF LIGHT.
“A RAY OF LIGHT”?
THAT'S SO GIRLIE.
GULP
AND WHAT ABOUT YOU?

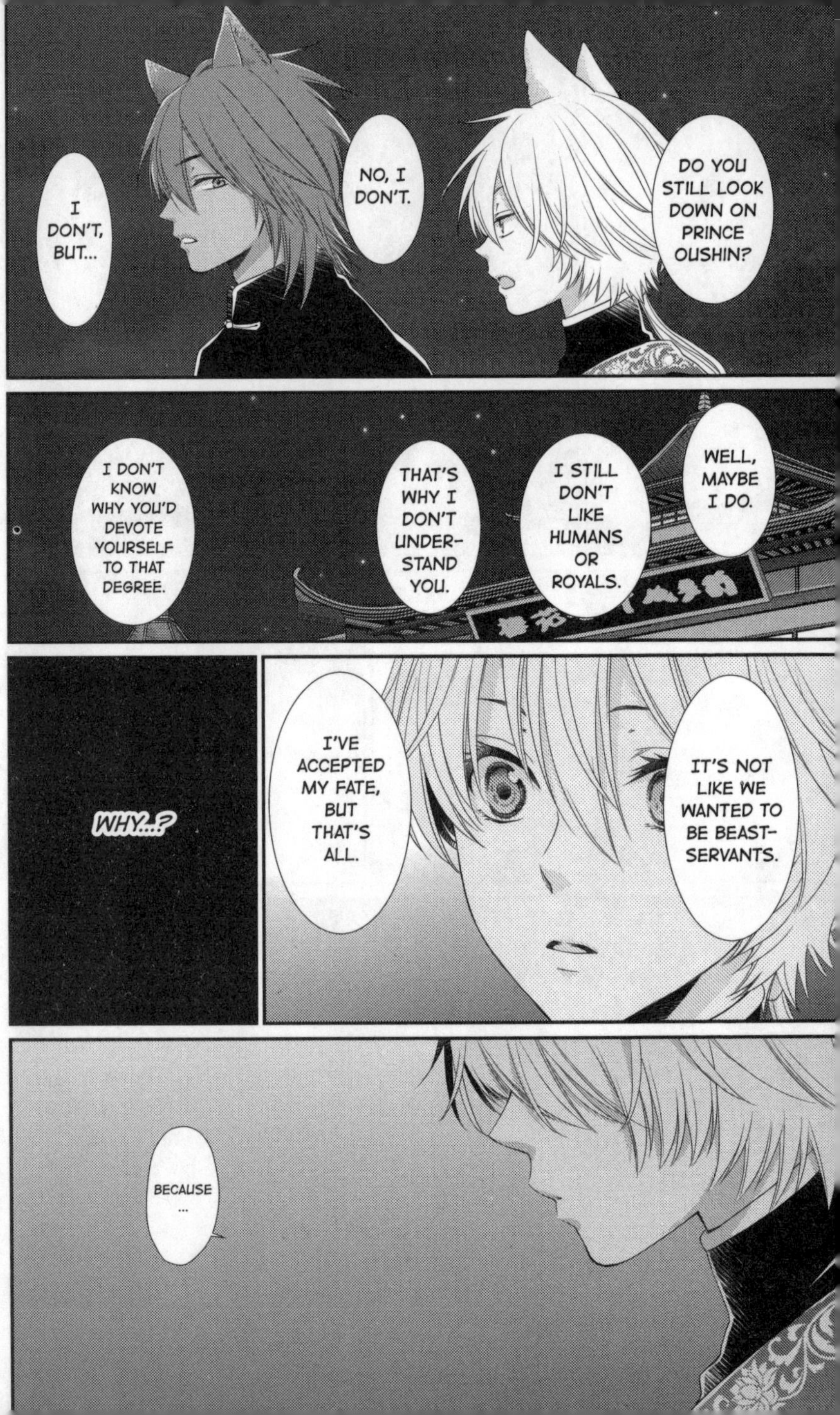
DO YOU STILL LOOK DOWN ON PRINCE OUSHIN?
NO, I DON'T.
I DON'T, BUT...
WELL, MAYBE I DO.
I STILL DON'T LIKE HUMANS OR ROYALS.
THAT'S WHY I DON'T UNDER-STAND YOU.
I DON'T KNOW WHY YOU'D DEVOTE YOURSELF TO THAT DEGREE.
IT'S NOT LIKE WE WANTED TO BE BEAST-SERVANTS.
I'VE ACCEPTED MY FATE, BUT THAT'S ALL.
WHY...?
BECAUSE...

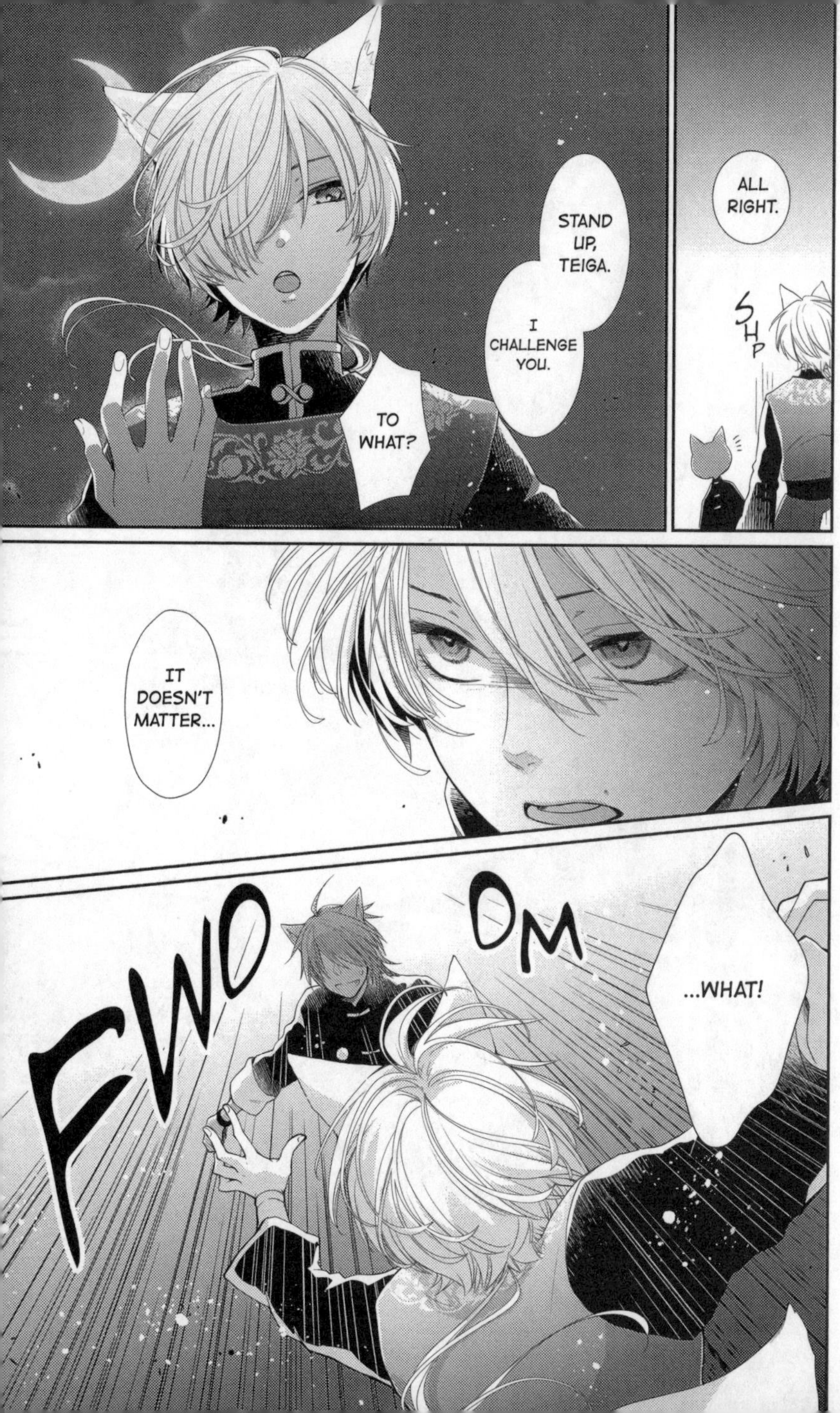

ALL RIGHT.
SHP
STAND UP, TEIGA.
I CHALLENGE YOU.
TO WHAT?
IT DOESN'T MATTER...
...WHAT!
FWOOM

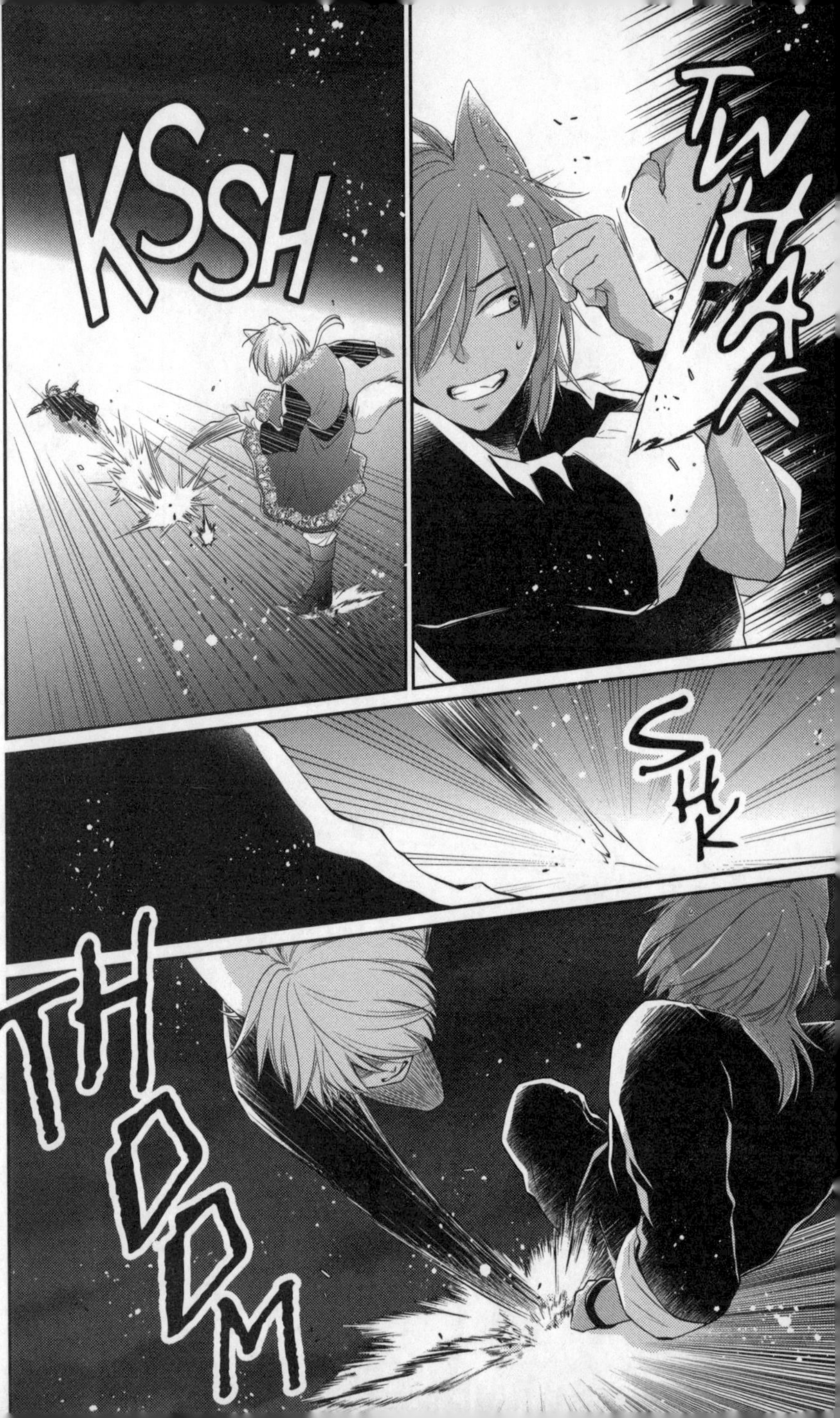
TWHAK
KSSH
SHK
THOOM

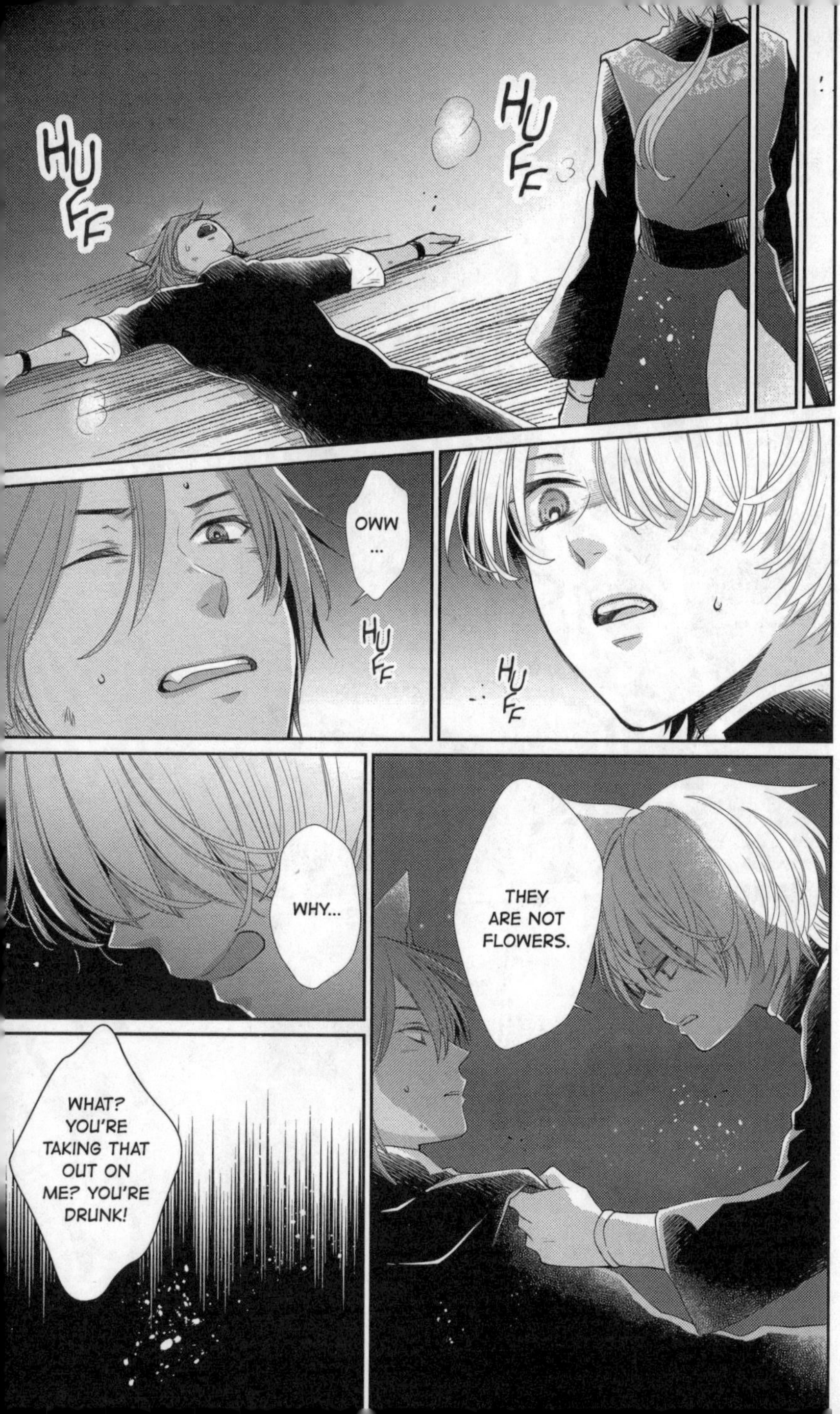
HUFF HUFF
HUFF HUFF
HUFF
OWW...
HUFF
WHY...
THEY ARE NOT FLOWERS.
WHAT? YOU'RE TAKING THAT OUT ON ME? YOU'RE DRUNK!

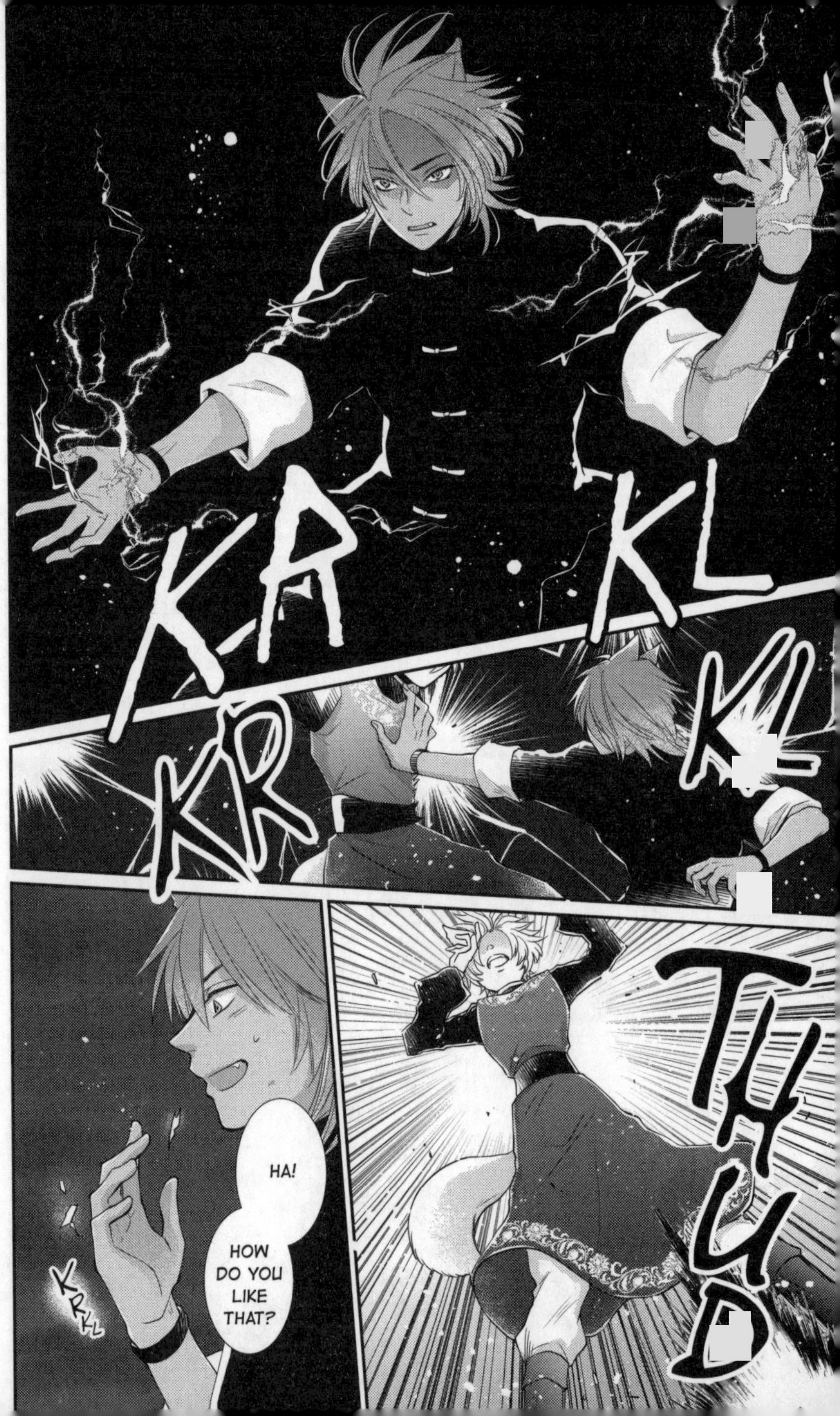
KRA KL
KR KL
THUD
HA!
HOW DO YOU LIKE THAT?
KRKL

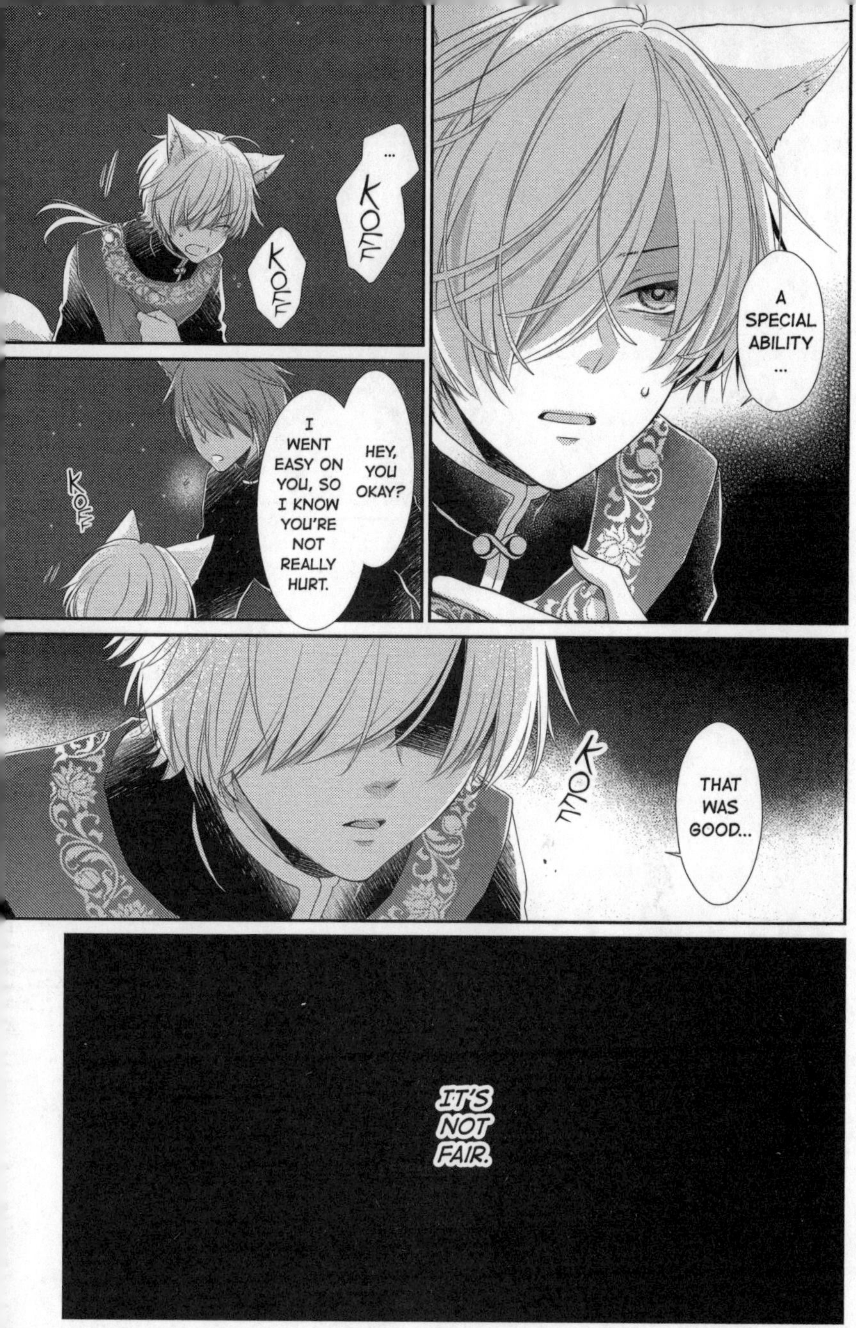
A SPECIAL ABILITY ...
...
KOFF
KOFF
HEY, YOU OKAY?
I WENT EASY ON YOU, SO I KNOW YOU'RE NOT REALLY HURT.
KOFF
THAT WAS GOOD...
KOFF
IT'S NOT FAIR.

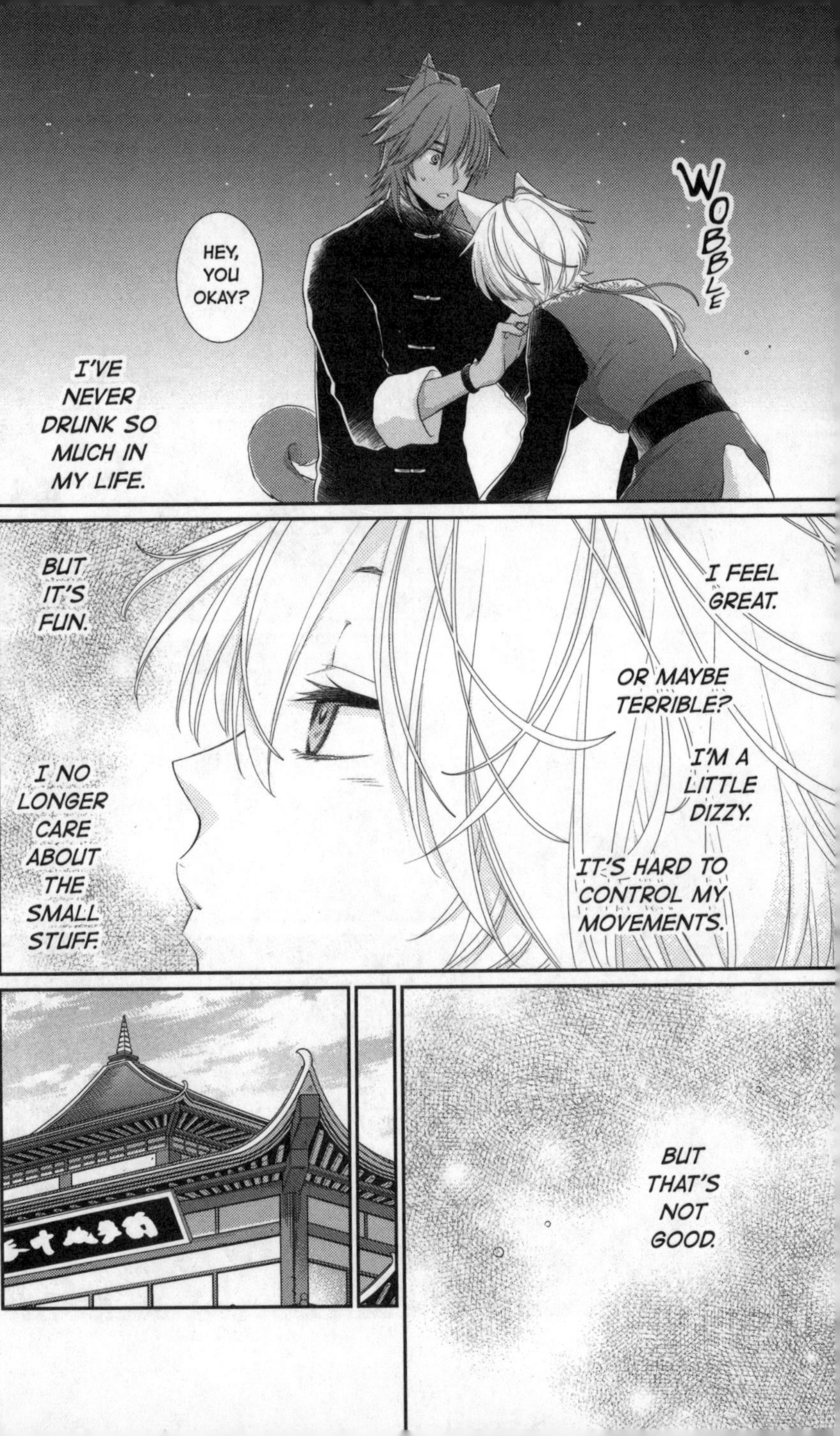
WOBBLE
HEY, YOU OKAY?
I'VE NEVER DRUNK SO MUCH IN MY LIFE.
I FEEL GREAT.
OR MAYBE TERRIBLE?
I'M A LITTLE DIZZY.
IT'S HARD TO CONTROL MY MOVEMENTS.
BUT IT'S FUN.
I NO LONGER CARE ABOUT THE SMALL STUFF.
BUT THAT'S NOT GOOD.

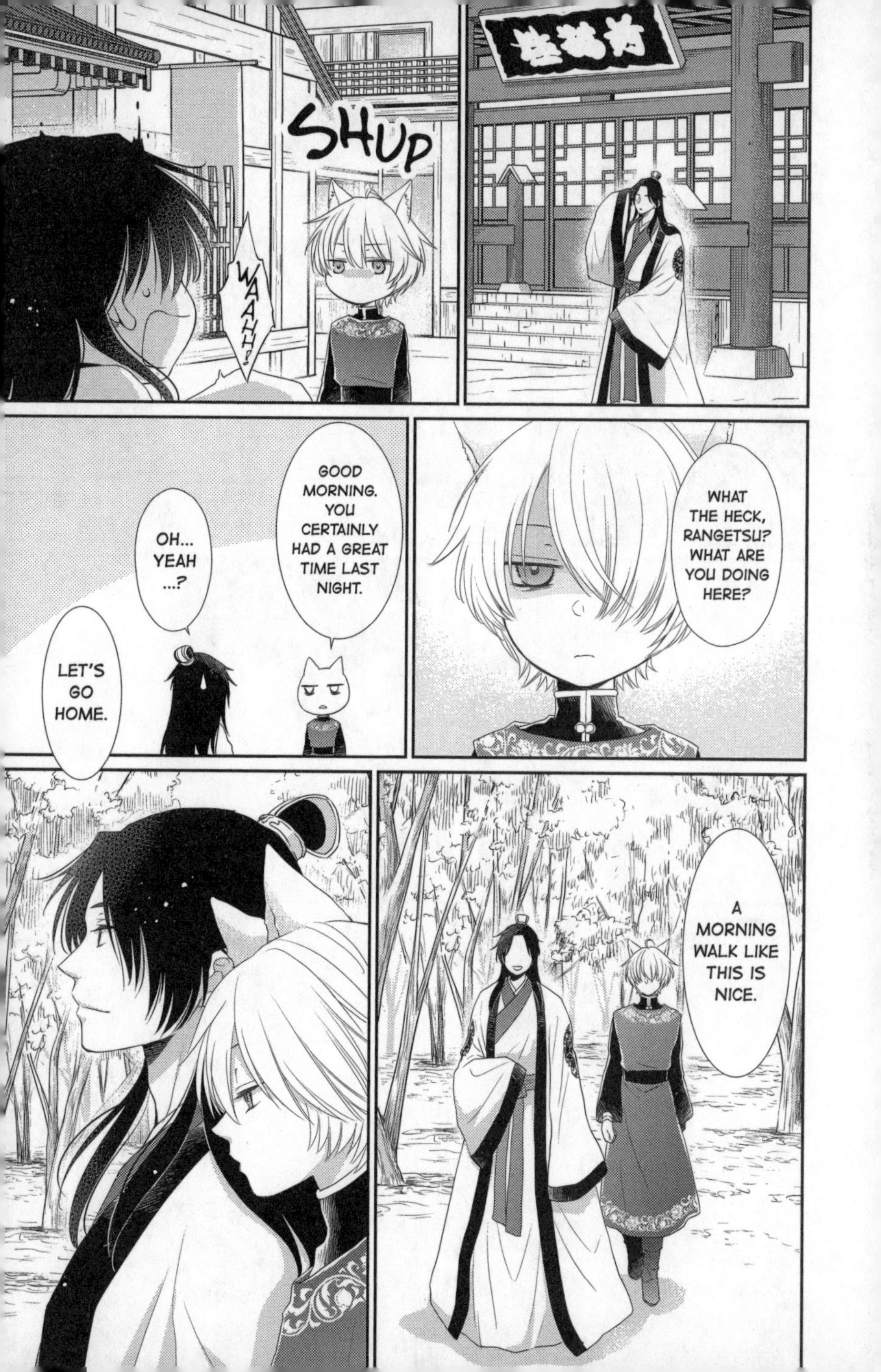
SHUP
WAAHH!?
WHAT THE HECK, RANGETSU? WHAT ARE YOU DOING HERE?
GOOD MORNING. YOU CERTAINLY HAD A GREAT TIME LAST NIGHT.
OH... YEAH ...?
LET'S GO HOME.
A MORNING WALK LIKE THIS IS NICE.

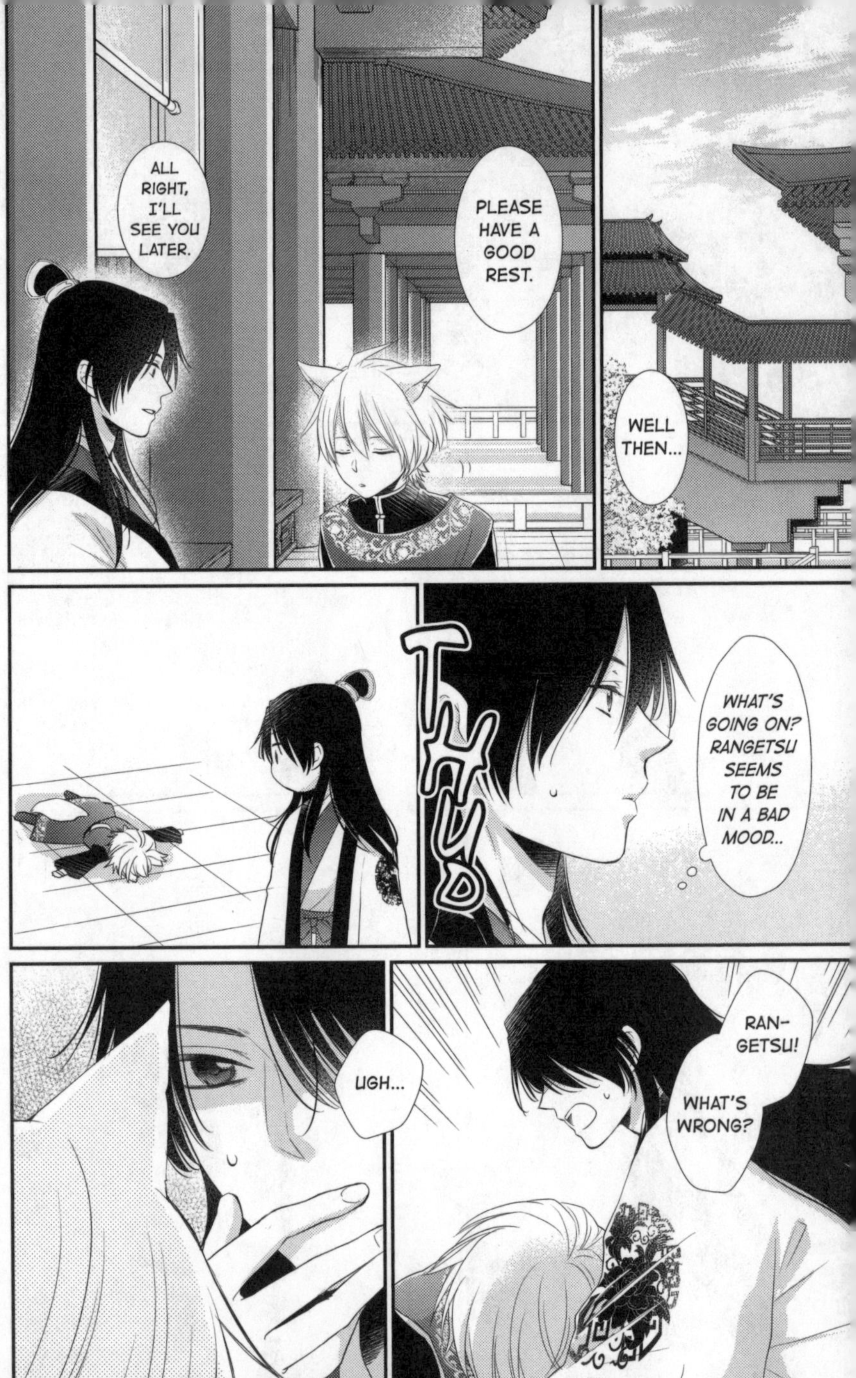
WELL THEN...
PLEASE HAVE A GOOD REST.
ALL RIGHT, I'LL SEE YOU LATER.
WHAT'S GOING ON? RANGETSU SEEMS TO BE IN A BAD MOOD...
THUD
RAN-GETSU!
WHAT'S WRONG?
UGH...

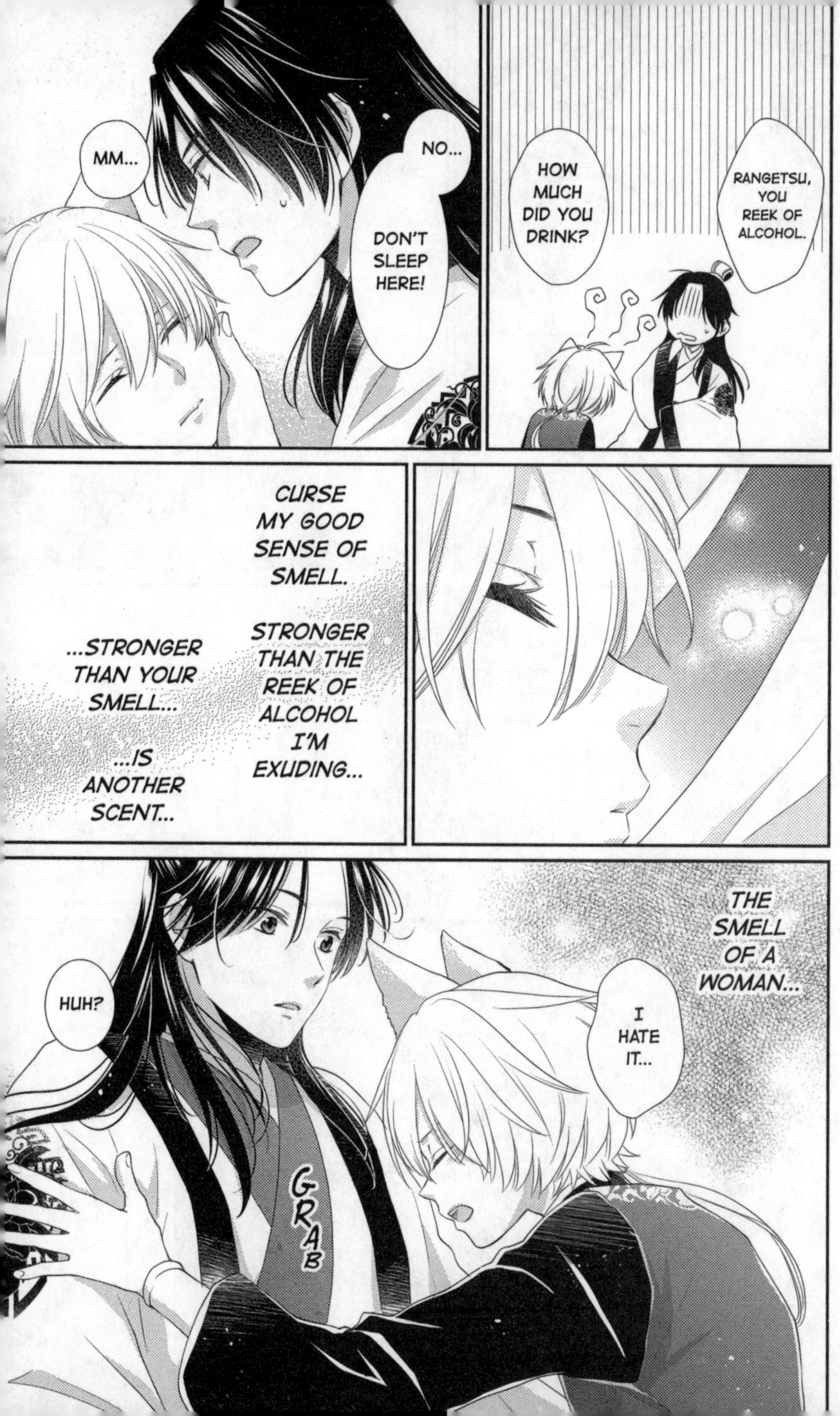
RANGETSU, YOU REEK OF ALCOHOL.
HOW MUCH DID YOU DRINK?
NO...
DON'T SLEEP HERE!
MM...
CURSE MY GOOD SENSE OF SMELL.
STRONGER THAN THE REEK OF ALCOHOL I'M EXUDING...
...STRONGER THAN YOUR SMELL...
...IS ANOTHER SCENT...
THE SMELL OF A WOMAN...
I HATE IT...
HUH?
GRAB

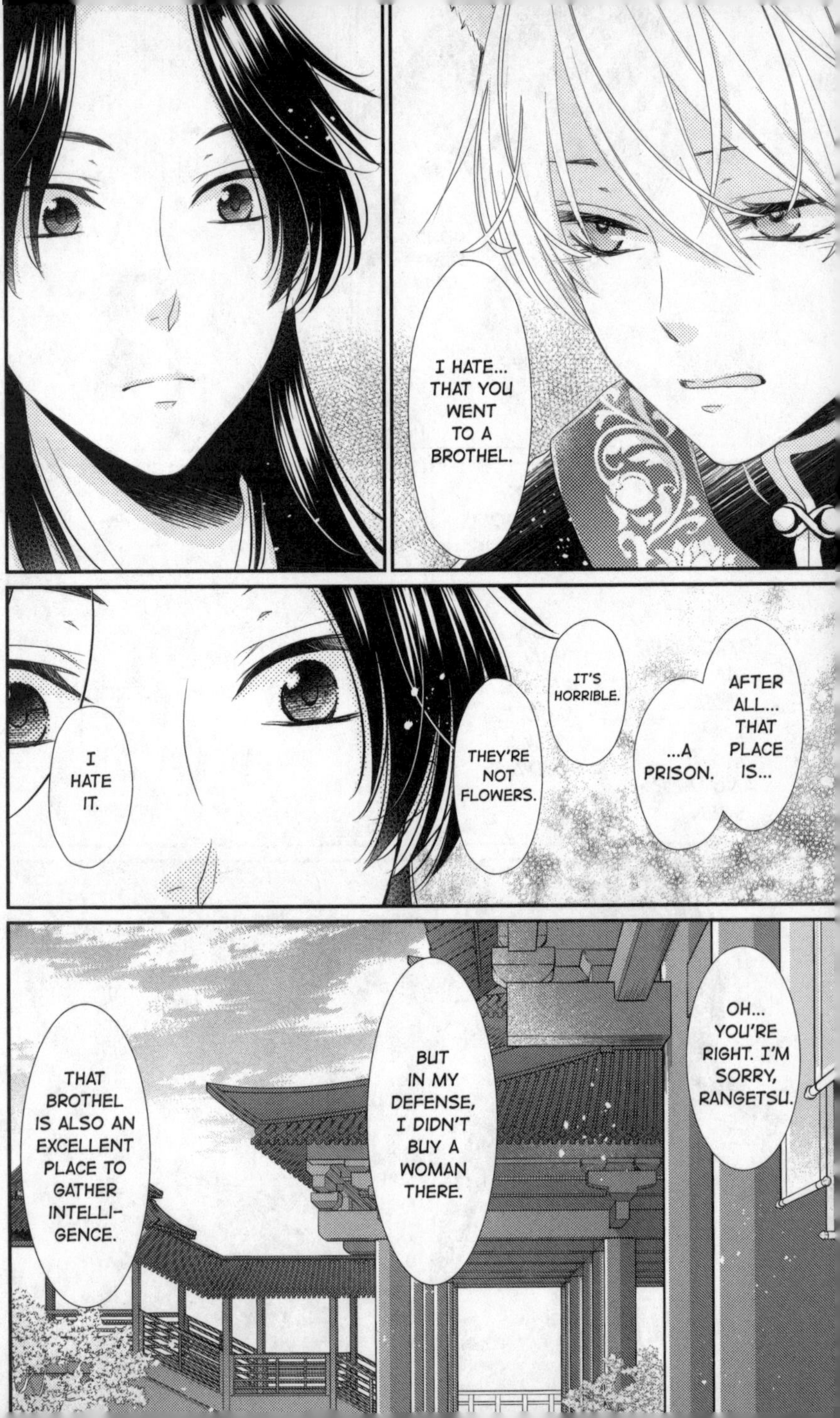
I HATE... THAT YOU WENT TO A BROTHEL.
AFTER ALL... THAT PLACE IS...
...A PRISON.
IT'S HORRIBLE.
THEY'RE NOT FLOWERS.
I HATE IT.
OH... YOU'RE RIGHT. I'M SORRY, RANGETSU.
BUT IN MY DEFENSE, I DIDN'T BUY A WOMAN THERE.
THAT BROTHEL IS ALSO AN EXCELLENT PLACE TO GATHER INTELLI-GENCE.

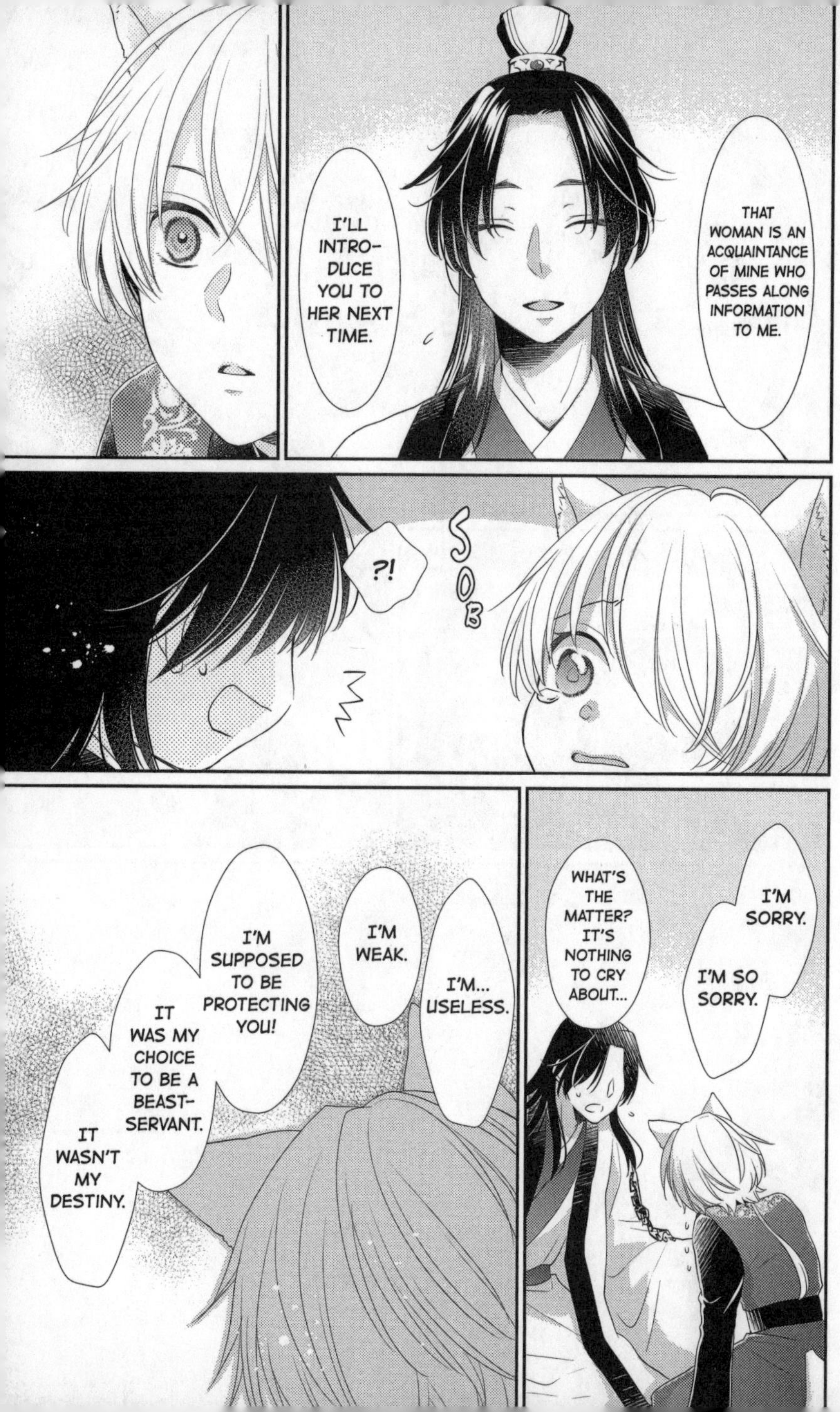
THAT WOMAN IS AN ACQUAINTANCE OF MINE WHO PASSES ALONG INFORMATION TO ME.
I'LL INTRO-DUCE YOU TO HER NEXT TIME.
SOB
?!
I'M SORRY.
I'M SO SORRY.
WHAT'S THE MATTER? IT'S NOTHING TO CRY ABOUT...
I'M... USELESS.
I'M WEAK.
I'M SUPPOSED TO BE PROTECTING YOU!
IT WAS MY CHOICE TO BE A BEAST-SERVANT.
IT WASN'T MY DESTINY.

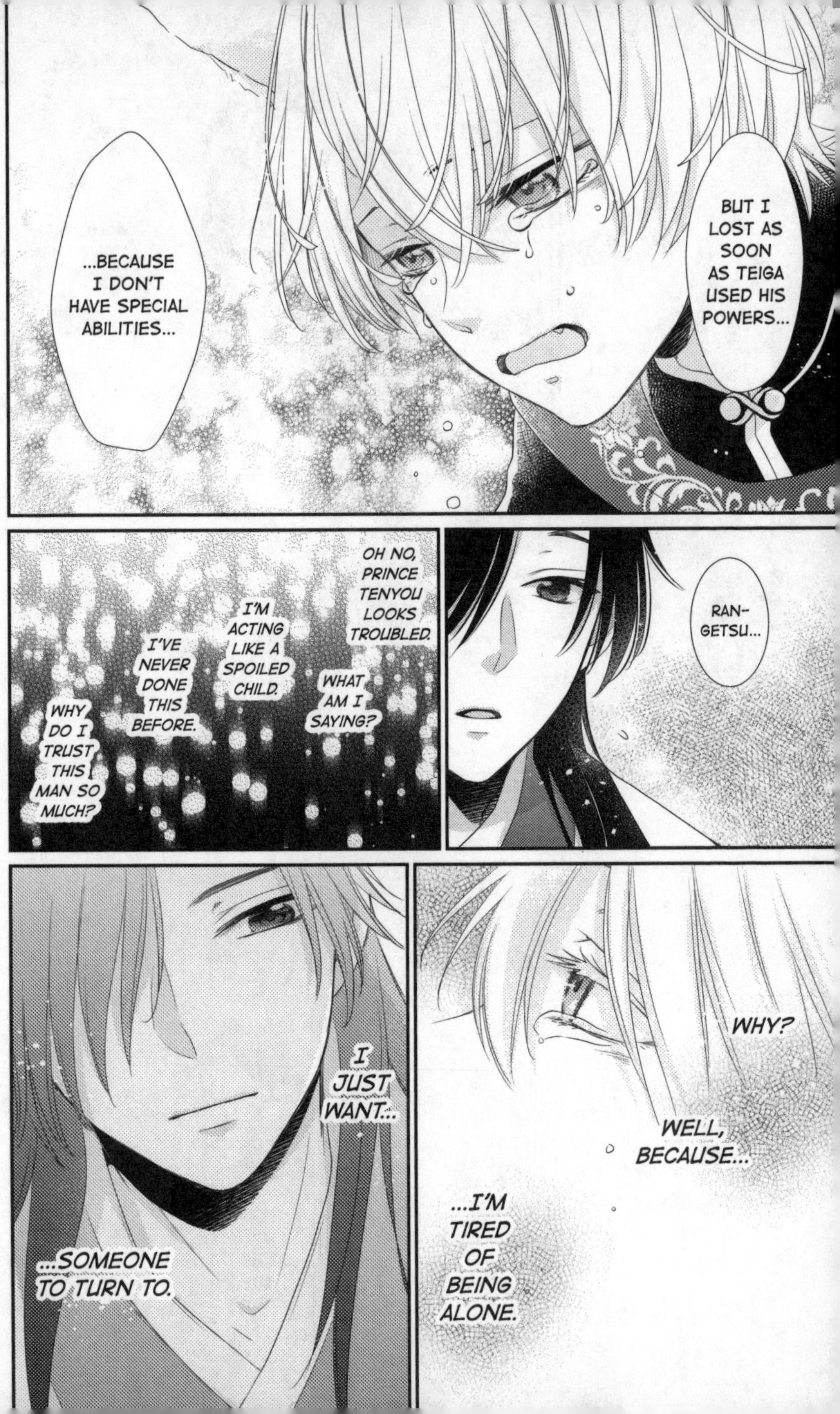
BUT I LOST AS SOON AS TEIGA USED HIS POWERS...
...BECAUSE I DON'T HAVE SPECIAL ABILITIES...
RAN-GETSU...
OH NO, PRINCE TENYOU LOOKS TROUBLED.
WHAT AM I SAYING?
I'M ACTING LIKE A SPOILED CHILD.
I'VE NEVER DONE THIS BEFORE.
WHY DO I TRUST THIS MAN SO MUCH?
WHY?
WELL, BECAUSE...
...I'M TIRED OF BEING ALONE.
I JUST WANT...
...SOMEONE TO TURN TO.

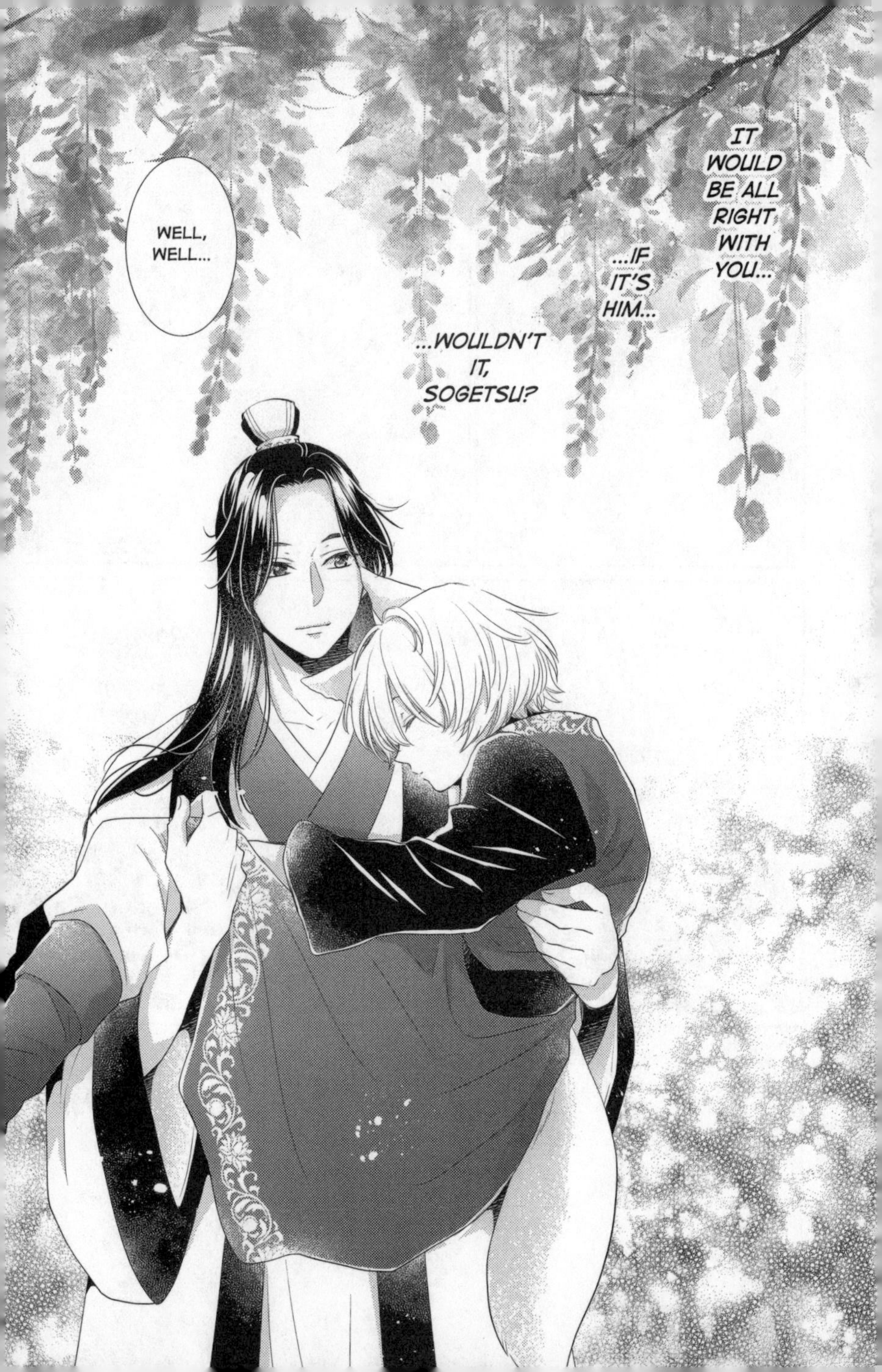
IT WOULD BE ALL RIGHT WITH YOU...
...IF IT'S HIM...
...WOULDN'T IT, SOGETSU?
WELL, WELL...

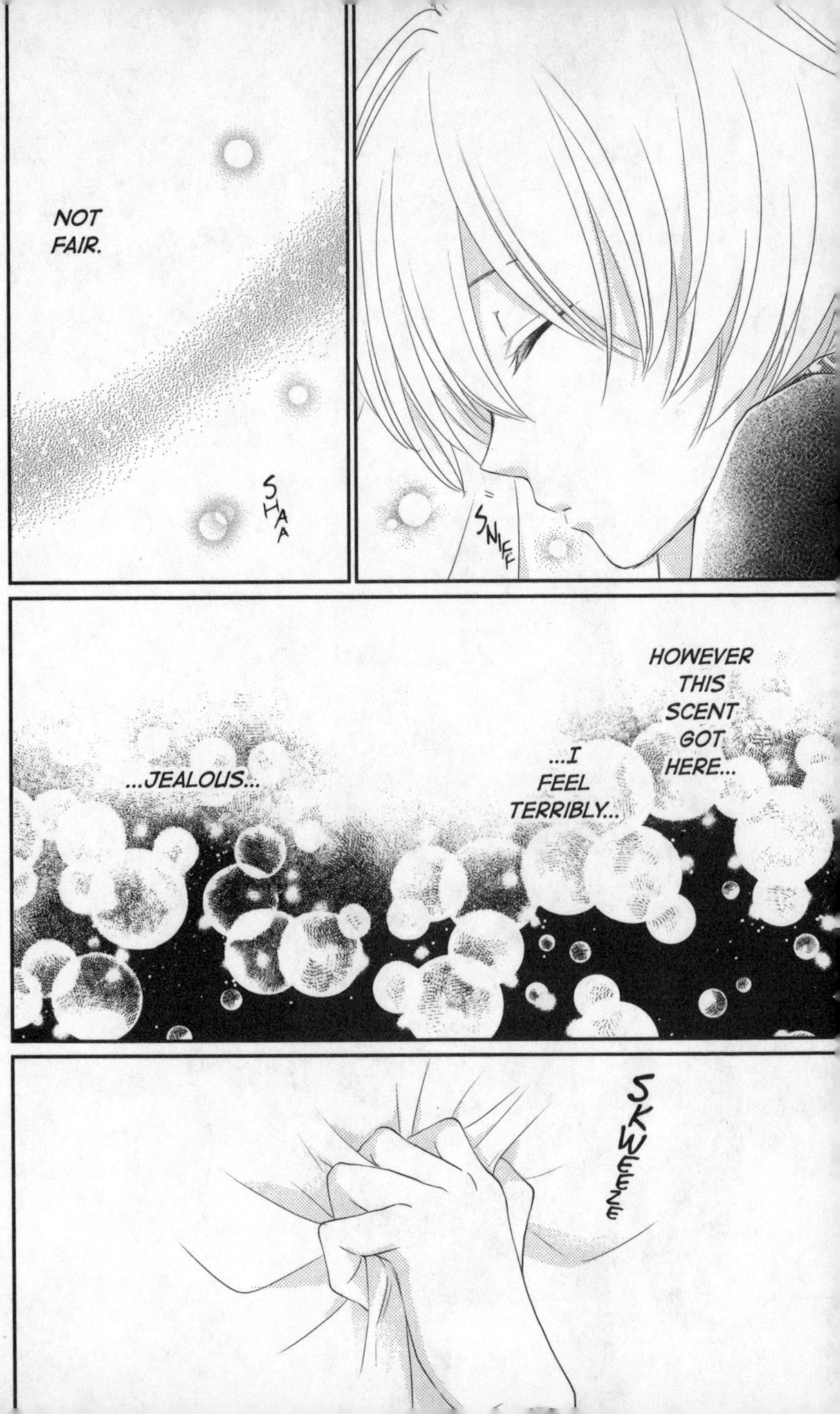
SNIFF
NOT FAIR.
SHAA
HOWEVER THIS SCENT GOT HERE...
...I FEEL TERRIBLY...
...JEALOUS...
SKWEEZE

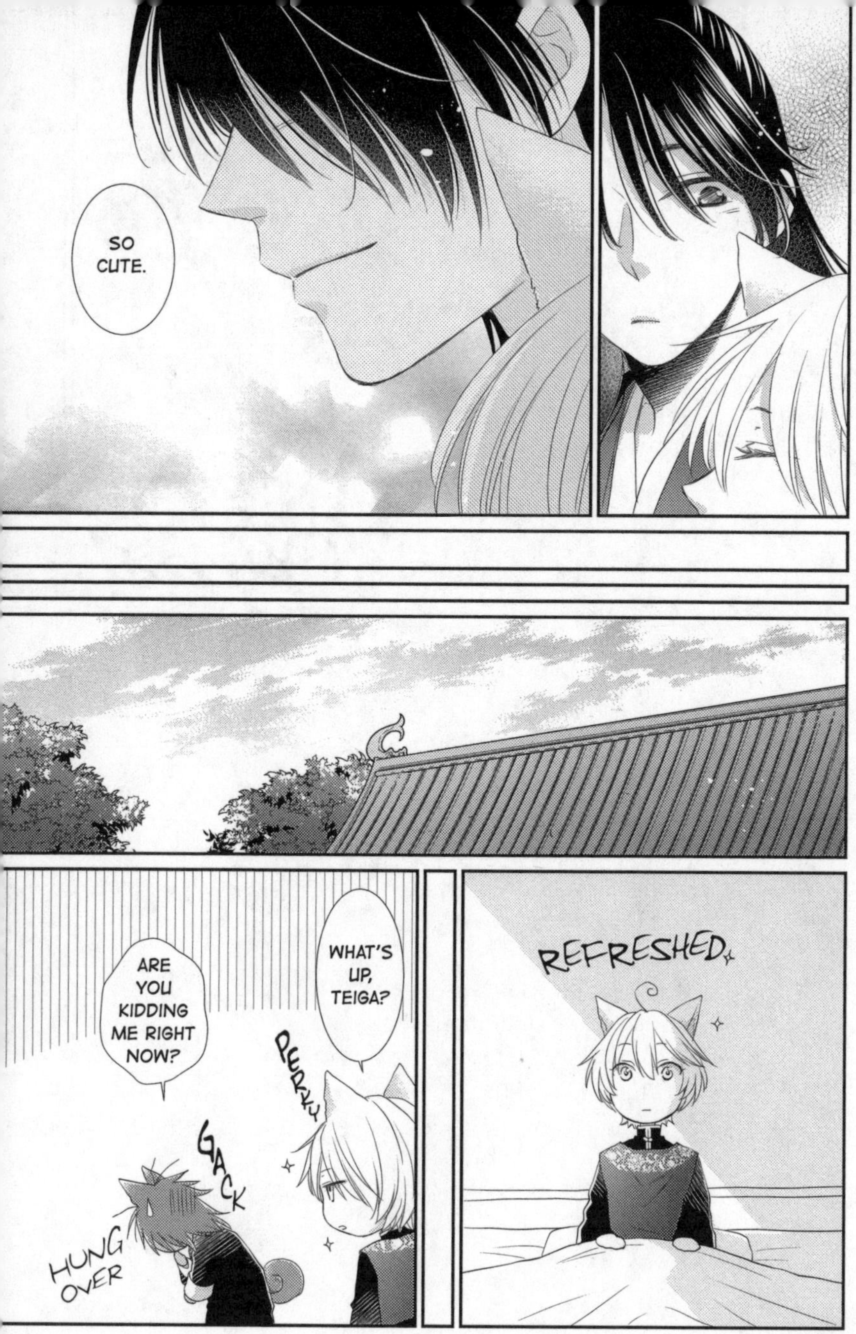
SO CUTE.
REFRESHED
WHAT'S UP, TEIGA?
PERKY
ARE YOU KIDDING ME RIGHT NOW?
GACK
HUNG OVER

THE KING'S *Beast*

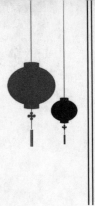

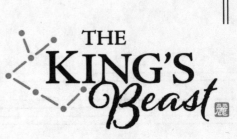

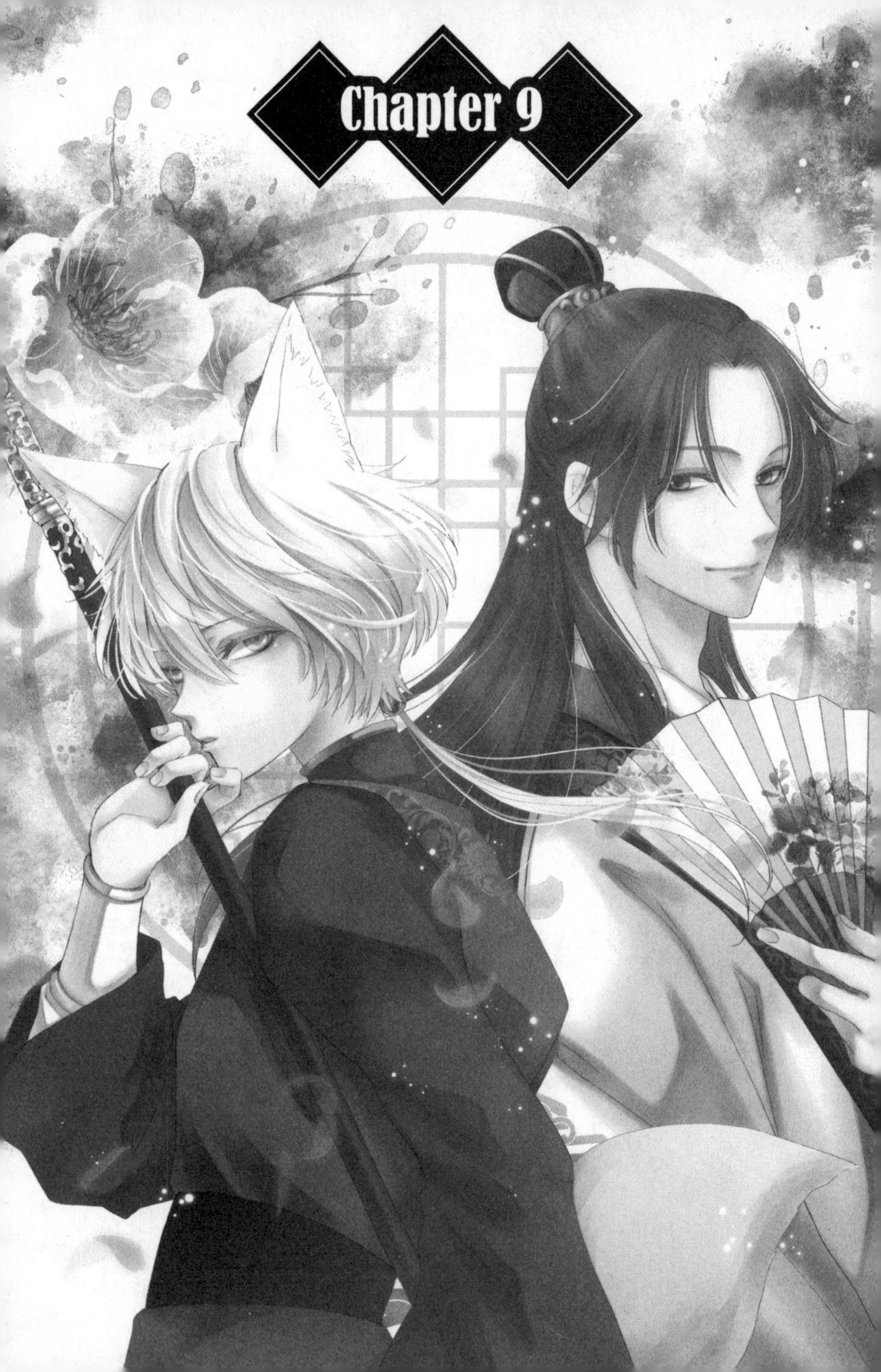
Chapter 9

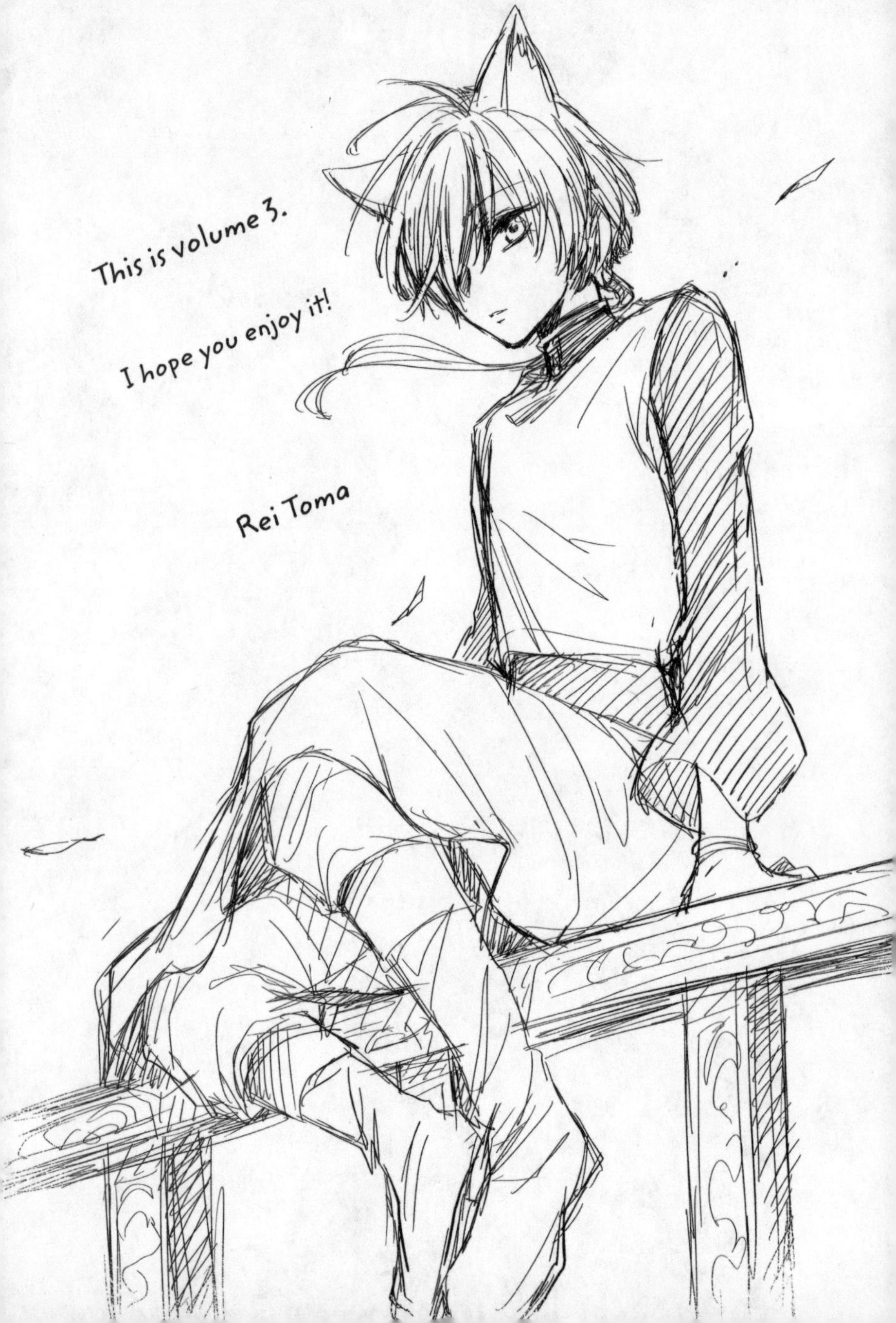
This is volume 3.
I hope you enjoy it!
Rei Toma

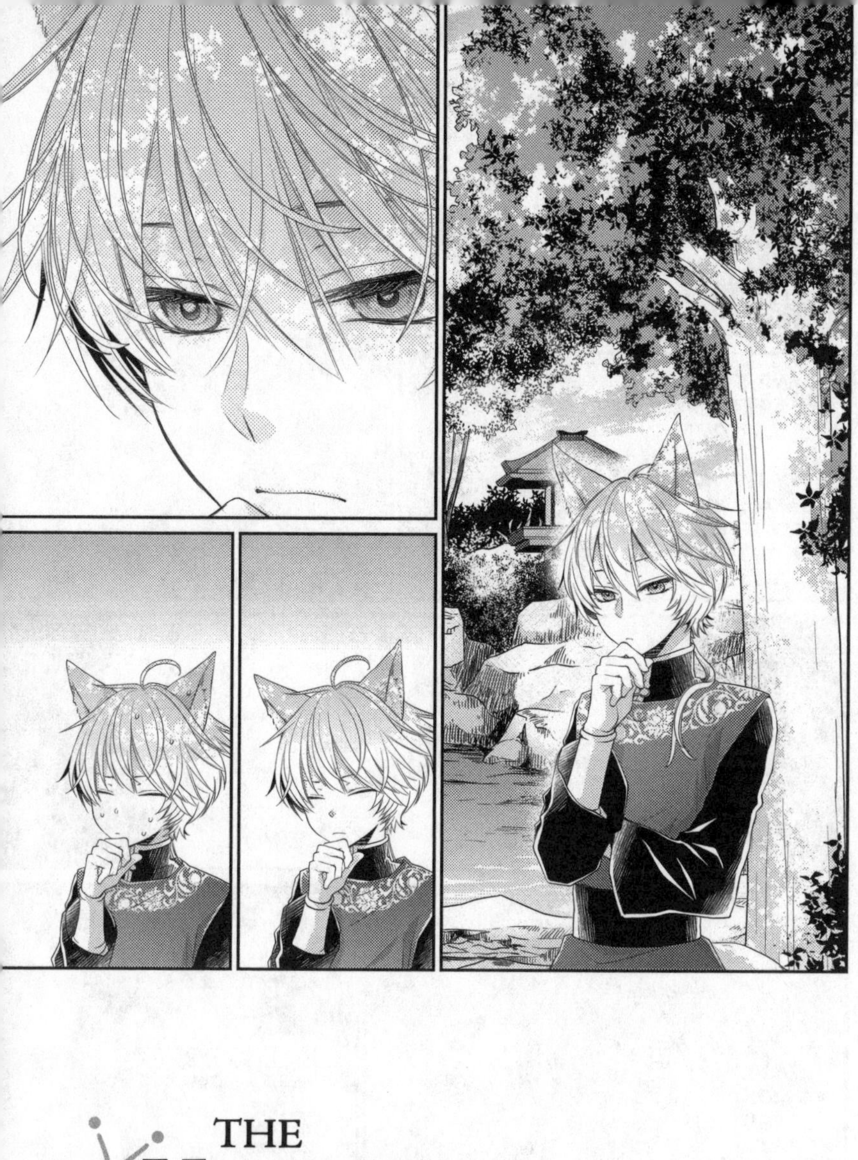

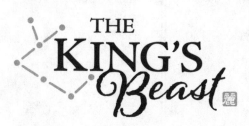

THE KING'S Beast

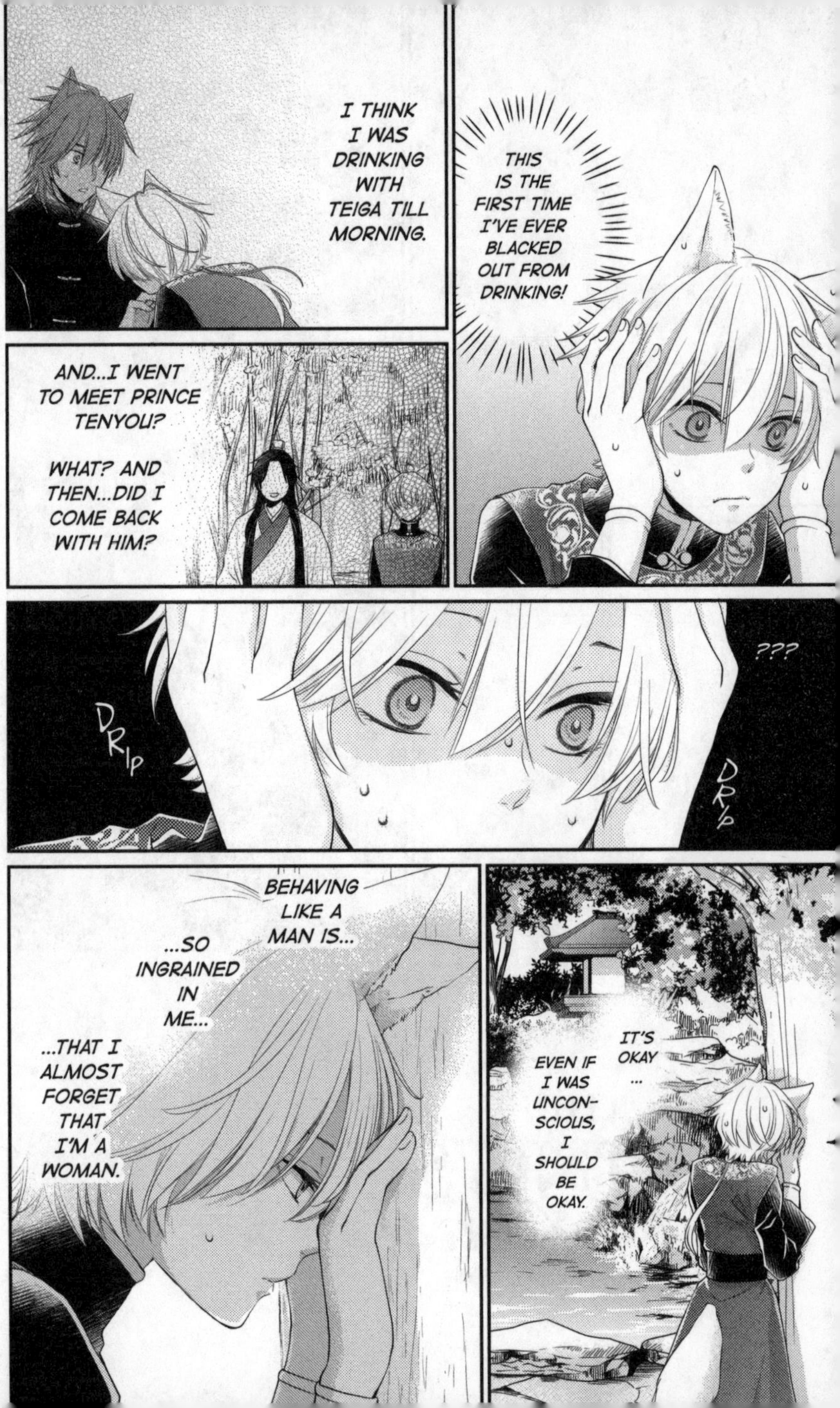
THIS IS THE FIRST TIME I'VE EVER BLACKED OUT FROM DRINKING!
I THINK I WAS DRINKING WITH TEIGA TILL MORNING.
AND...I WENT TO MEET PRINCE TENYOU?
WHAT? AND THEN...DID I COME BACK WITH HIM?
???
DRIP
DRIP
IT'S OKAY...
EVEN IF I WAS UNCON-SCIOUS, I SHOULD BE OKAY.
BEHAVING LIKE A MAN IS...
...SO INGRAINED IN ME...
...THAT I ALMOST FORGET THAT I'M A WOMAN.

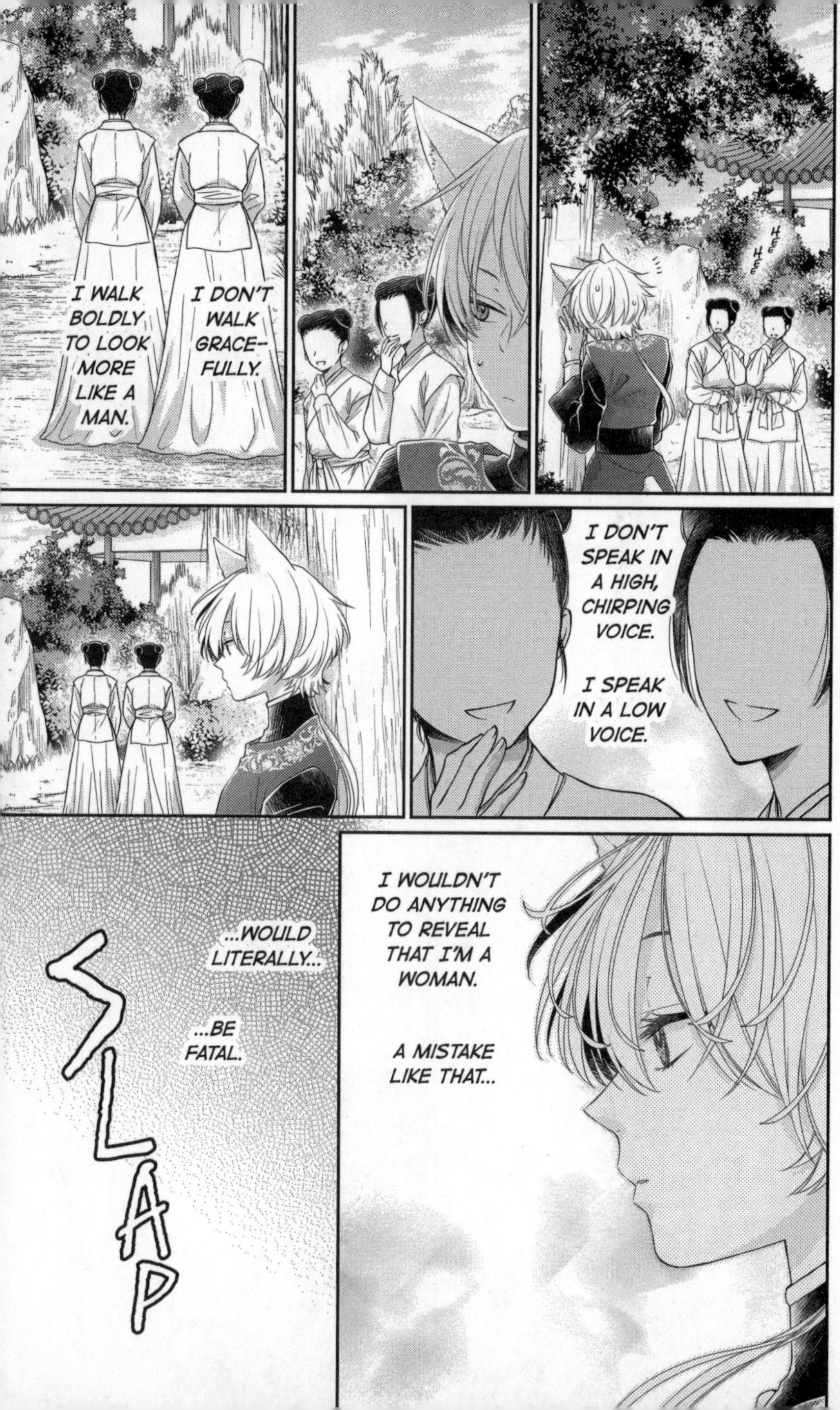
HEE HEE
I DON'T WALK GRACEFULLY.
I WALK BOLDLY TO LOOK MORE LIKE A MAN.
I DON'T SPEAK IN A HIGH, CHIRPING VOICE.
I SPEAK IN A LOW VOICE.
I WOULDN'T DO ANYTHING TO REVEAL THAT I'M A WOMAN.
A MISTAKE LIKE THAT...
...WOULD LITERALLY...
...BE FATAL.
SLAP

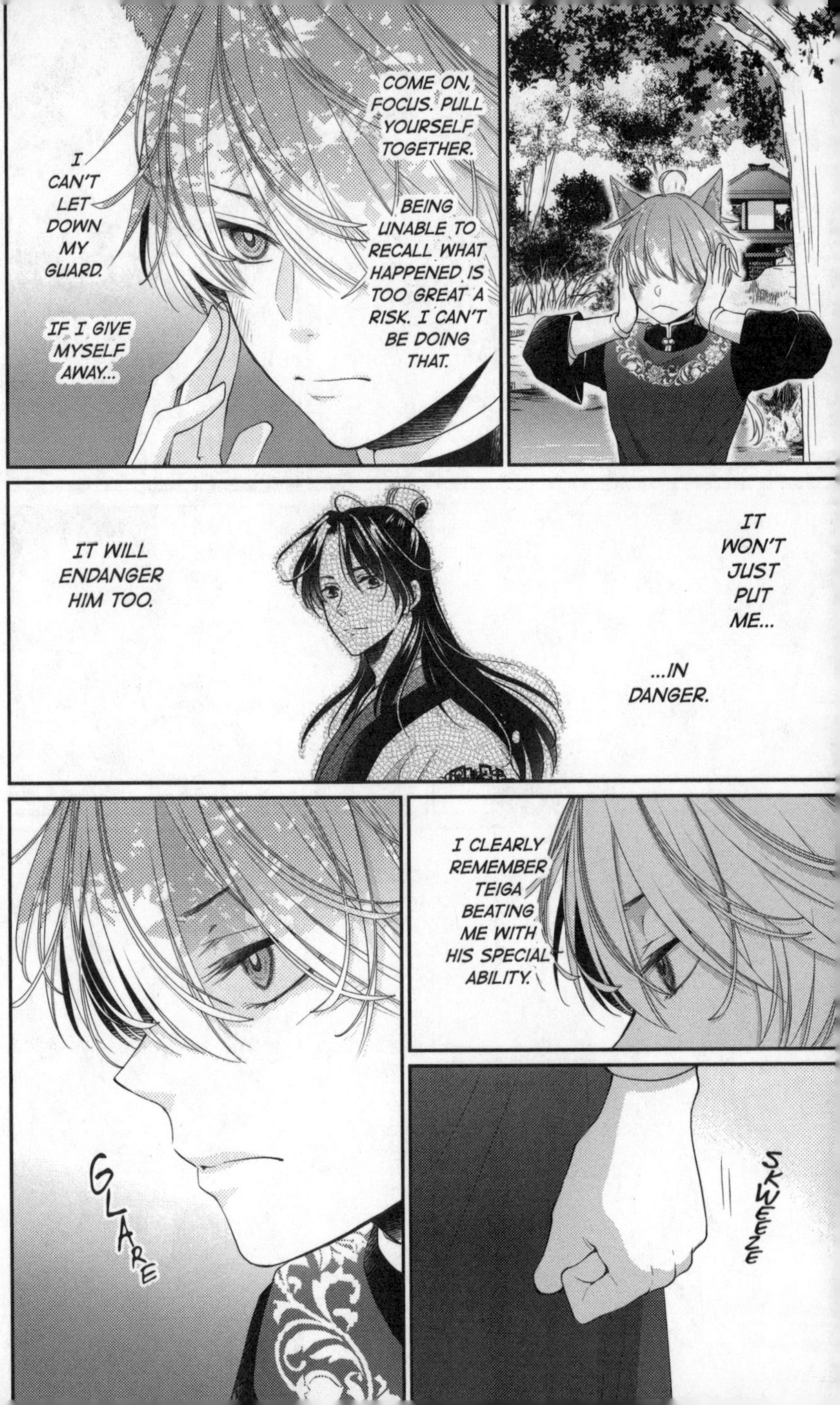
COME ON, FOCUS. PULL YOURSELF TOGETHER.
BEING UNABLE TO RECALL WHAT HAPPENED IS TOO GREAT A RISK. I CAN'T BE DOING THAT.
I CAN'T LET DOWN MY GUARD.
IF I GIVE MYSELF AWAY...
IT WON'T JUST PUT ME...
...IN DANGER.
IT WILL ENDANGER HIM TOO.
I CLEARLY REMEMBER TEIGA BEATING ME WITH HIS SPECIAL ABILITY.
SKWEEZE
GLARE

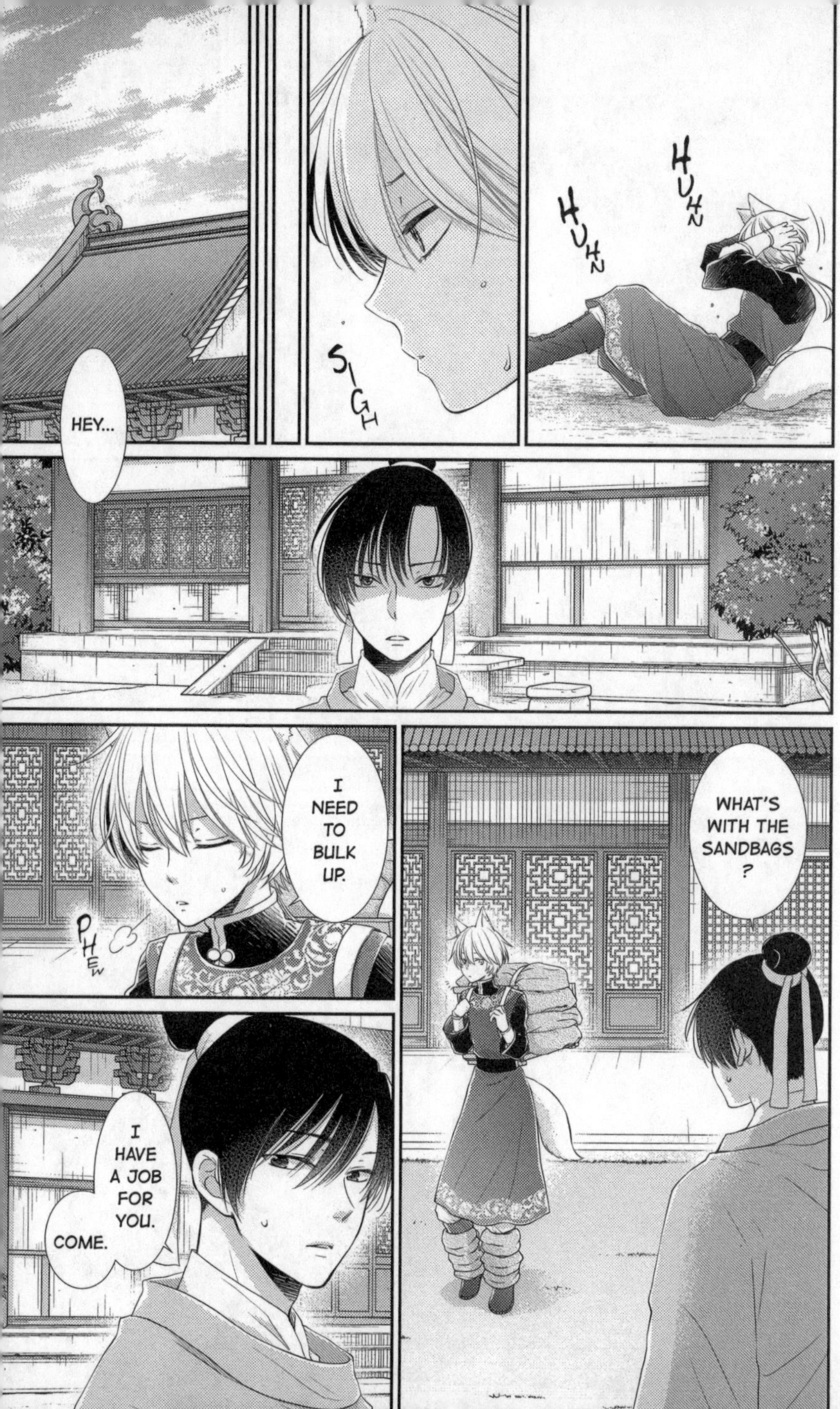
HUHN
HUHN
SIGH
HEY...
WHAT'S WITH THE SANDBAGS ?
I NEED TO BULK UP.
PHEW
I HAVE A JOB FOR YOU.
COME.

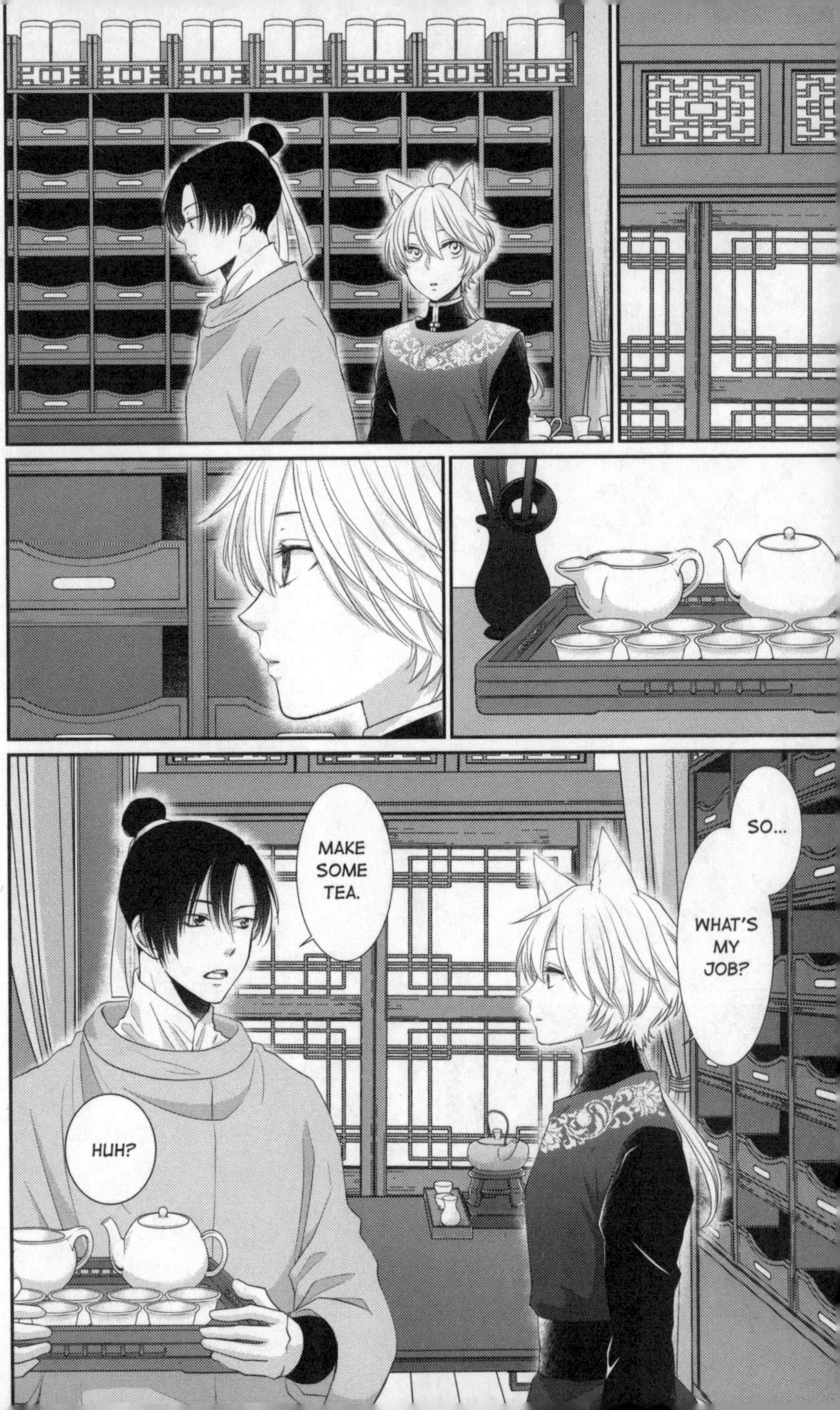
SO...
WHAT'S MY JOB?
MAKE SOME TEA.
HUH?

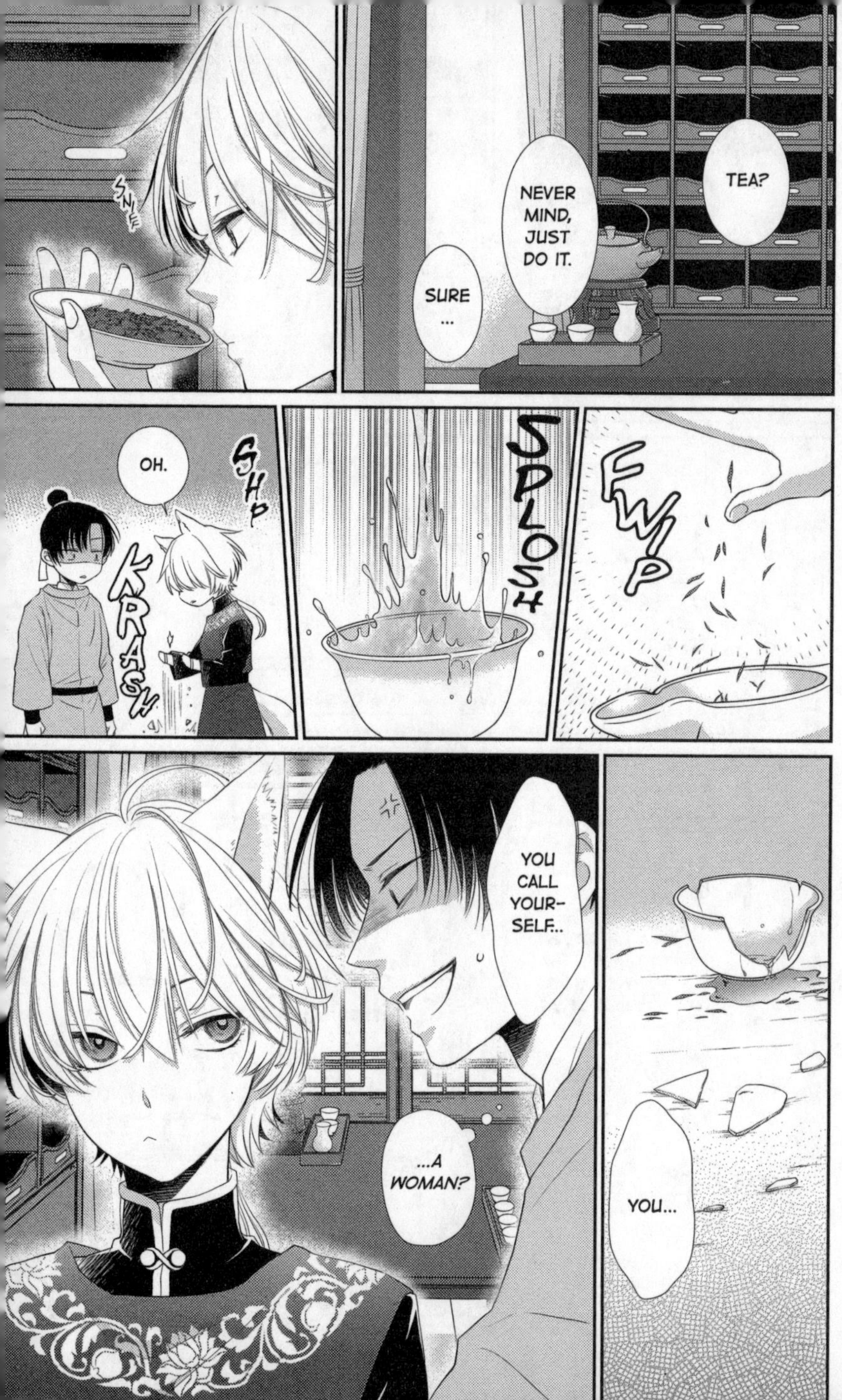
TEA?
NEVER MIND, JUST DO IT.
SURE ...
SNIF
FWIP
SPLOSH
OH.
SHP
KRASH
YOU...
YOU CALL YOUR-SELF...
...A WOMAN?

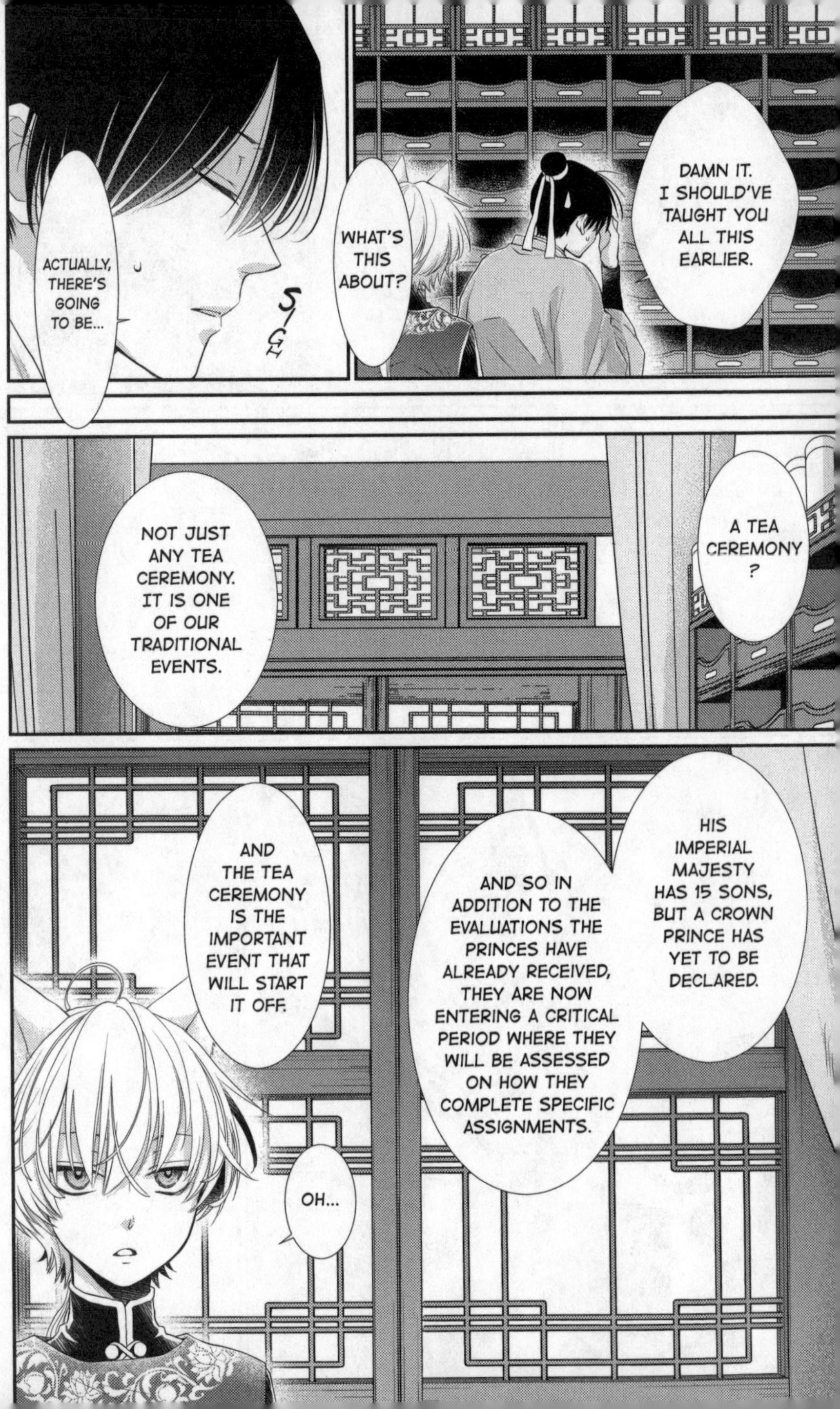
DAMN IT. I SHOULD'VE TAUGHT YOU ALL THIS EARLIER.
WHAT'S THIS ABOUT?
ACTUALLY, THERE'S GOING TO BE...
SIGH
A TEA CEREMONY?
NOT JUST ANY TEA CEREMONY. IT IS ONE OF OUR TRADITIONAL EVENTS.
HIS IMPERIAL MAJESTY HAS 15 SONS, BUT A CROWN PRINCE HAS YET TO BE DECLARED.
AND SO IN ADDITION TO THE EVALUATIONS THE PRINCES HAVE ALREADY RECEIVED, THEY ARE NOW ENTERING A CRITICAL PERIOD WHERE THEY WILL BE ASSESSED ON HOW THEY COMPLETE SPECIFIC ASSIGNMENTS.
AND THE TEA CEREMONY IS THE IMPORTANT EVENT THAT WILL START IT OFF.
OH...

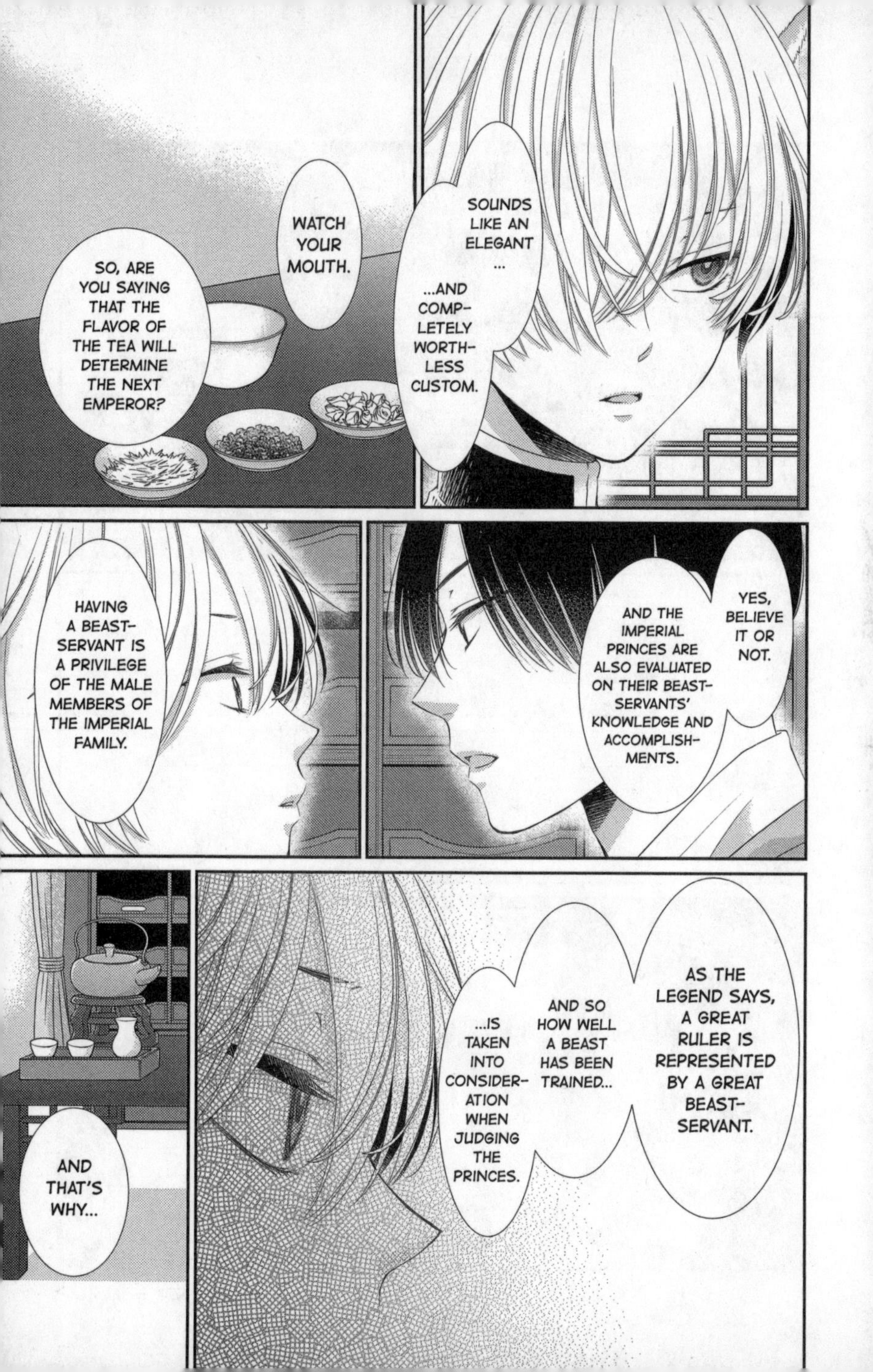
SOUNDS LIKE AN ELEGANT ...
...AND COMPLETELY WORTHLESS CUSTOM.
WATCH YOUR MOUTH.
SO, ARE YOU SAYING THAT THE FLAVOR OF THE TEA WILL DETERMINE THE NEXT EMPEROR?
YES, BELIEVE IT OR NOT.
AND THE IMPERIAL PRINCES ARE ALSO EVALUATED ON THEIR BEAST-SERVANTS' KNOWLEDGE AND ACCOMPLISH-MENTS.
HAVING A BEAST-SERVANT IS A PRIVILEGE OF THE MALE MEMBERS OF THE IMPERIAL FAMILY.
AS THE LEGEND SAYS, A GREAT RULER IS REPRESENTED BY A GREAT BEAST-SERVANT.
AND SO HOW WELL A BEAST HAS BEEN TRAINED...
...IS TAKEN INTO CONSIDER-ATION WHEN JUDGING THE PRINCES.
AND THAT'S WHY...

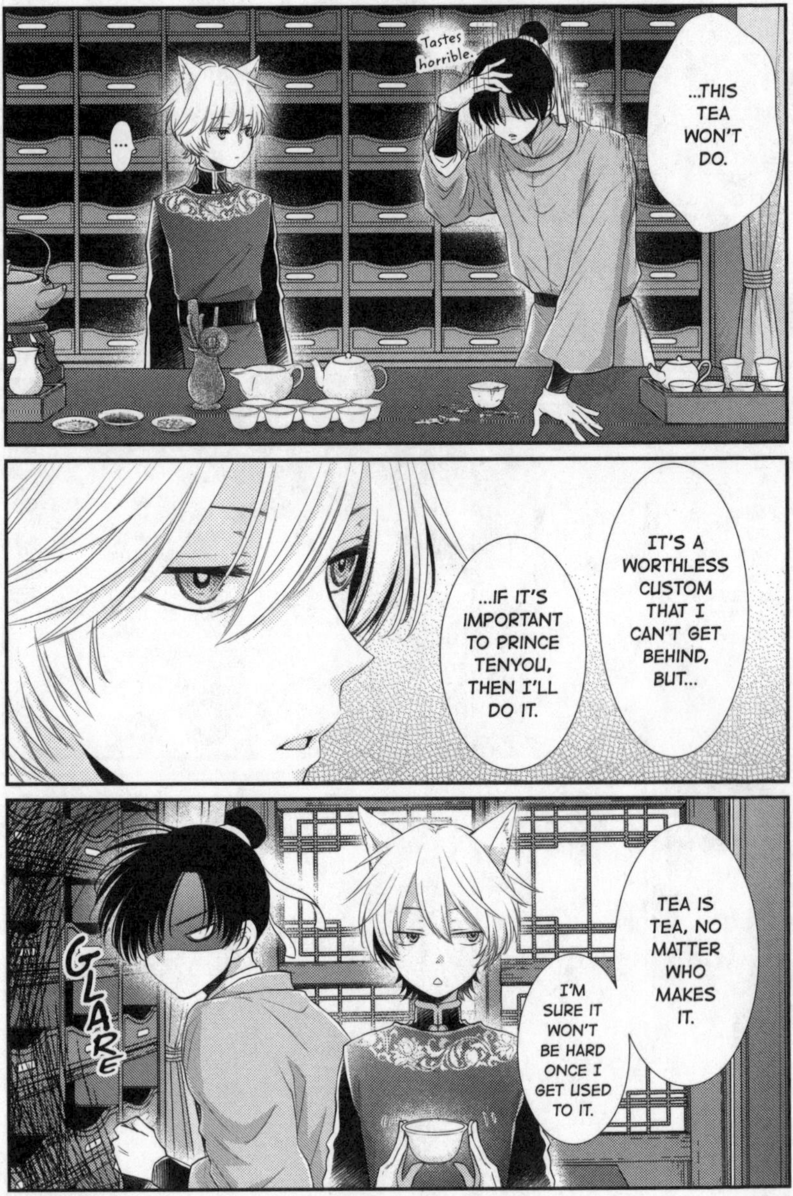
...THIS TEA WON'T DO.
Tastes horrible.
...
IT'S A WORTHLESS CUSTOM THAT I CAN'T GET BEHIND, BUT...
...IF IT'S IMPORTANT TO PRINCE TENYOU, THEN I'LL DO IT.
TEA IS TEA, NO MATTER WHO MAKES IT.
I'M SURE IT WON'T BE HARD ONCE I GET USED TO IT.
GLARE

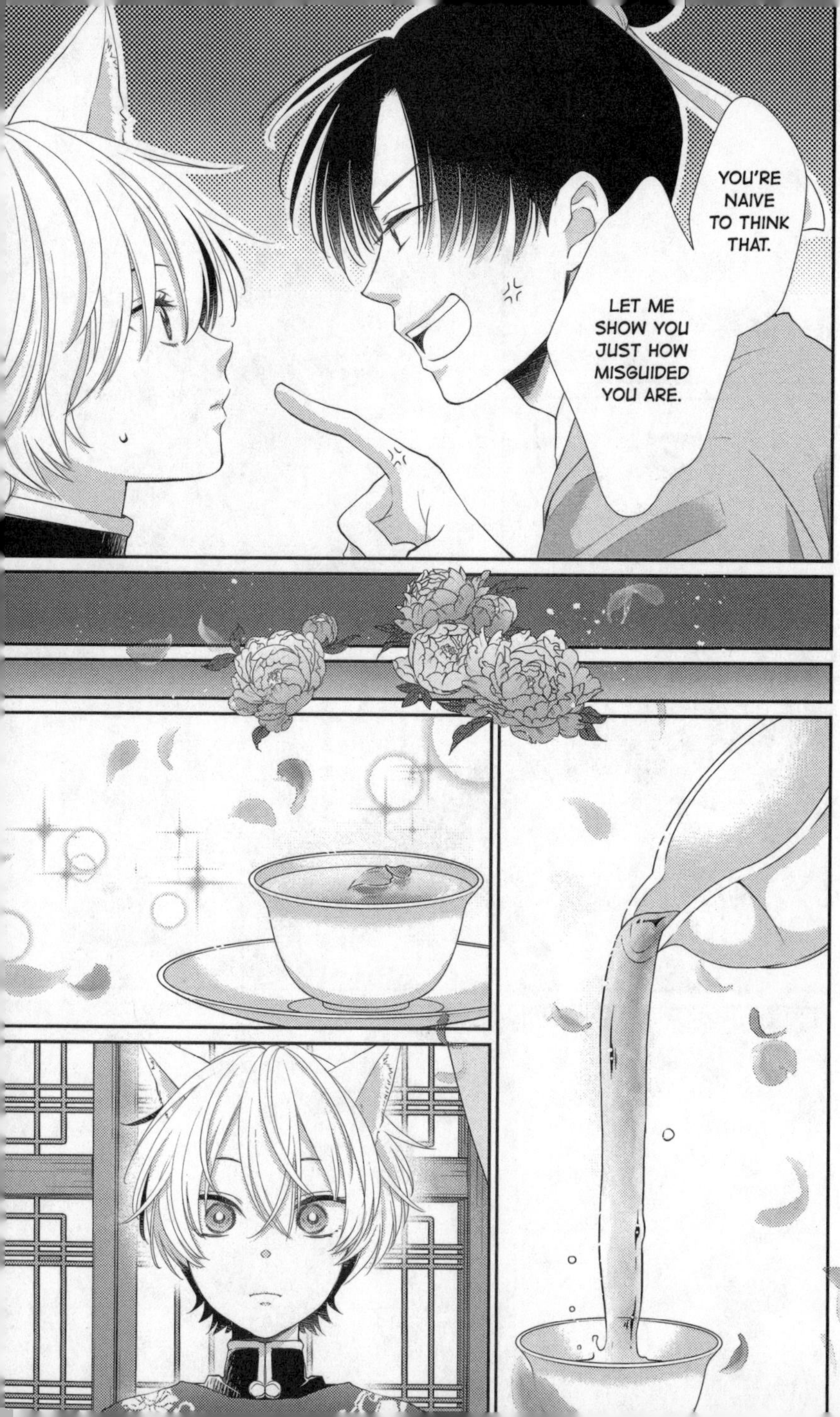
YOU'RE NAIVE TO THINK THAT.
LET ME SHOW YOU JUST HOW MISGUIDED YOU ARE.

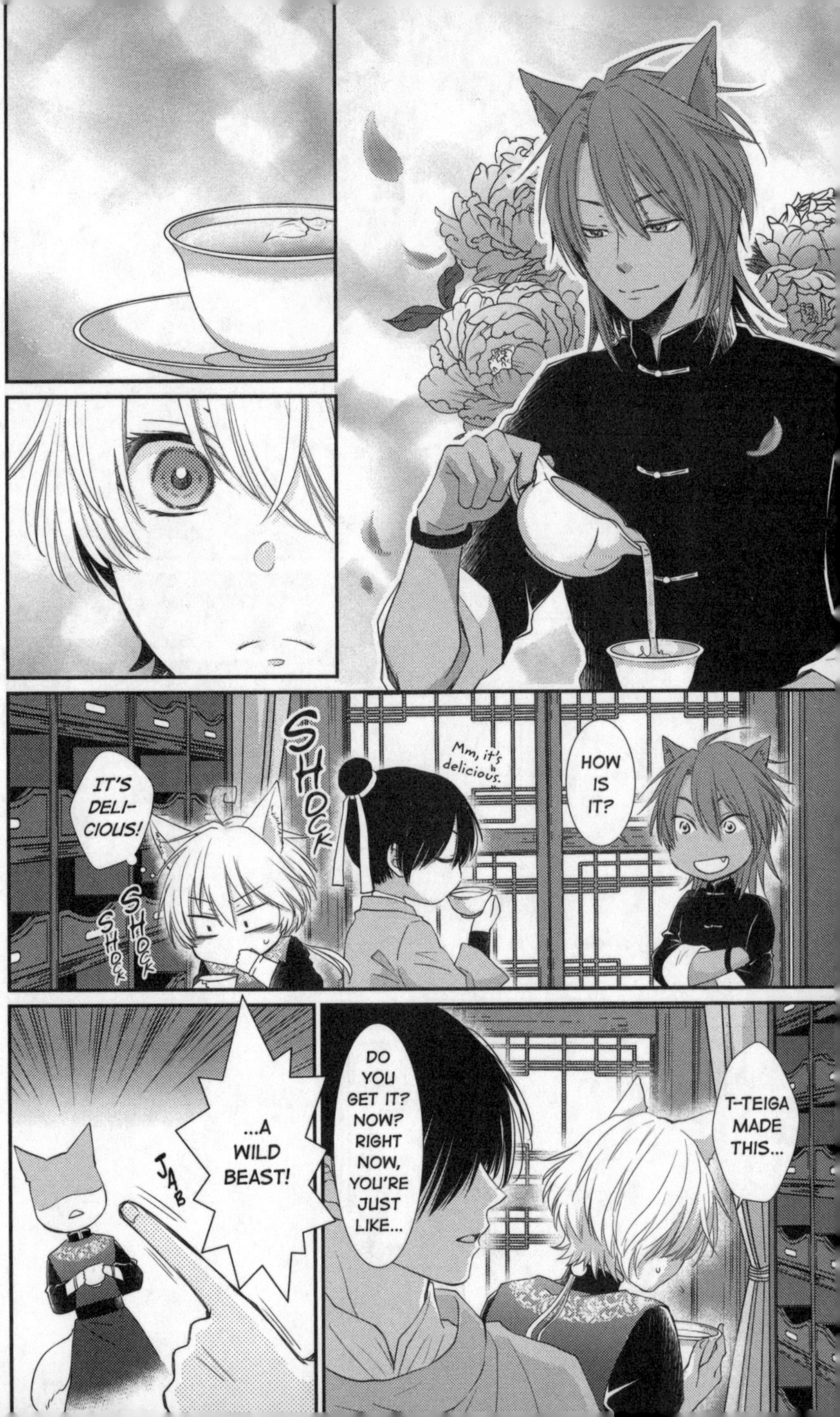
HOW IS IT?
Mm, it's delicious.
SHOCK
IT'S DELICIOUS!
SHOCK SHOCK
T-TEIGA MADE THIS...
DO YOU GET IT? NOW? RIGHT NOW, YOU'RE JUST LIKE...
...A WILD BEAST!
JAB

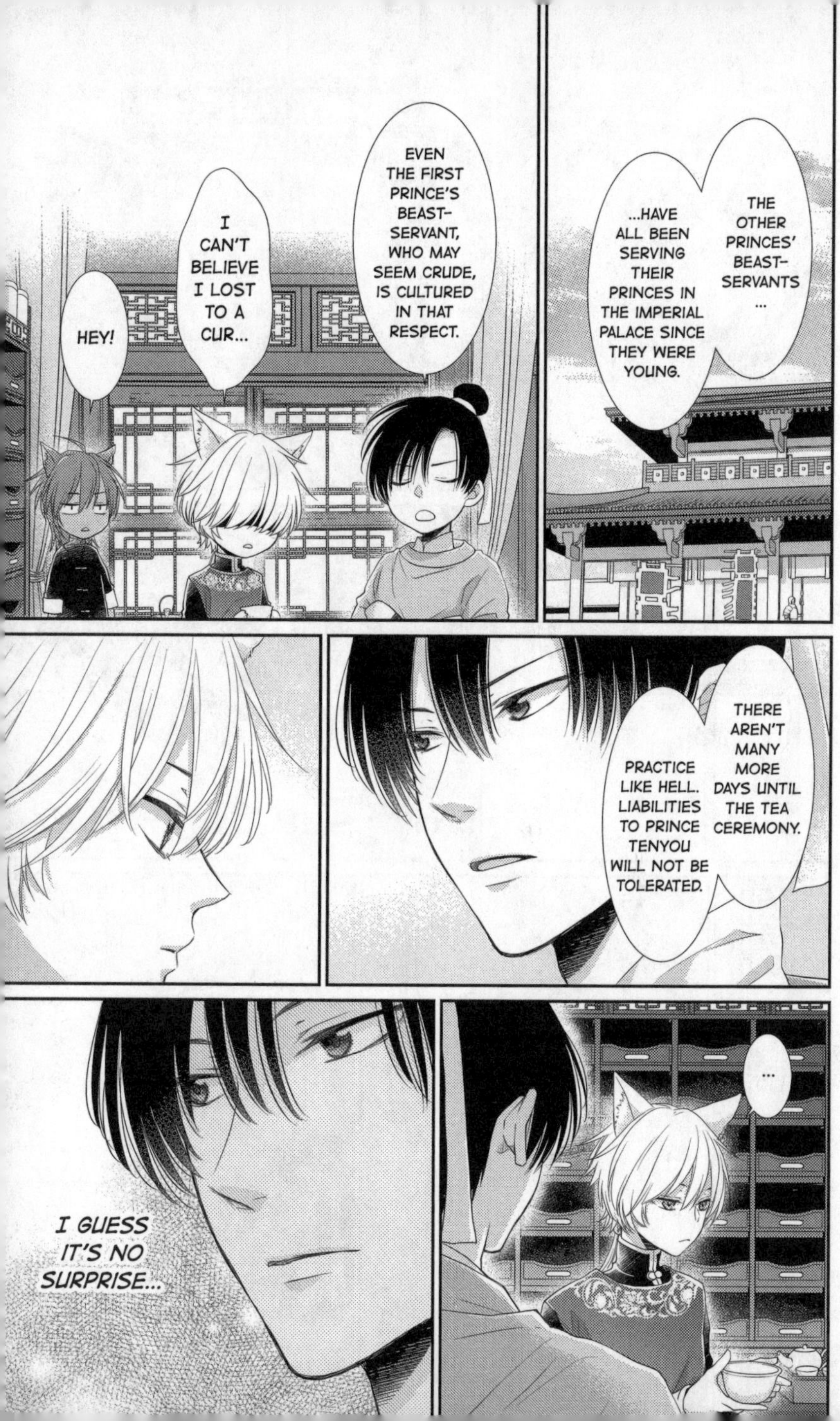
THE OTHER PRINCES' BEAST-SERVANTS...
...HAVE ALL BEEN SERVING THEIR PRINCES IN THE IMPERIAL PALACE SINCE THEY WERE YOUNG.
EVEN THE FIRST PRINCE'S BEAST-SERVANT, WHO MAY SEEM CRUDE, IS CULTURED IN THAT RESPECT.
I CAN'T BELIEVE I LOST TO A CUR...
HEY!
THERE AREN'T MANY MORE DAYS UNTIL THE TEA CEREMONY.
PRACTICE LIKE HELL. LIABILITIES TO PRINCE TENYOU WILL NOT BE TOLERATED.
...
I GUESS IT'S NO SURPRISE...

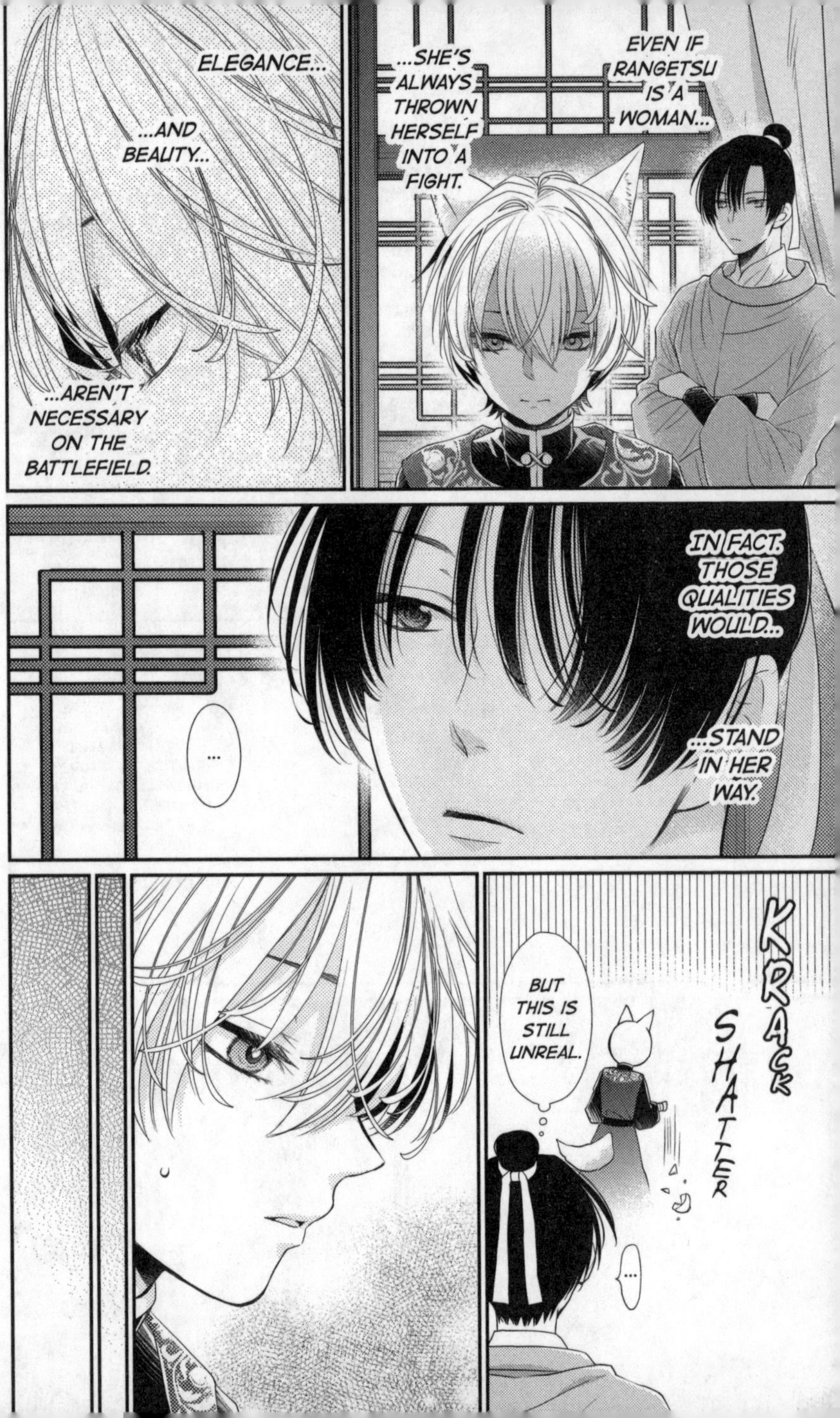
EVEN IF RANGETSU IS A WOMAN...
...SHE'S ALWAYS THROWN HERSELF INTO A FIGHT.
ELEGANCE...
...AND BEAUTY...
...AREN'T NECESSARY ON THE BATTLEFIELD.
IN FACT, THOSE QUALITIES WOULD...
...STAND IN HER WAY.
...
KRACK
SHATTER
BUT THIS IS STILL UNREAL.
...

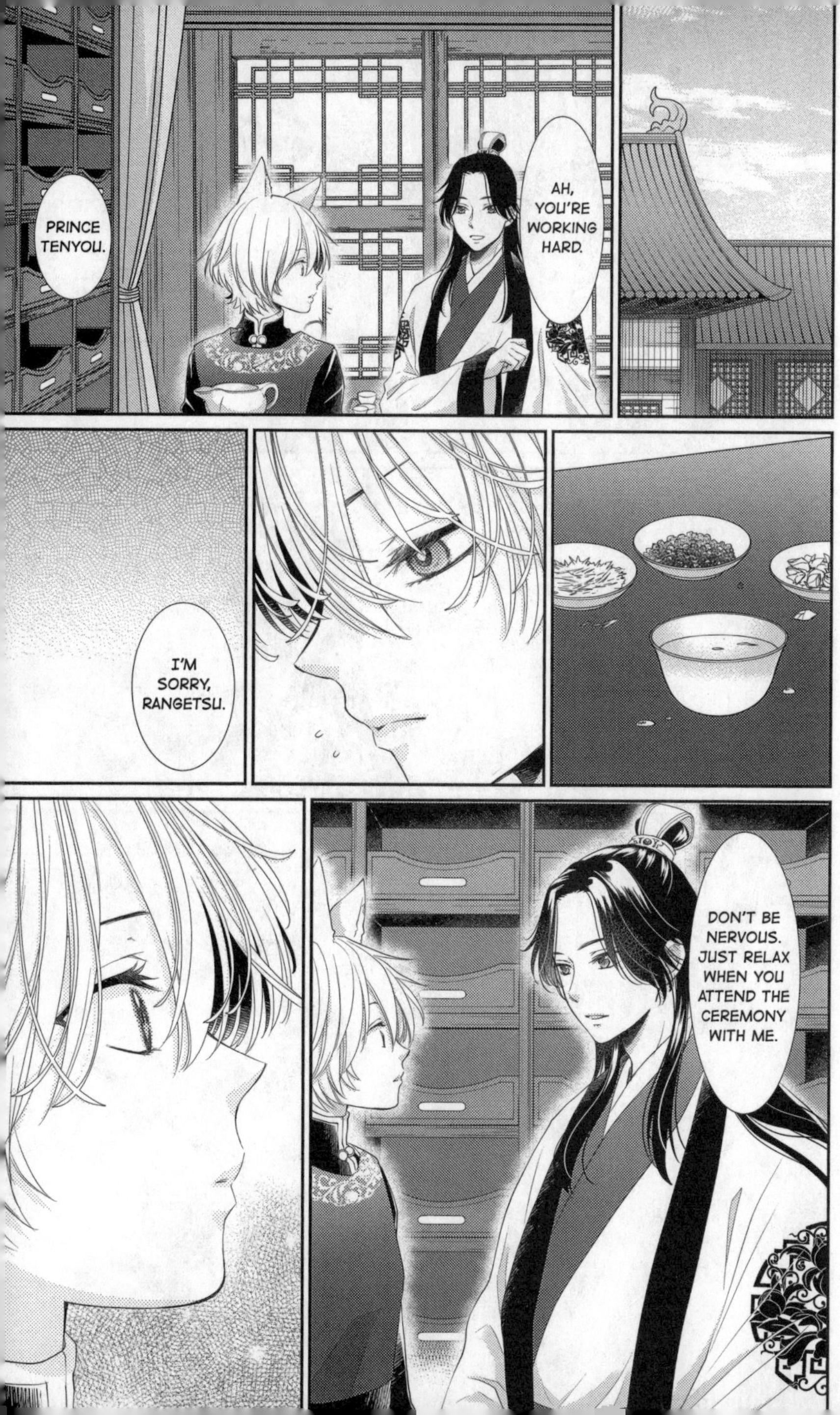
AH, YOU'RE WORKING HARD.
PRINCE TENYOU.
I'M SORRY, RANGETSU.
DON'T BE NERVOUS. JUST RELAX WHEN YOU ATTEND THE CEREMONY WITH ME.

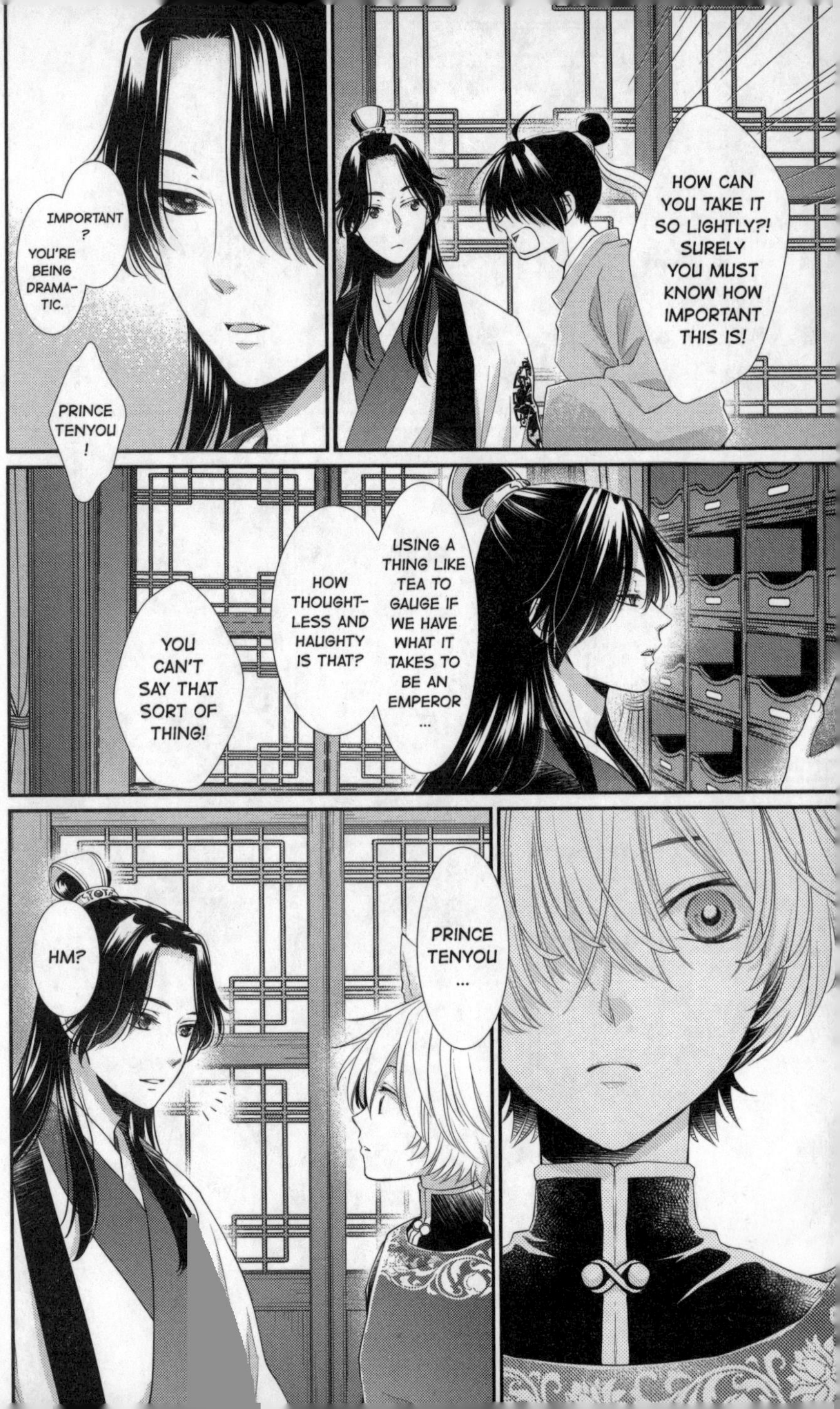
HOW CAN YOU TAKE IT SO LIGHTLY?! SURELY YOU MUST KNOW HOW IMPORTANT THIS IS!
IMPORTANT? YOU'RE BEING DRAMA-TIC.
PRINCE TENYOU!
USING A THING LIKE TEA TO GAUGE IF WE HAVE WHAT IT TAKES TO BE AN EMPEROR...
HOW THOUGHT-LESS AND HAUGHTY IS THAT?
YOU CAN'T SAY THAT SORT OF THING!
PRINCE TENYOU...
HM?

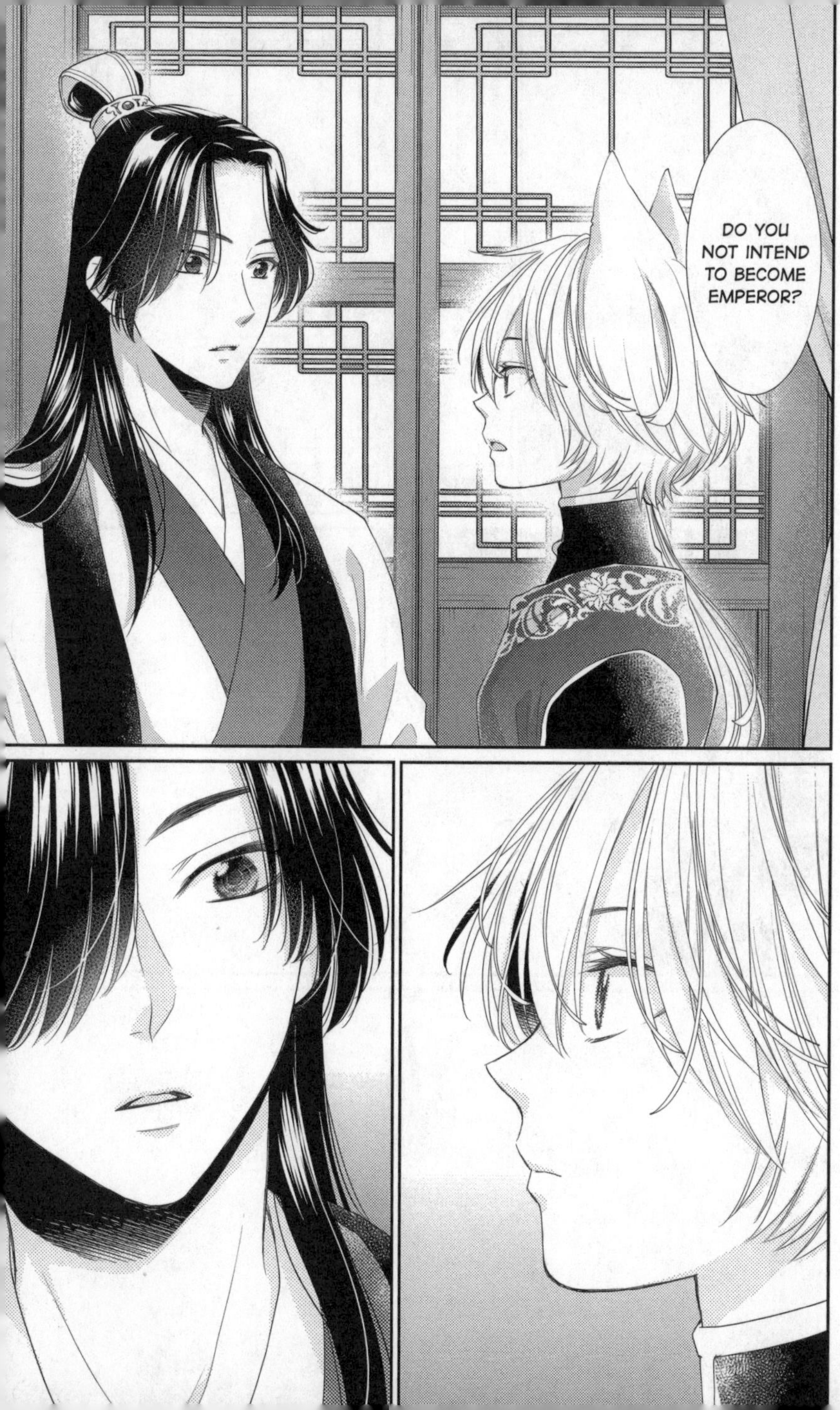
DO YOU NOT INTEND TO BECOME EMPEROR?

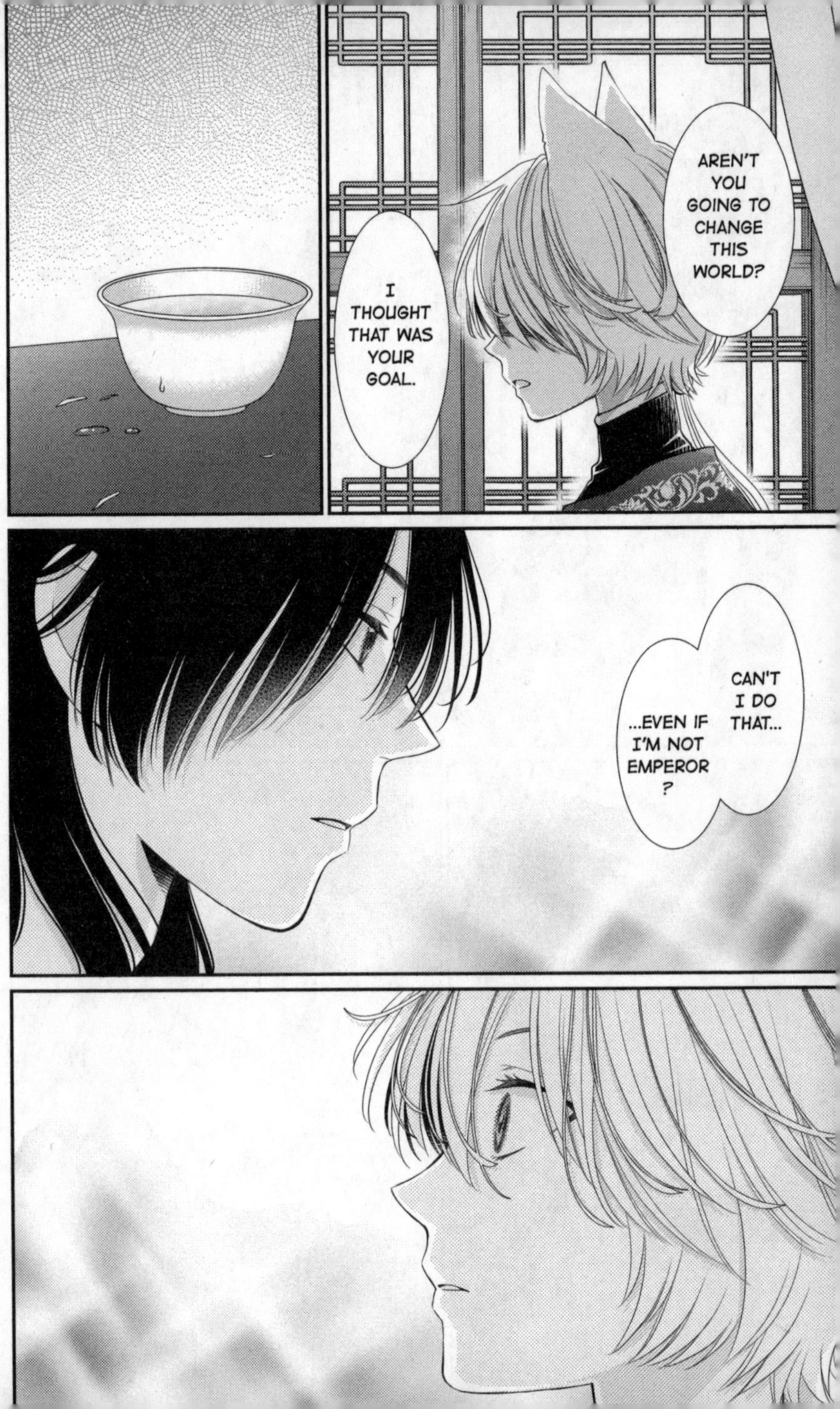
AREN'T YOU GOING TO CHANGE THIS WORLD?
I THOUGHT THAT WAS YOUR GOAL.
CAN'T I DO THAT...
...EVEN IF I'M NOT EMPEROR?

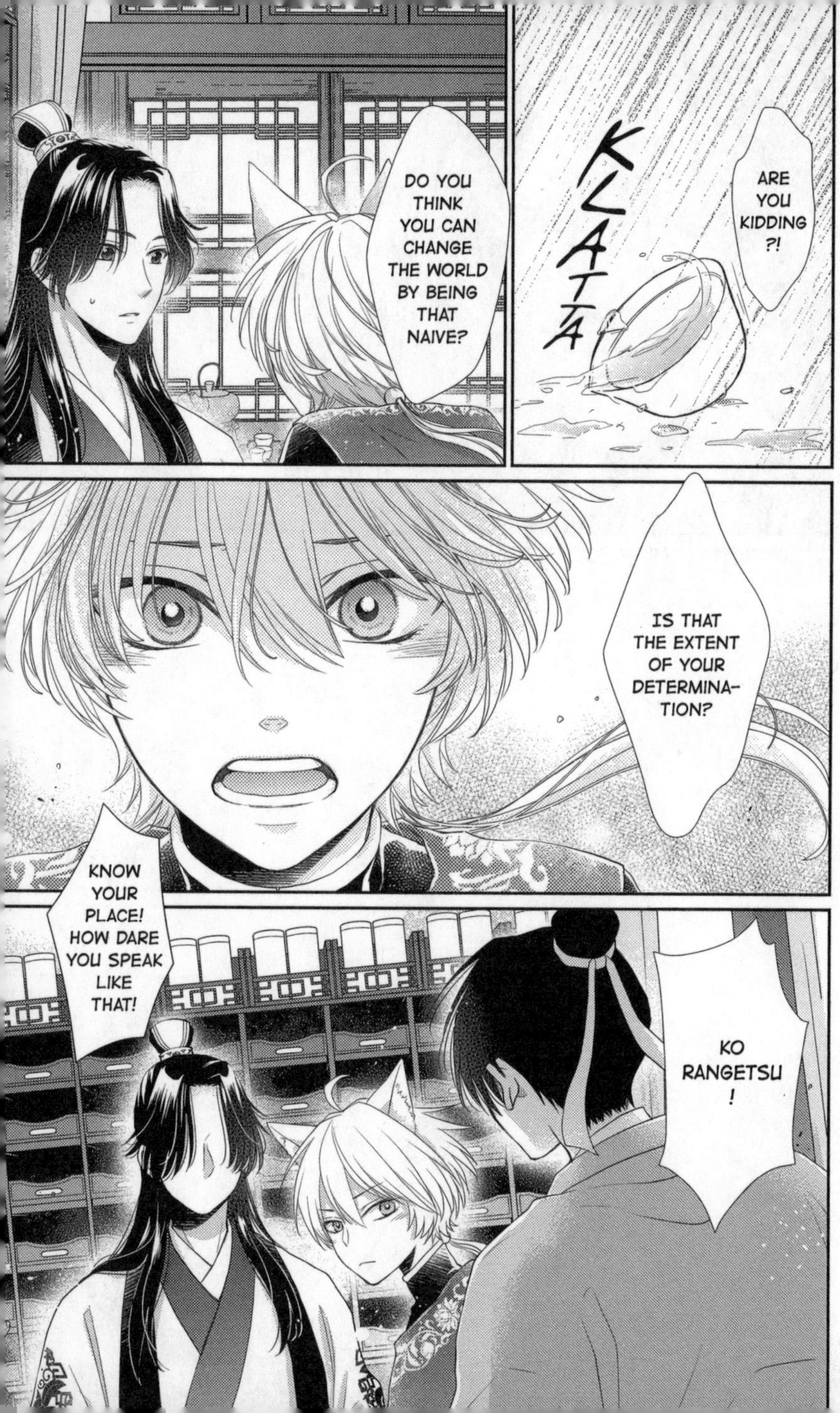
ARE YOU KIDDING?!
KLATTA
DO YOU THINK YOU CAN CHANGE THE WORLD BY BEING THAT NAIVE?
IS THAT THE EXTENT OF YOUR DETERMINATION?
KO RANGETSU!
KNOW YOUR PLACE! HOW DARE YOU SPEAK LIKE THAT!

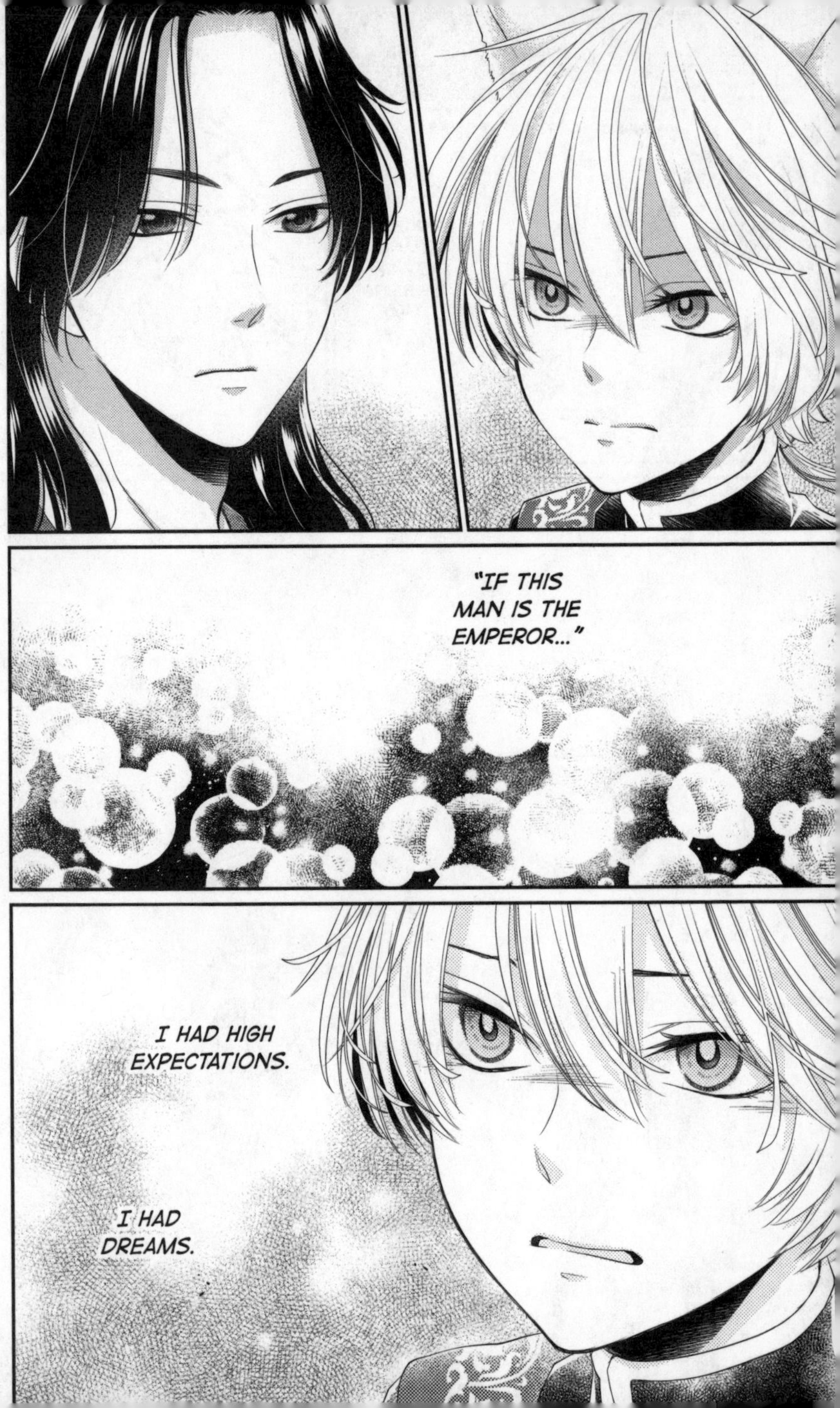
"IF THIS MAN IS THE EMPEROR..."
I HAD HIGH EXPECTATIONS.
I HAD DREAMS.

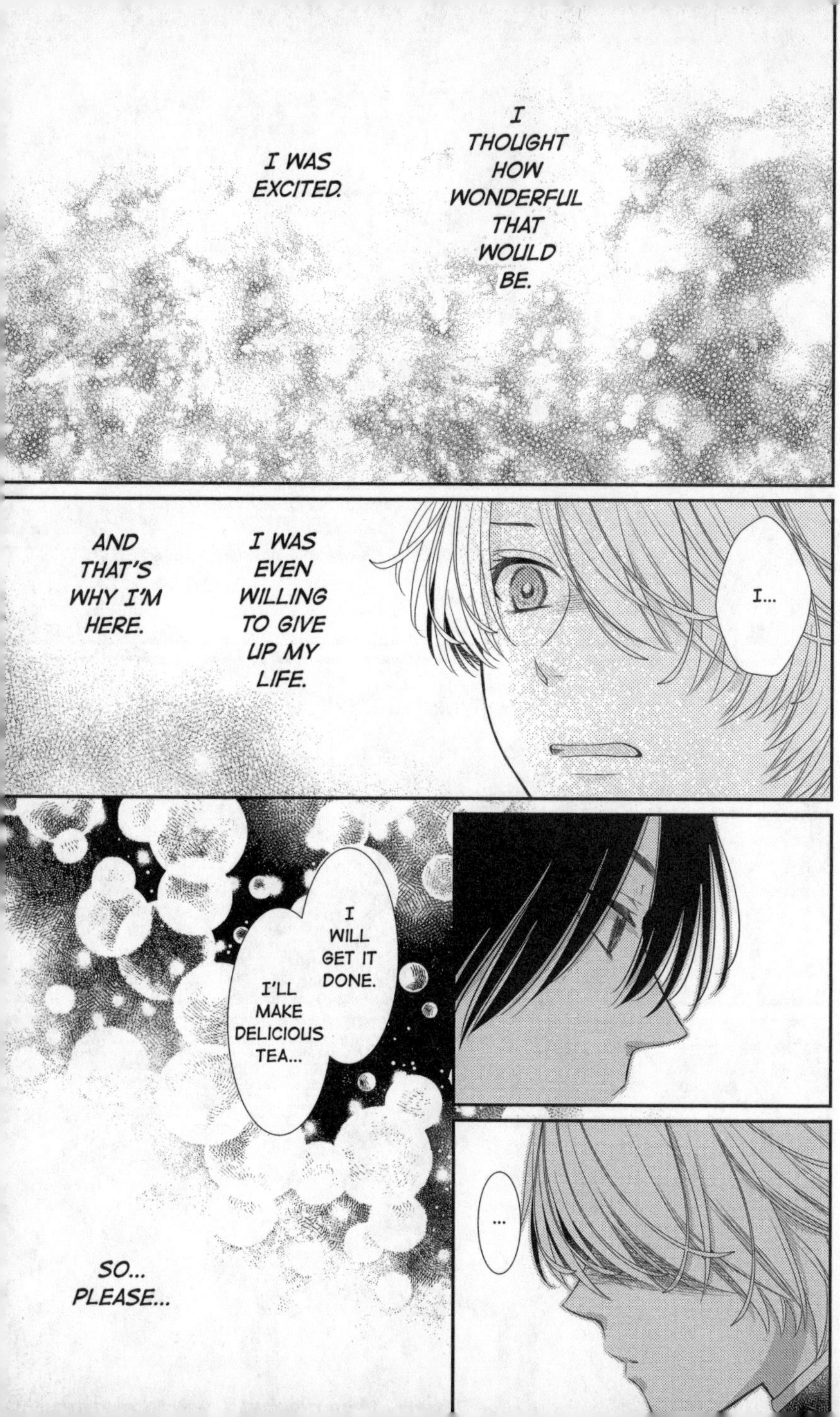
I THOUGHT HOW WONDERFUL THAT WOULD BE.
I WAS EXCITED.
I...
I WAS EVEN WILLING TO GIVE UP MY LIFE.
AND THAT'S WHY I'M HERE.
...
I WILL GET IT DONE.
I'LL MAKE DELICIOUS TEA...
SO... PLEASE...

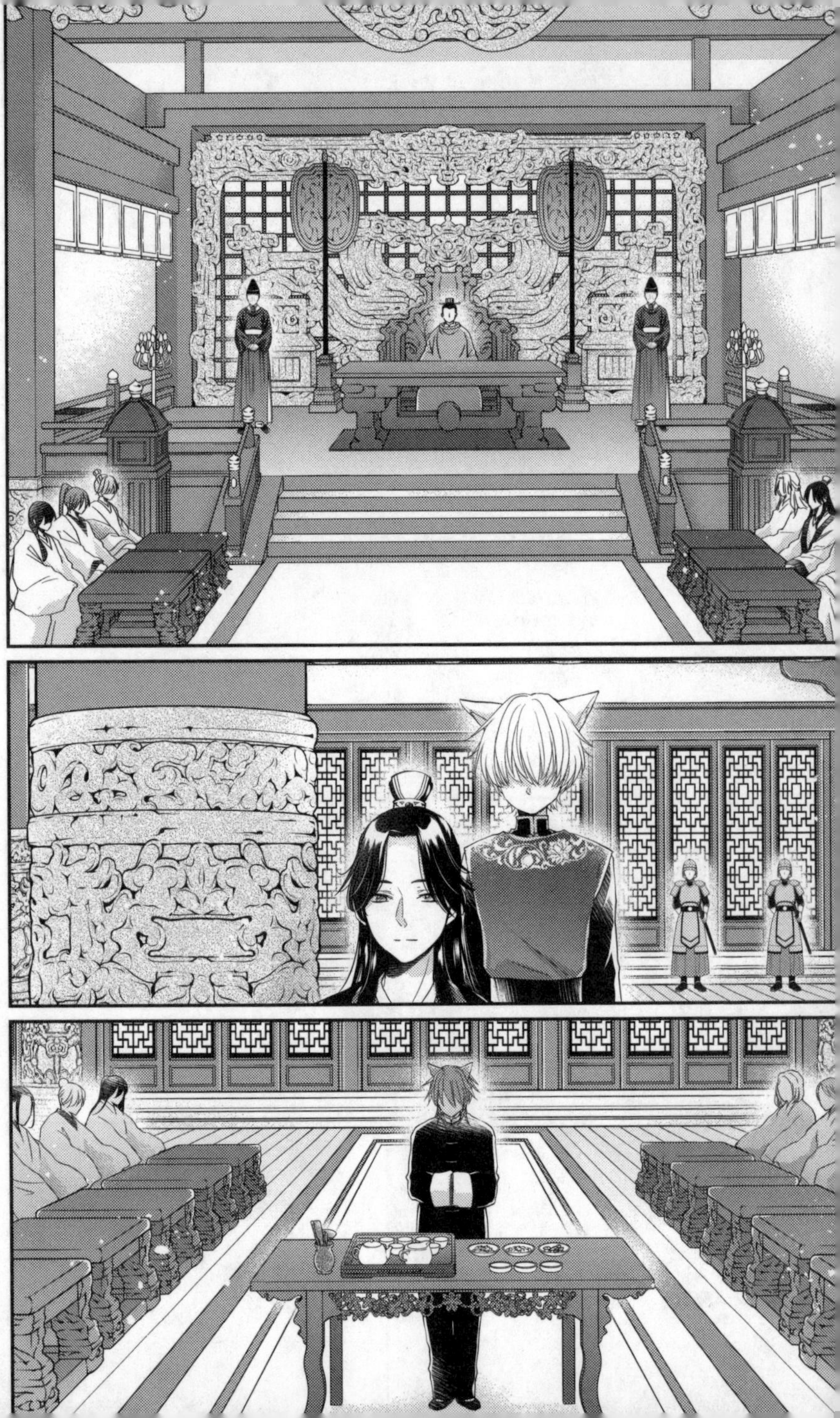

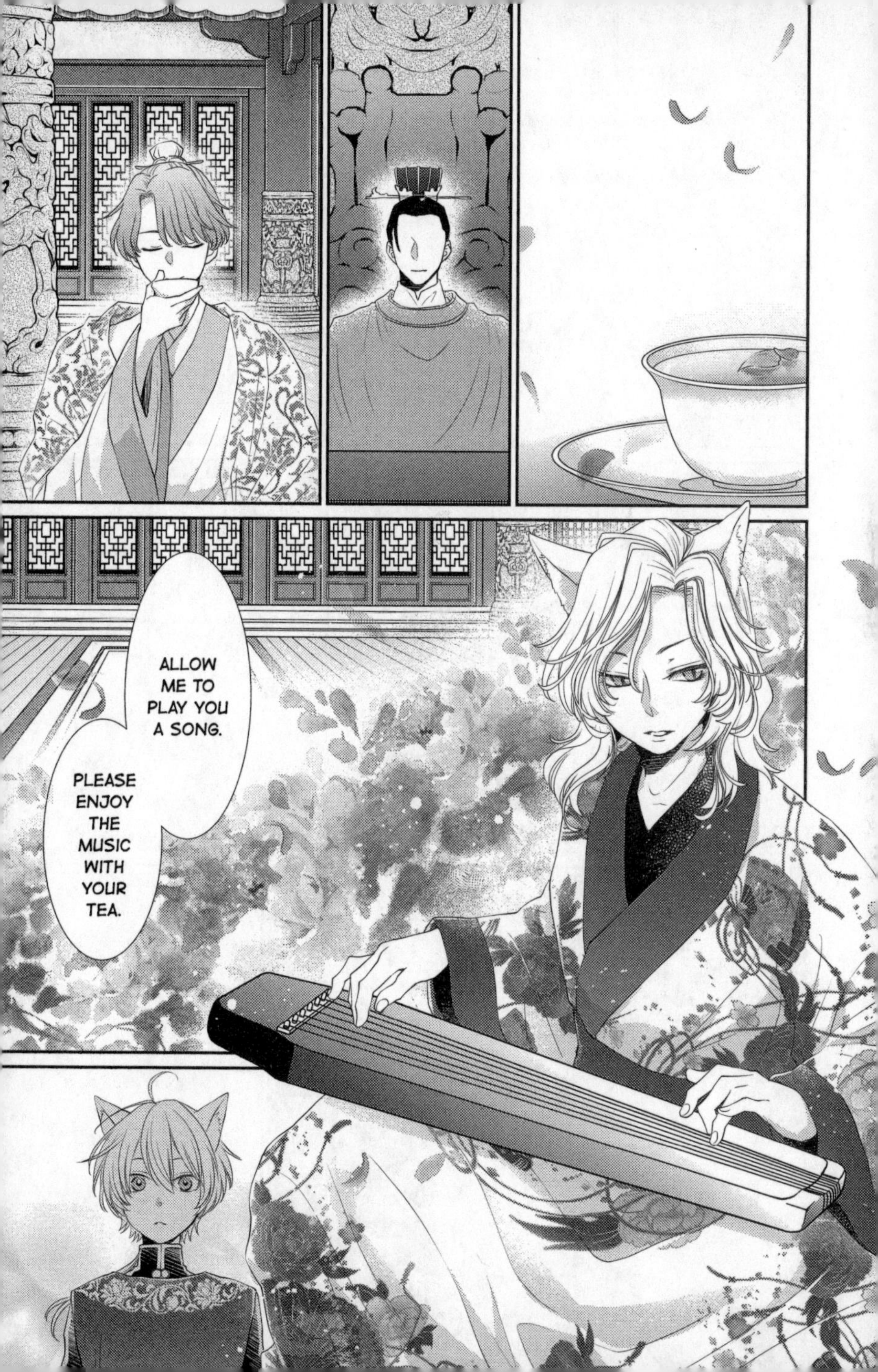
ALLOW ME TO PLAY YOU A SONG.
PLEASE ENJOY THE MUSIC WITH YOUR TEA.

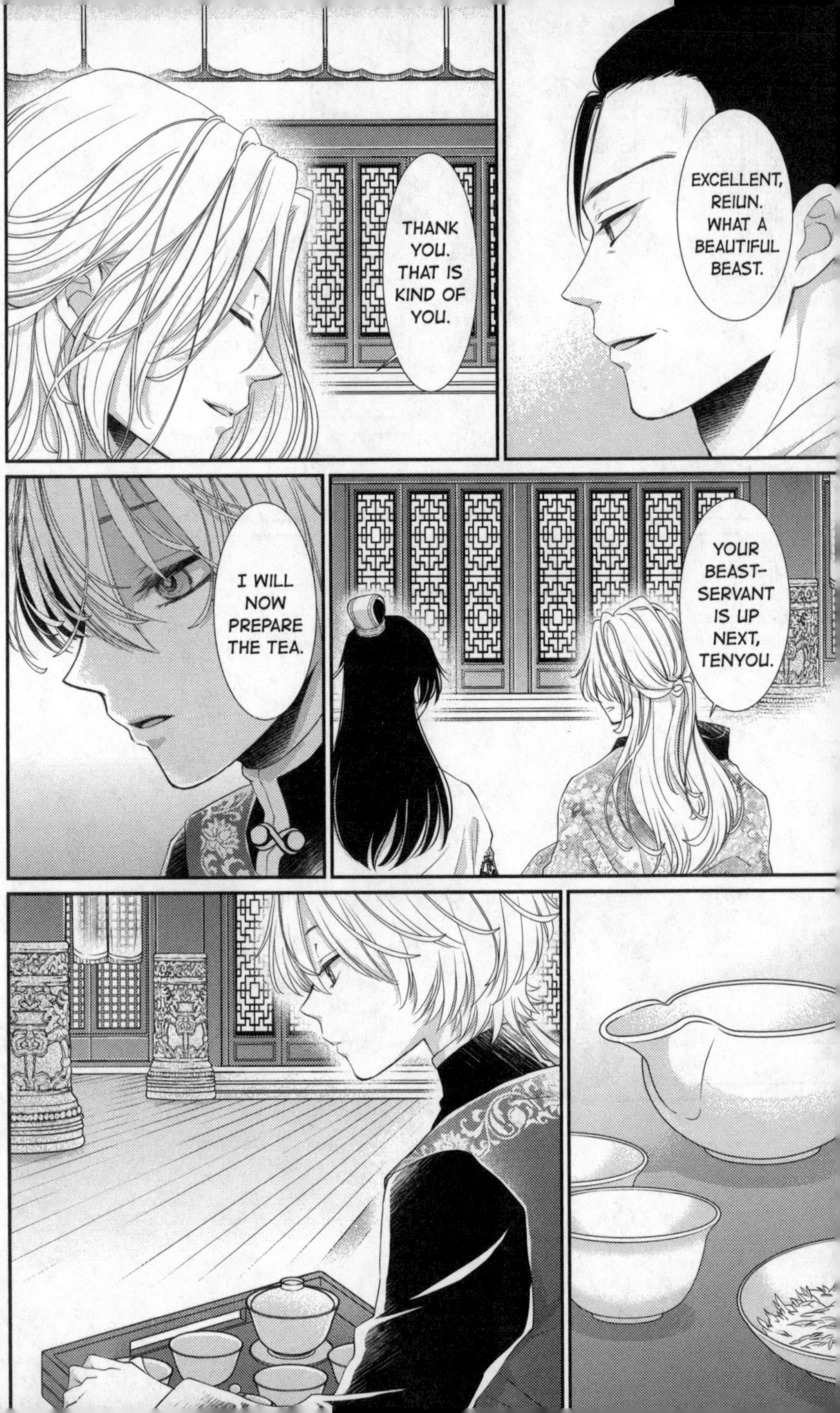
EXCELLENT, REIUN. WHAT A BEAUTIFUL BEAST.
THANK YOU. THAT IS KIND OF YOU.
YOUR BEAST-SERVANT IS UP NEXT, TENYOU.
I WILL NOW PREPARE THE TEA.

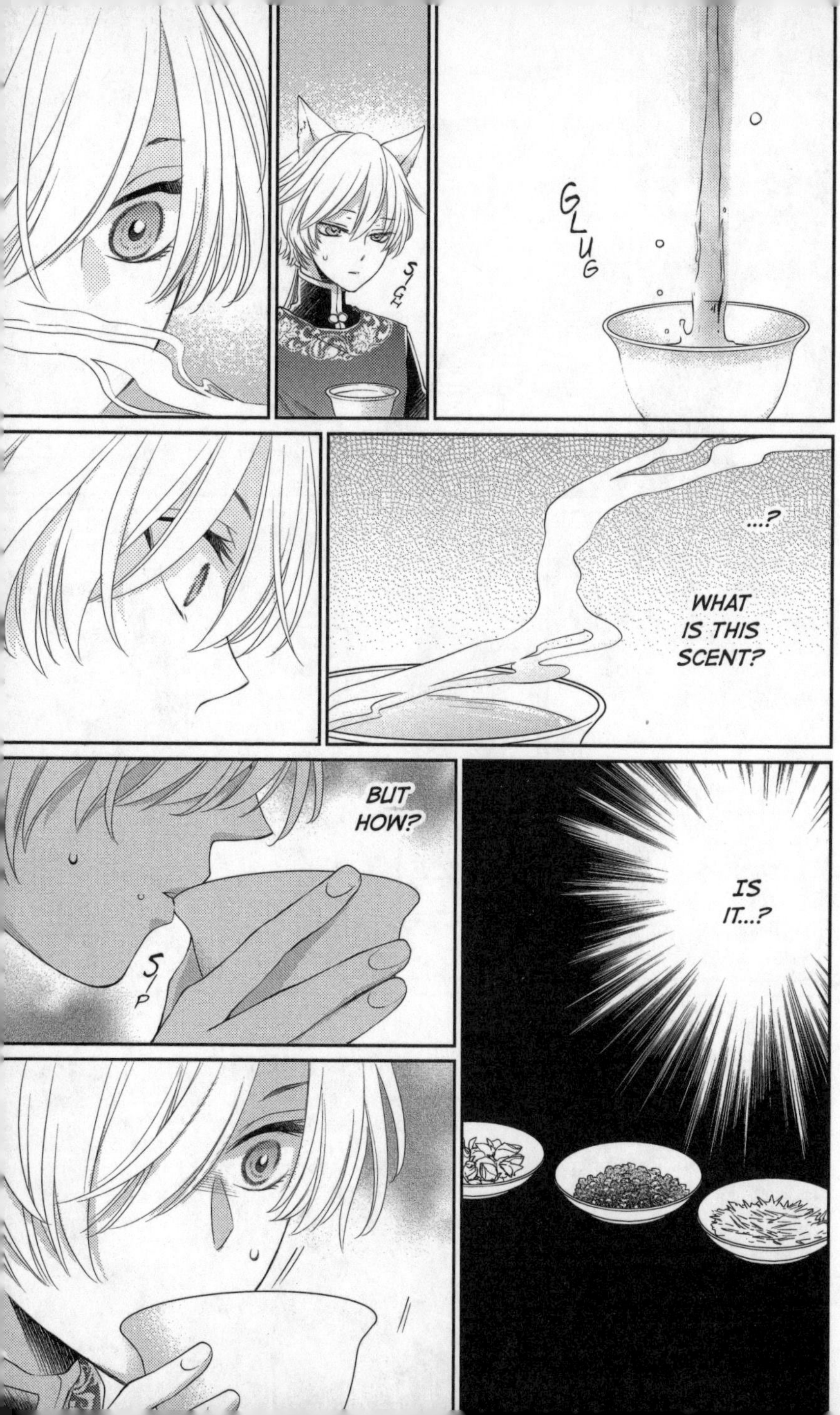
GLUG
SIGH
...?
WHAT IS THIS SCENT?
IS IT...?
BUT HOW?
SIP

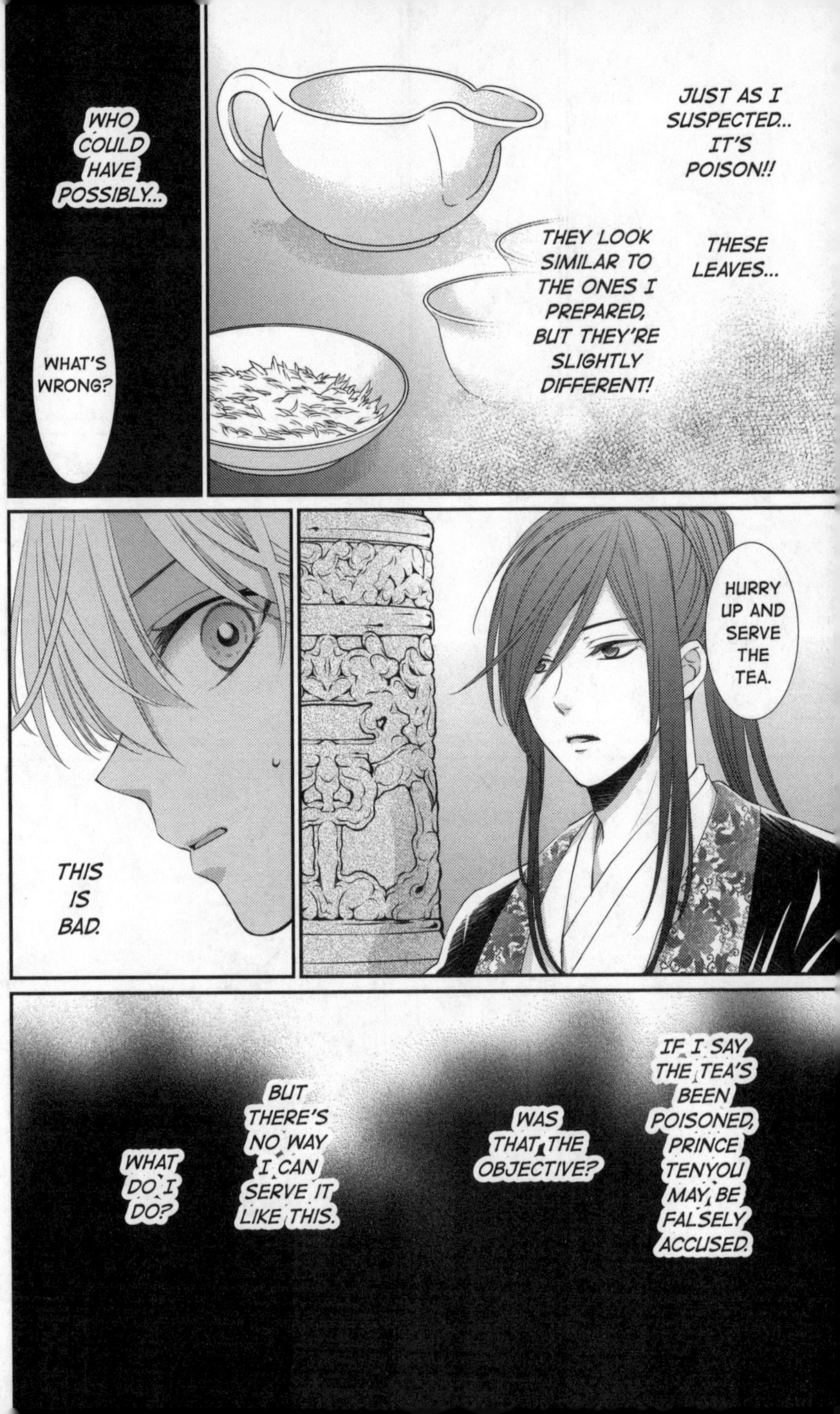
JUST AS I SUSPECTED... IT'S POISON!!
THESE LEAVES...
THEY LOOK SIMILAR TO THE ONES I PREPARED, BUT THEY'RE SLIGHTLY DIFFERENT!
WHO COULD HAVE POSSIBLY...
WHAT'S WRONG?
HURRY UP AND SERVE THE TEA.
THIS IS BAD.
IF I SAY THE TEA'S BEEN POISONED, PRINCE TENYOU MAY BE FALSELY ACCUSED.
WAS THAT THE OBJECTIVE?
BUT THERE'S NO WAY I CAN SERVE IT LIKE THIS.
WHAT DO I DO?

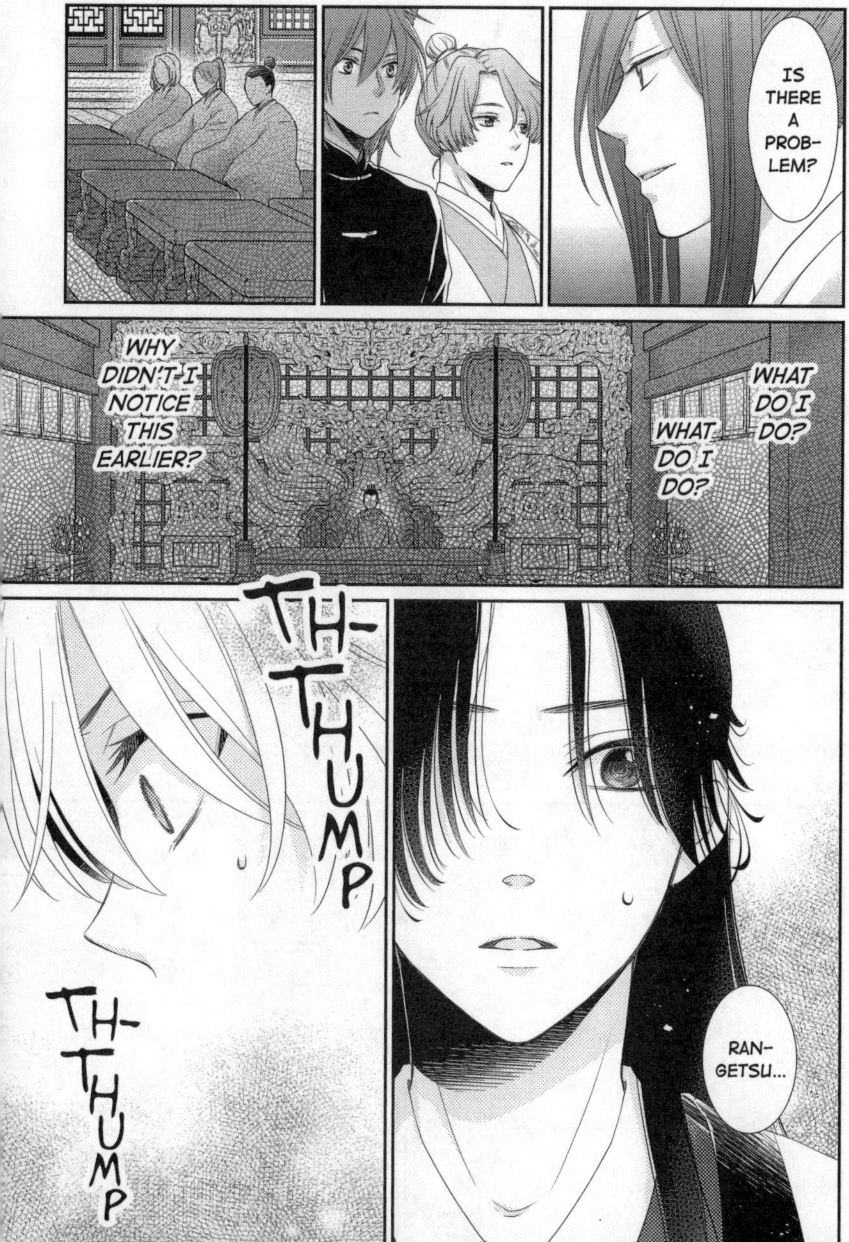
IS THERE A PROB-LEM?
WHAT DO I DO?
WHAT DO I DO?
WHY DIDN'T I NOTICE THIS EARLIER?
TH-THUMP
RAN-GETSU...
TH-THUMP

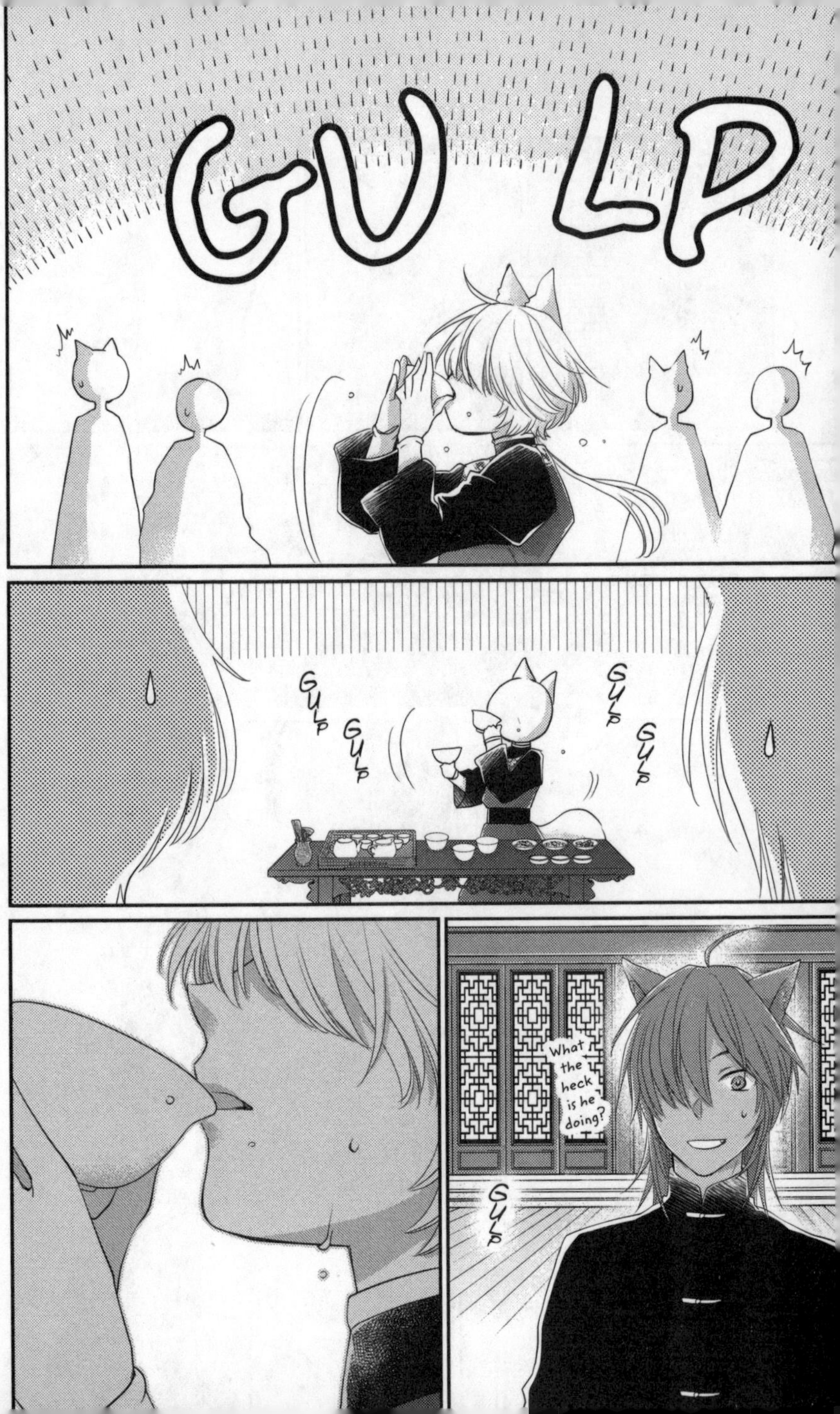
GULP
GULP
GULP
GULP
GULP
What the heck is he doing?
GULP

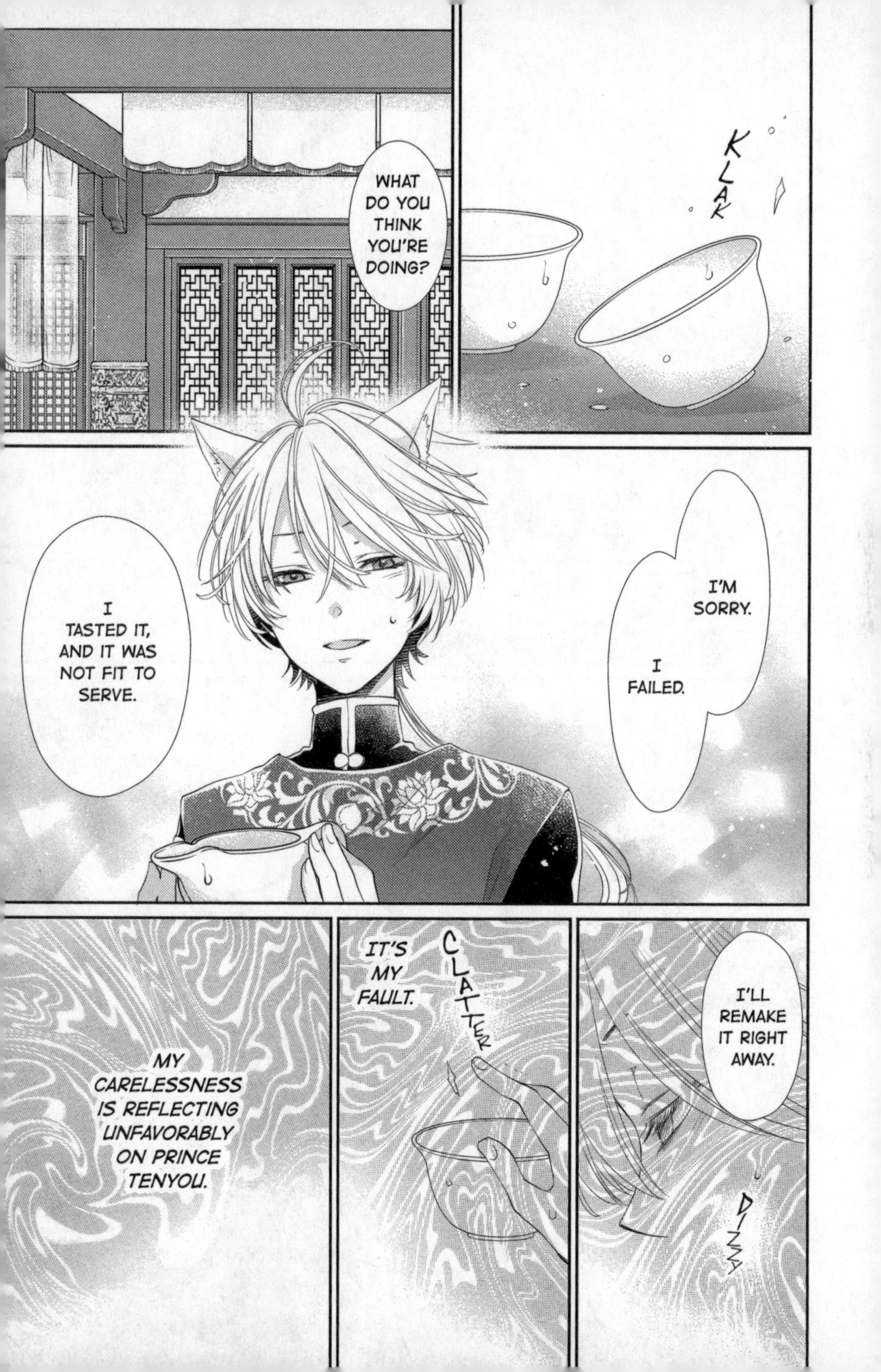
KLAK
WHAT DO YOU THINK YOU'RE DOING?
I'M SORRY.
I FAILED.
I TASTED IT, AND IT WAS NOT FIT TO SERVE.
I'LL REMAKE IT RIGHT AWAY.
DIZZY
CLATTER
IT'S MY FAULT.
MY CARELESSNESS IS REFLECTING UNFAVORABLY ON PRINCE TENYOU.

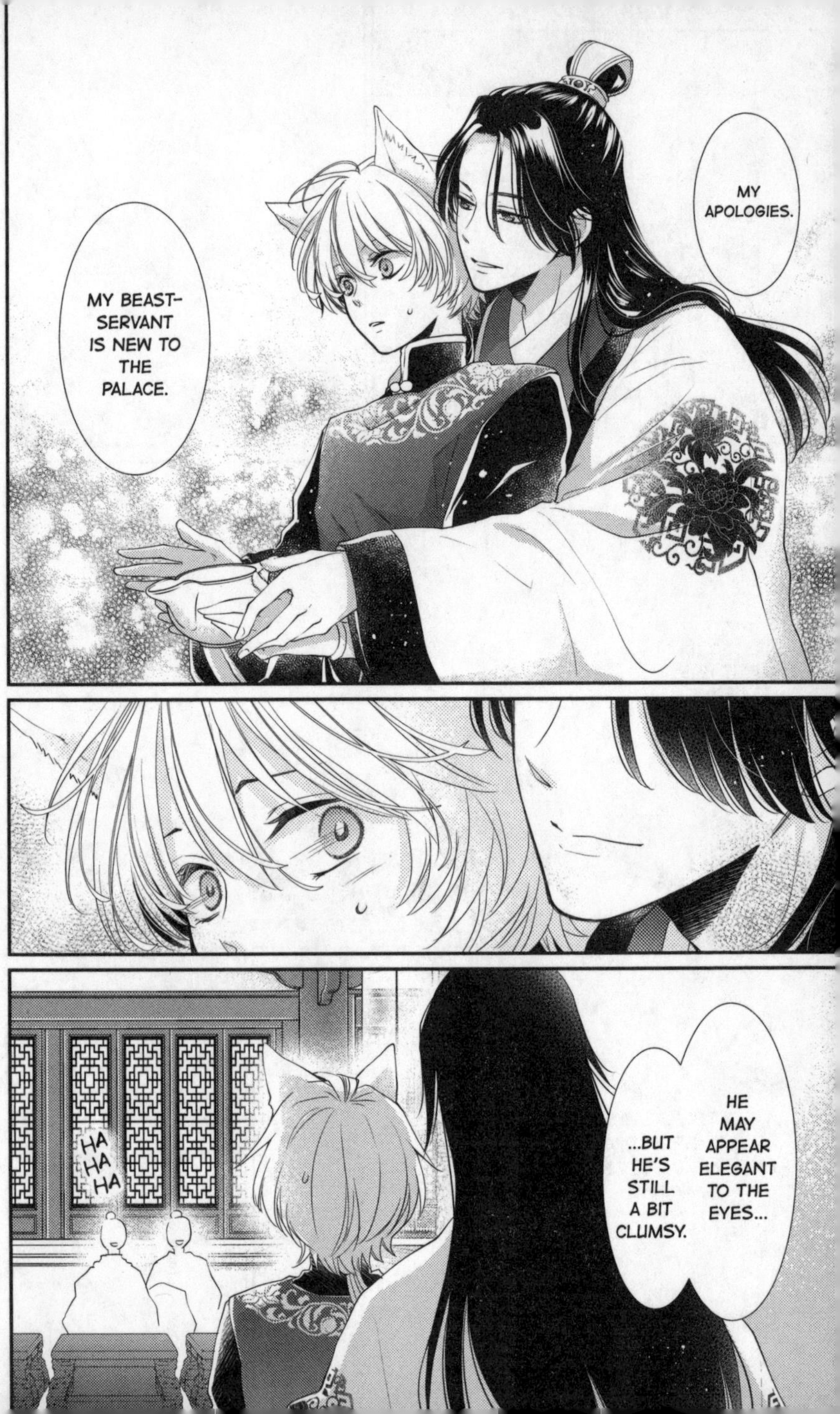
MY APOLOGIES.
MY BEAST-SERVANT IS NEW TO THE PALACE.
HE MAY APPEAR ELEGANT TO THE EYES...
...BUT HE'S STILL A BIT CLUMSY.
HA HA HA

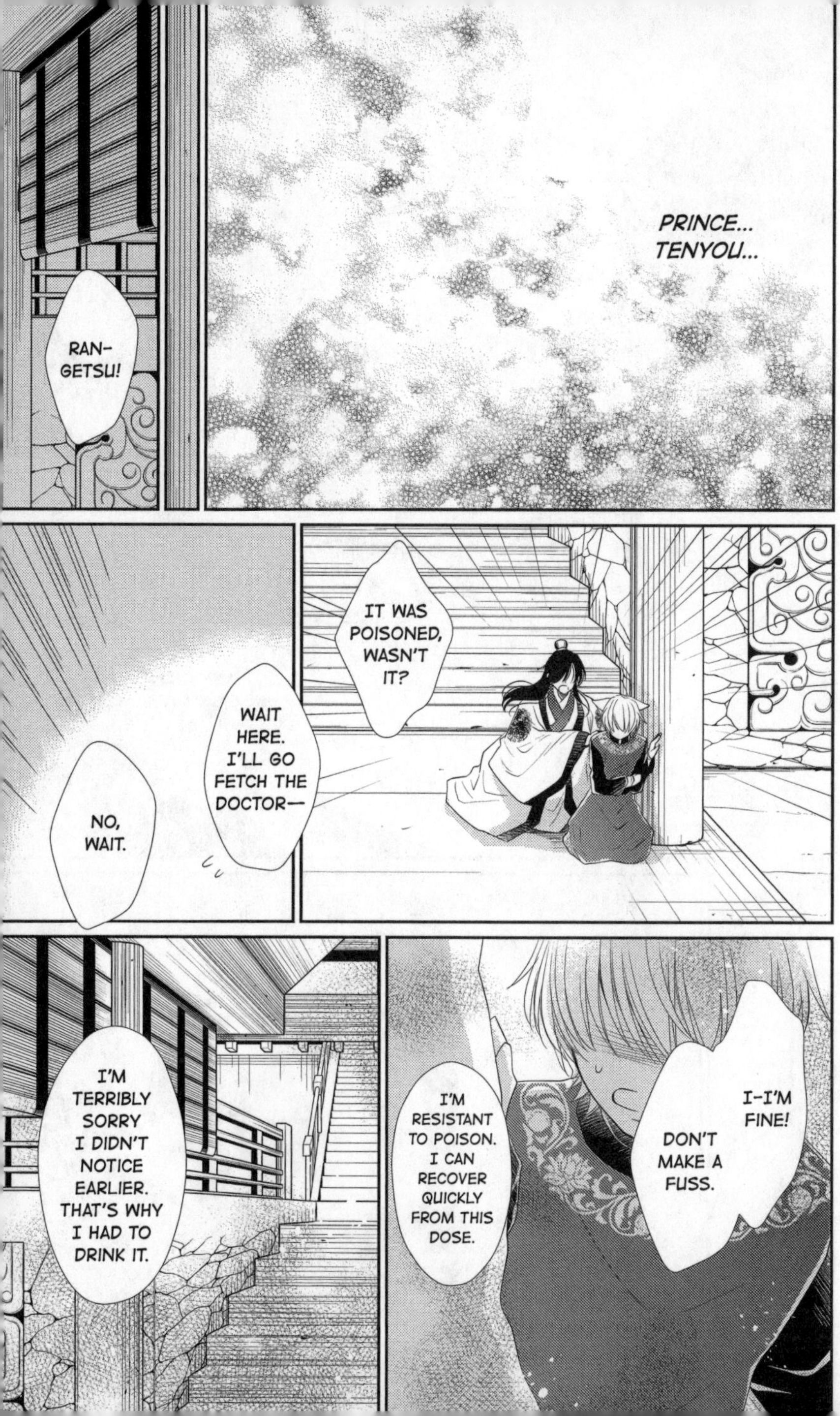
PRINCE... TENYOU...
RAN-GETSU!
IT WAS POISONED, WASN'T IT?
WAIT HERE. I'LL GO FETCH THE DOCTOR—
NO, WAIT.
I-I'M FINE!
DON'T MAKE A FUSS.
I'M RESISTANT TO POISON. I CAN RECOVER QUICKLY FROM THIS DOSE.
I'M TERRIBLY SORRY I DIDN'T NOTICE EARLIER. THAT'S WHY I HAD TO DRINK IT.

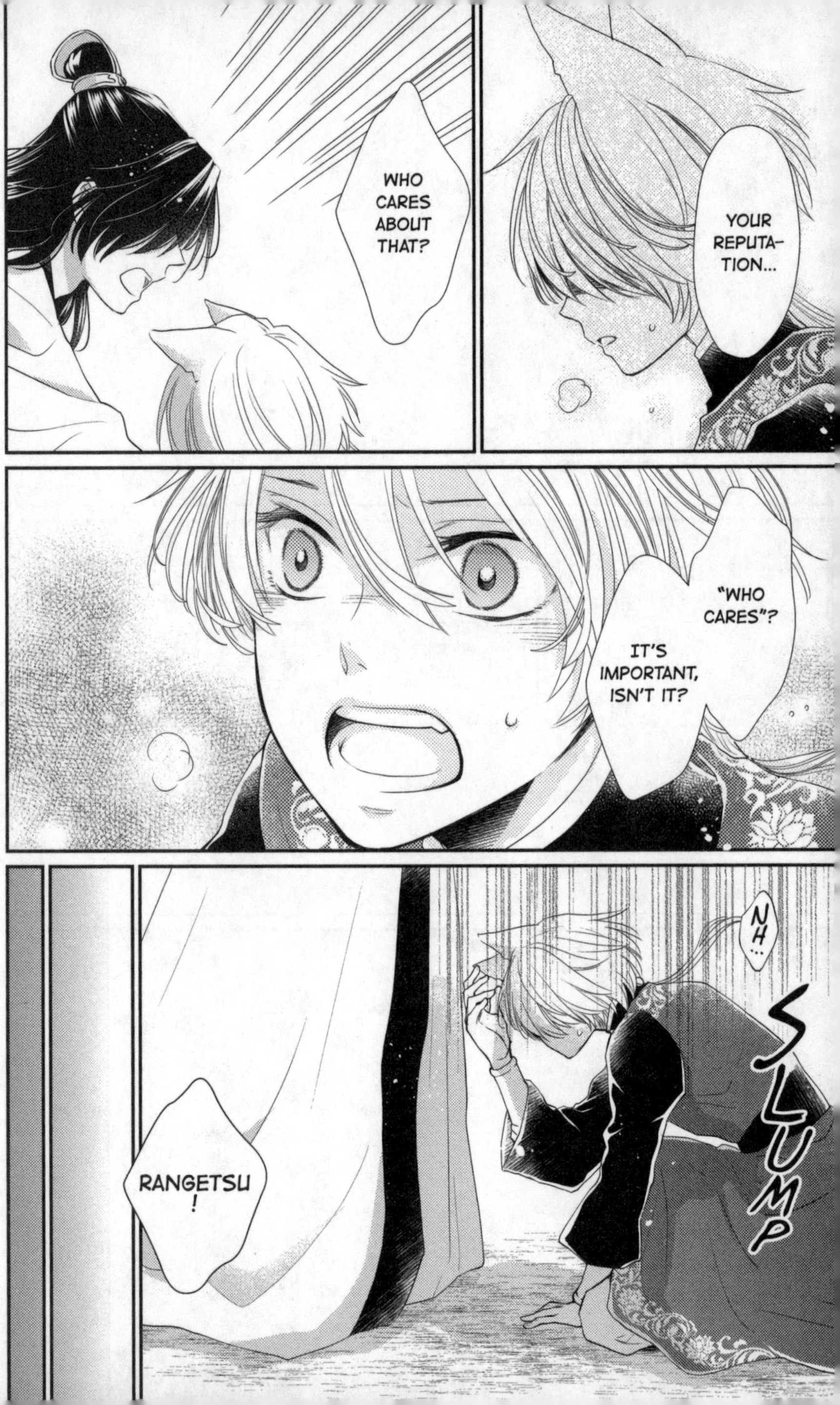
YOUR REPUTATION...
WHO CARES ABOUT THAT?
"WHO CARES"?
IT'S IMPORTANT, ISN'T IT?
NH...
SLUMP
RANGETSU!

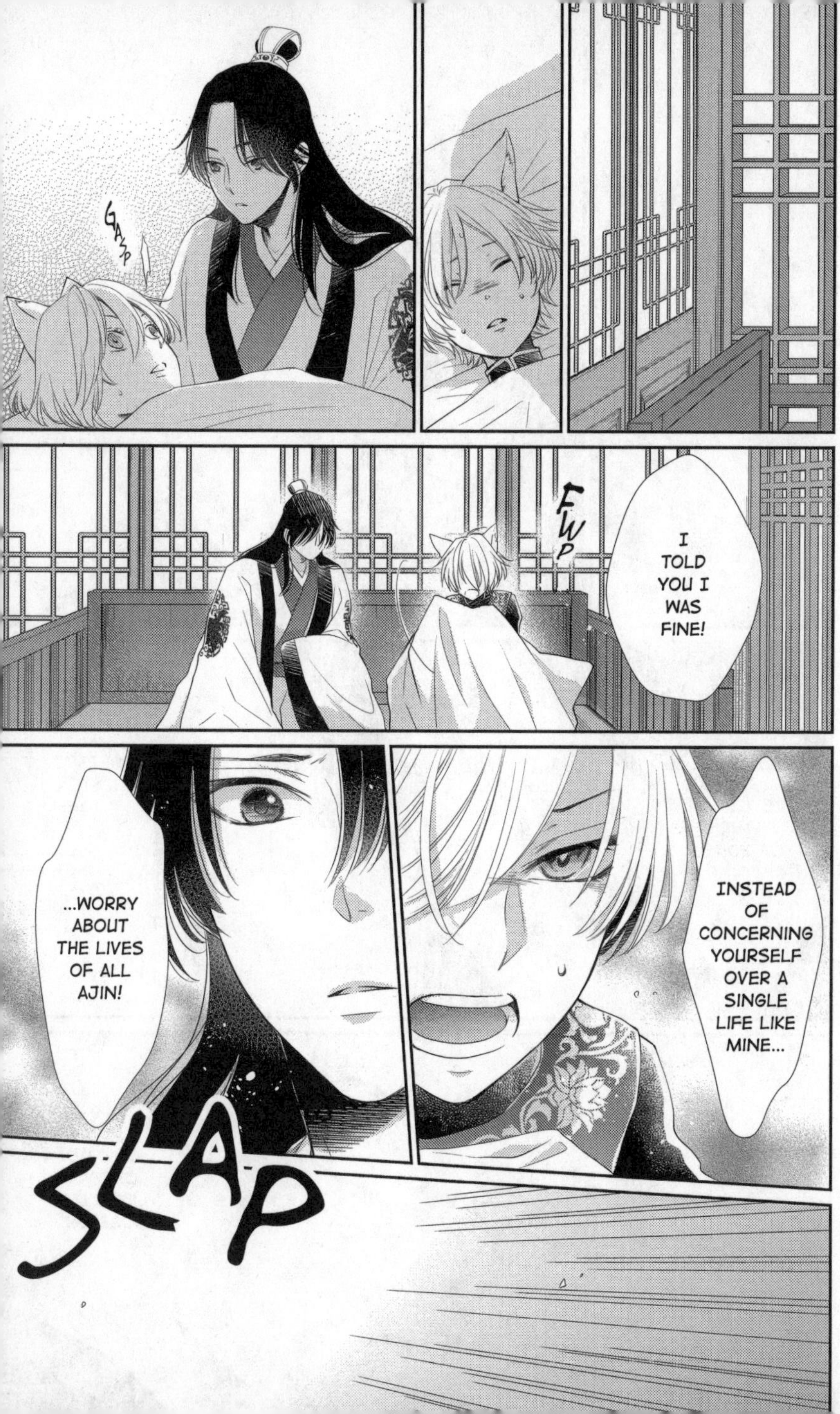
GASP
I TOLD YOU I WAS FINE!
FWP
INSTEAD OF CONCERNING YOURSELF OVER A SINGLE LIFE LIKE MINE...
...WORRY ABOUT THE LIVES OF ALL AJIN!
SLAP

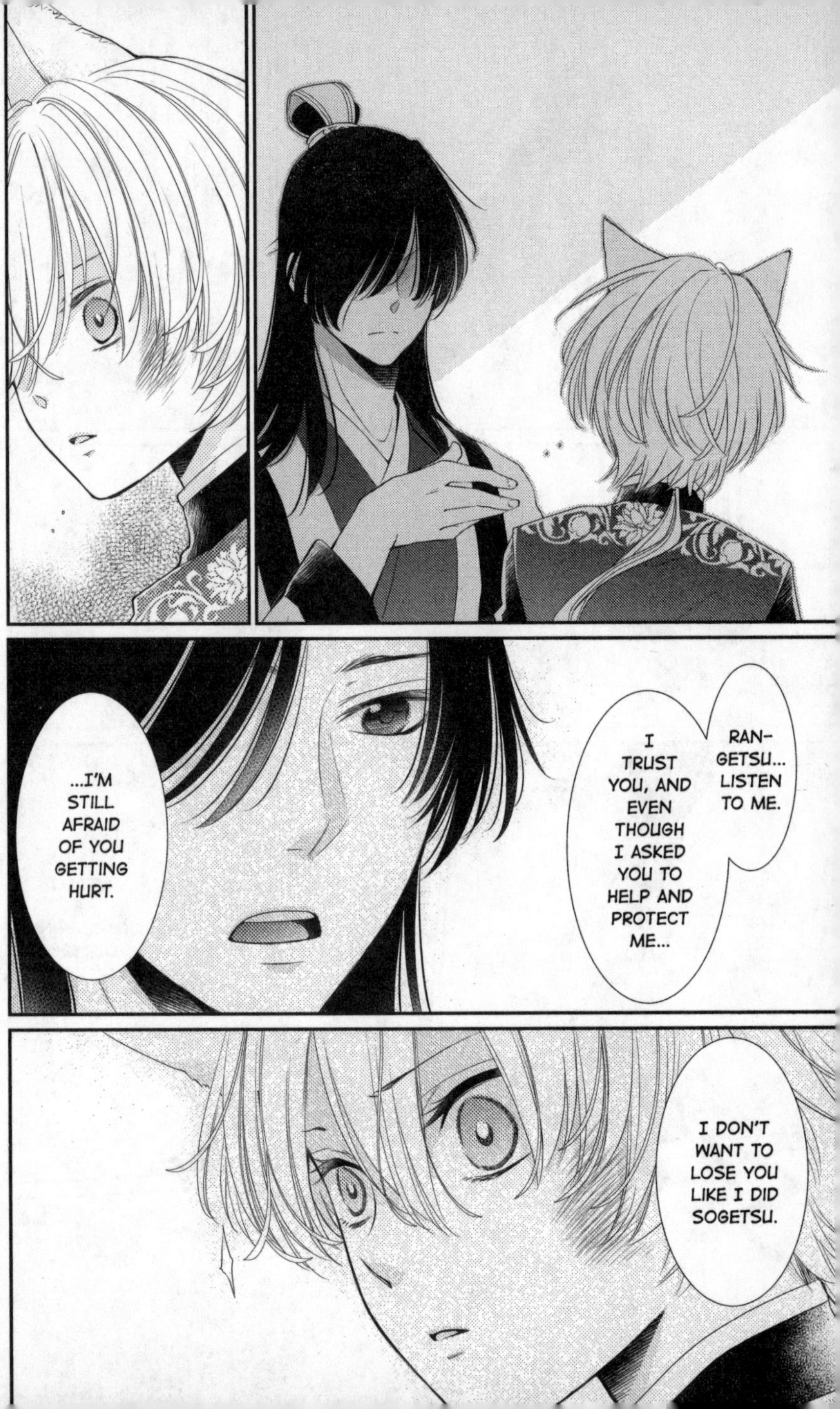
RAN-GETSU... LISTEN TO ME.
I TRUST YOU, AND EVEN THOUGH I ASKED YOU TO HELP AND PROTECT ME...
...I'M STILL AFRAID OF YOU GETTING HURT.
I DON'T WANT TO LOSE YOU LIKE I DID SOGETSU.

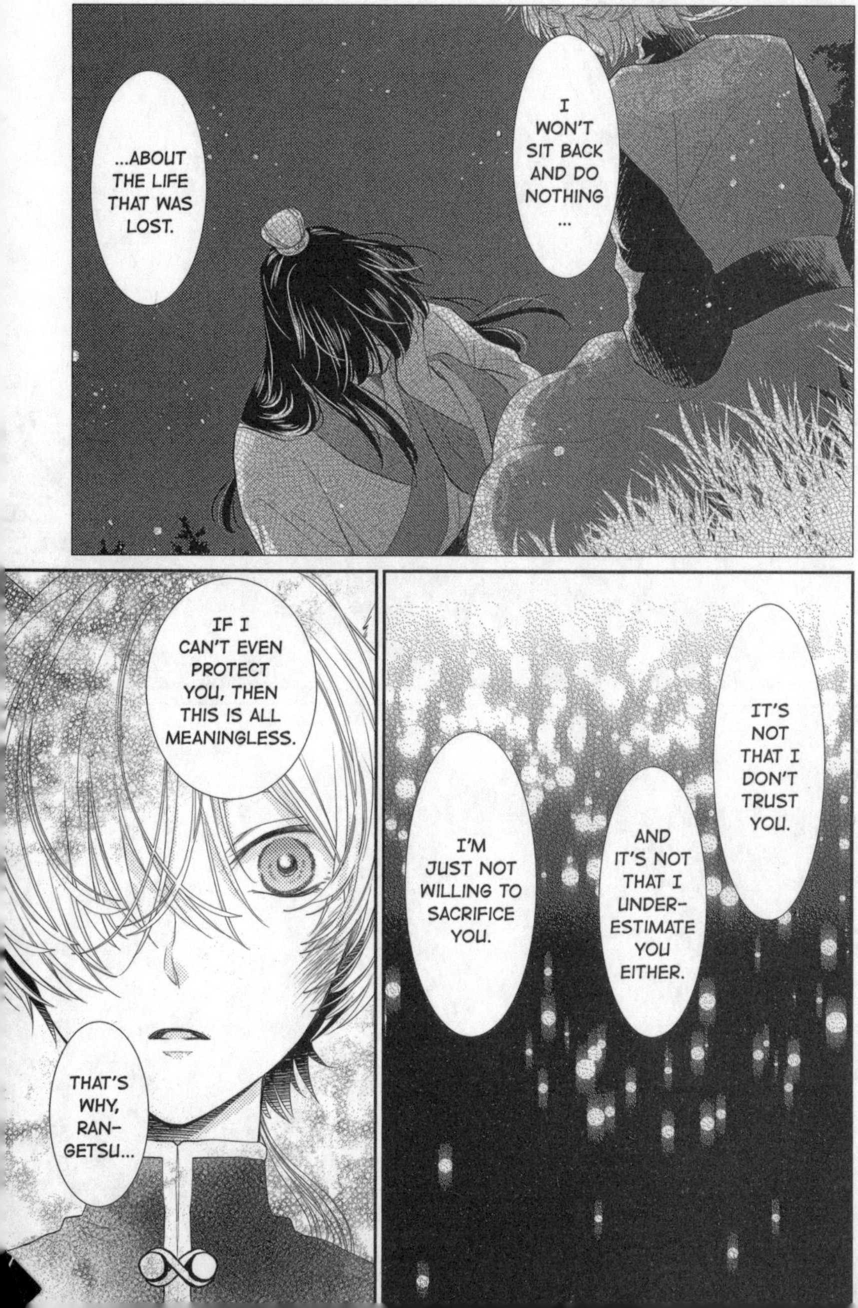
I WON'T SIT BACK AND DO NOTHING...
...ABOUT THE LIFE THAT WAS LOST.
IT'S NOT THAT I DON'T TRUST YOU.
AND IT'S NOT THAT I UNDER-ESTIMATE YOU EITHER.
I'M JUST NOT WILLING TO SACRIFICE YOU.
IF I CAN'T EVEN PROTECT YOU, THEN THIS IS ALL MEANINGLESS.
THAT'S WHY, RAN-GETSU...

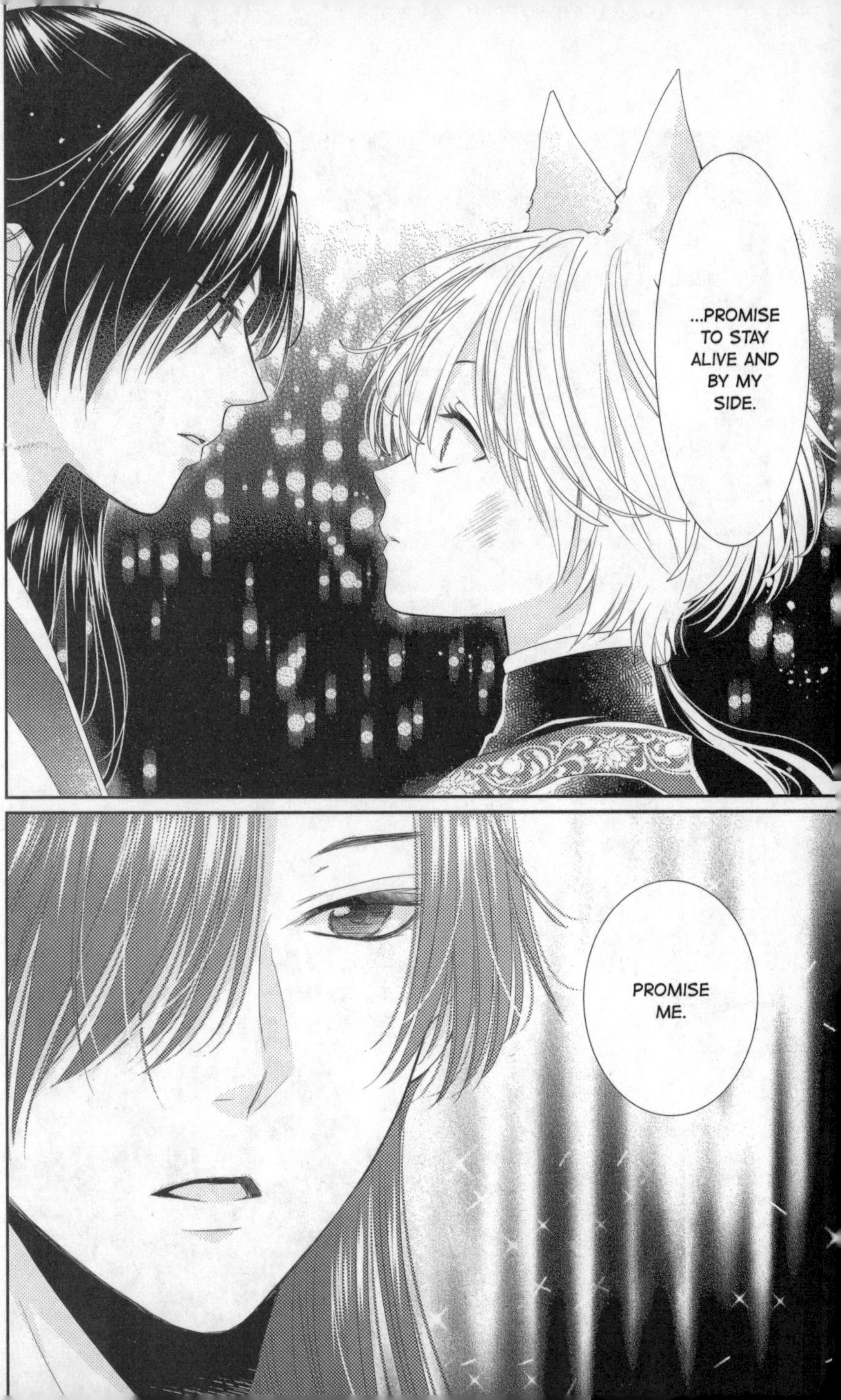
...PROMISE TO STAY ALIVE AND BY MY SIDE.
PROMISE ME.

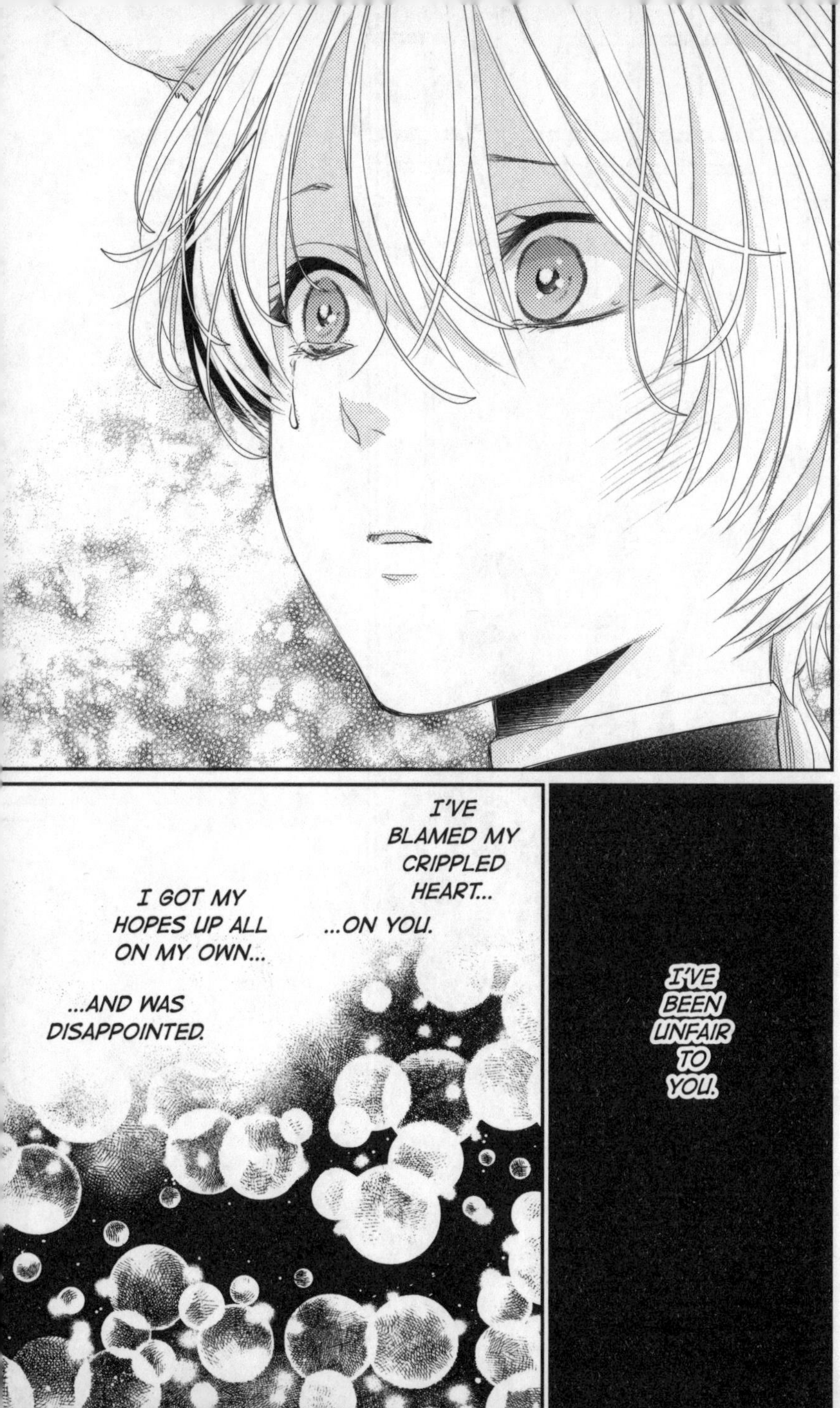
I'VE BEEN UNFAIR TO YOU.
I'VE BLAMED MY CRIPPLED HEART...
...ON YOU.
I GOT MY HOPES UP ALL ON MY OWN...
...AND WAS DISAPPOINTED.

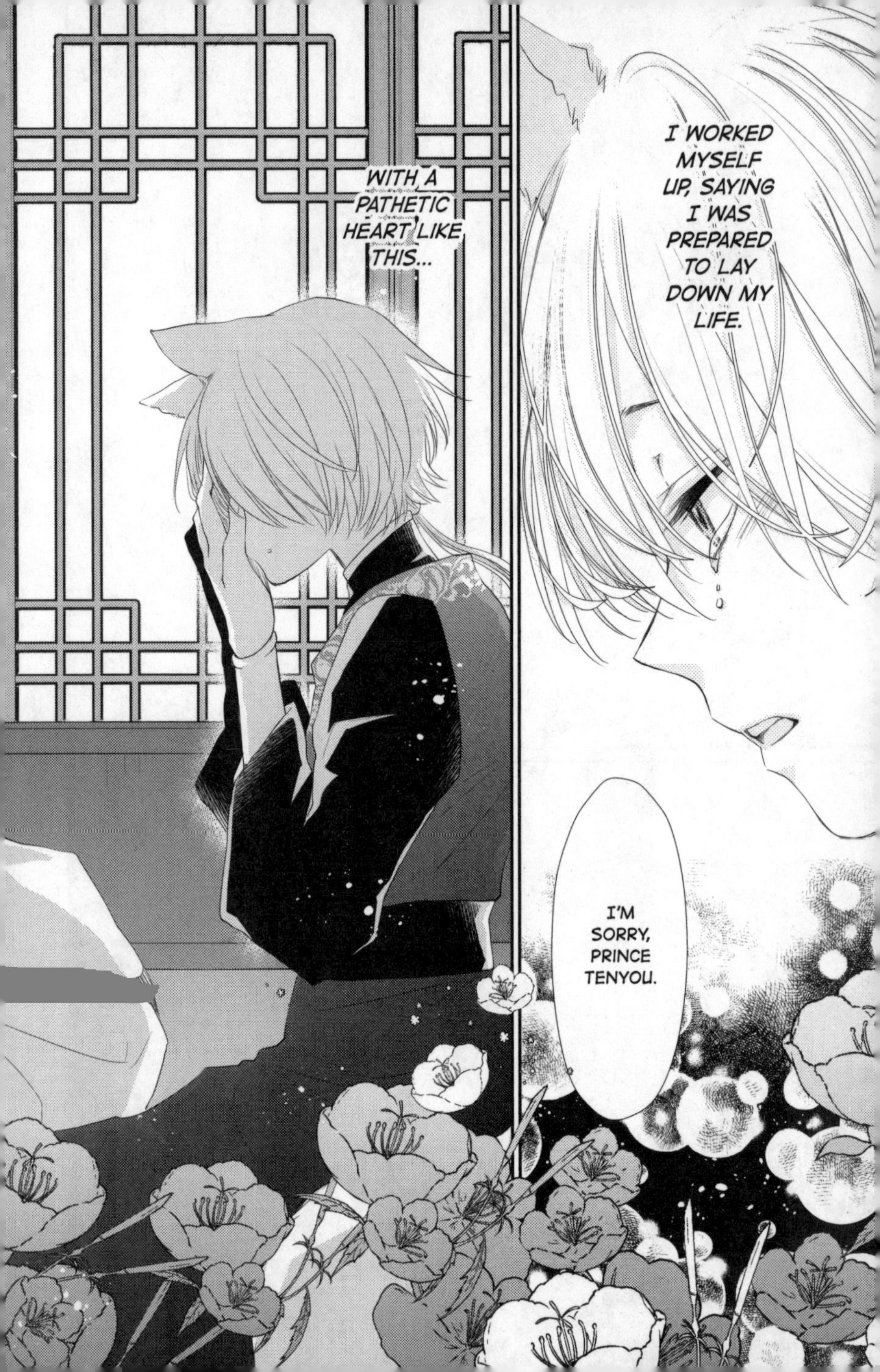
I WORKED MYSELF UP, SAYING I WAS PREPARED TO LAY DOWN MY LIFE.
I'M SORRY, PRINCE TENYOU.
WITH A PATHETIC HEART LIKE THIS...

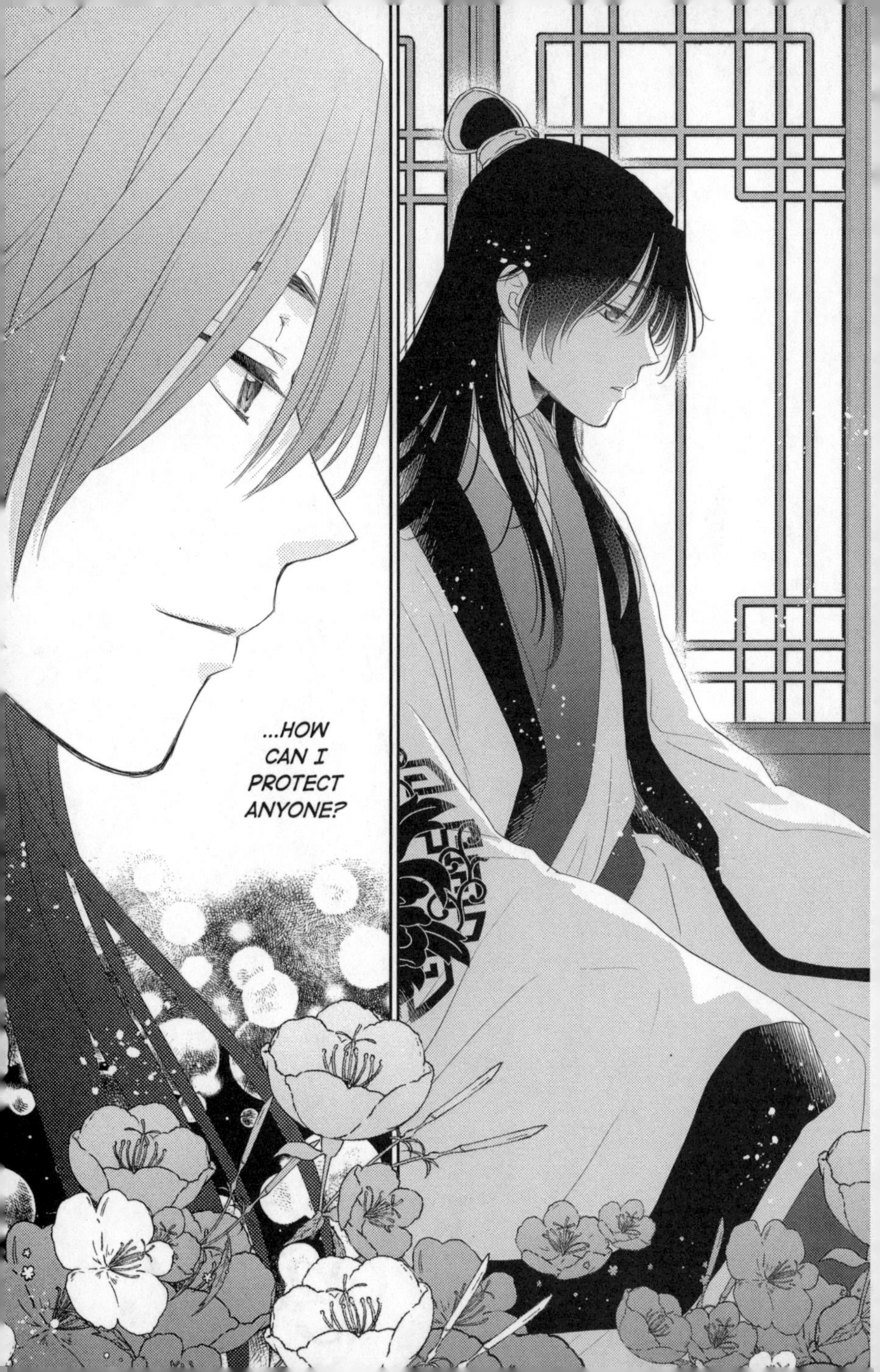
...HOW CAN I PROTECT ANYONE?

THE KING'S *Beast* 麗

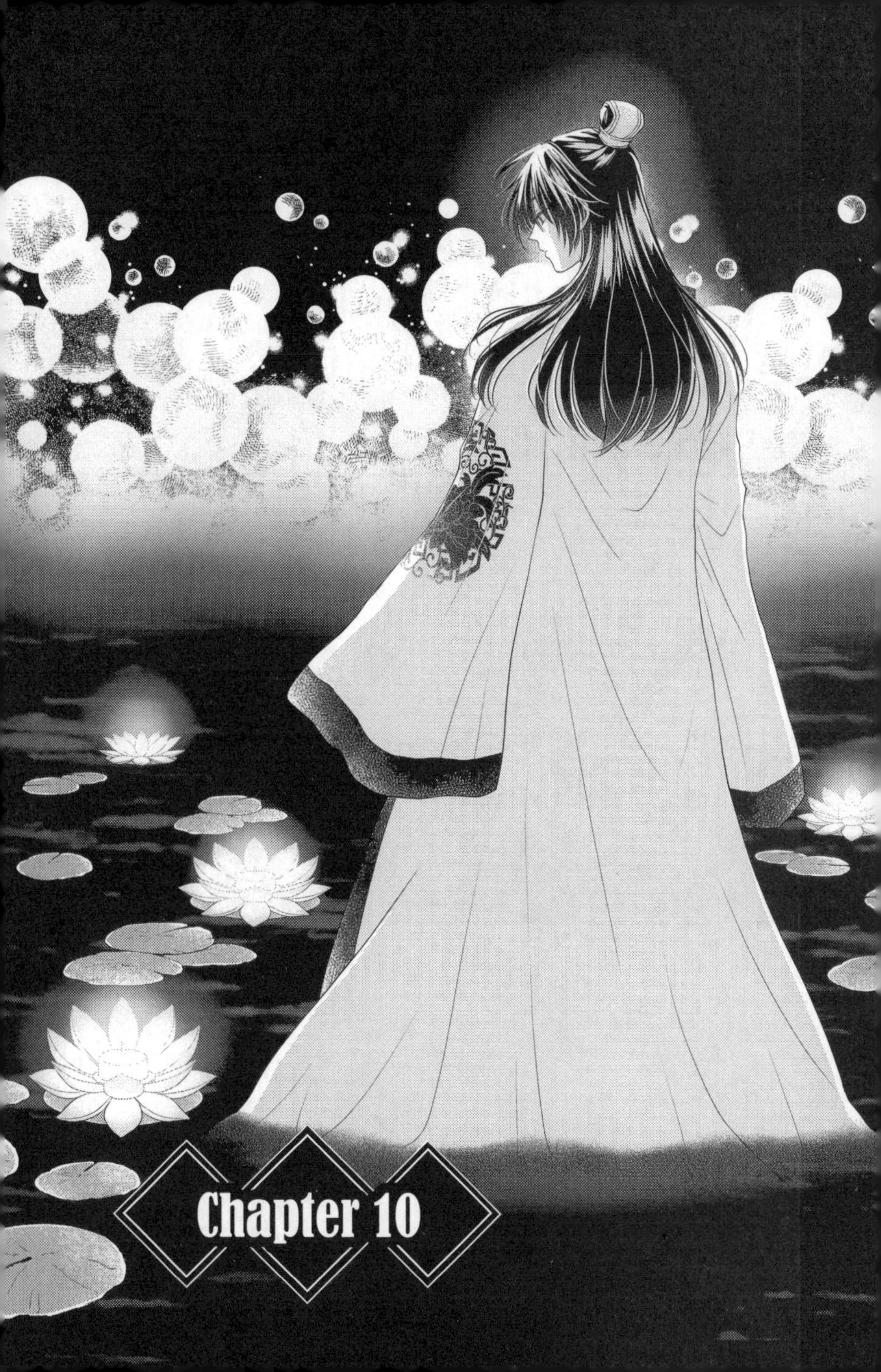
Chapter 10

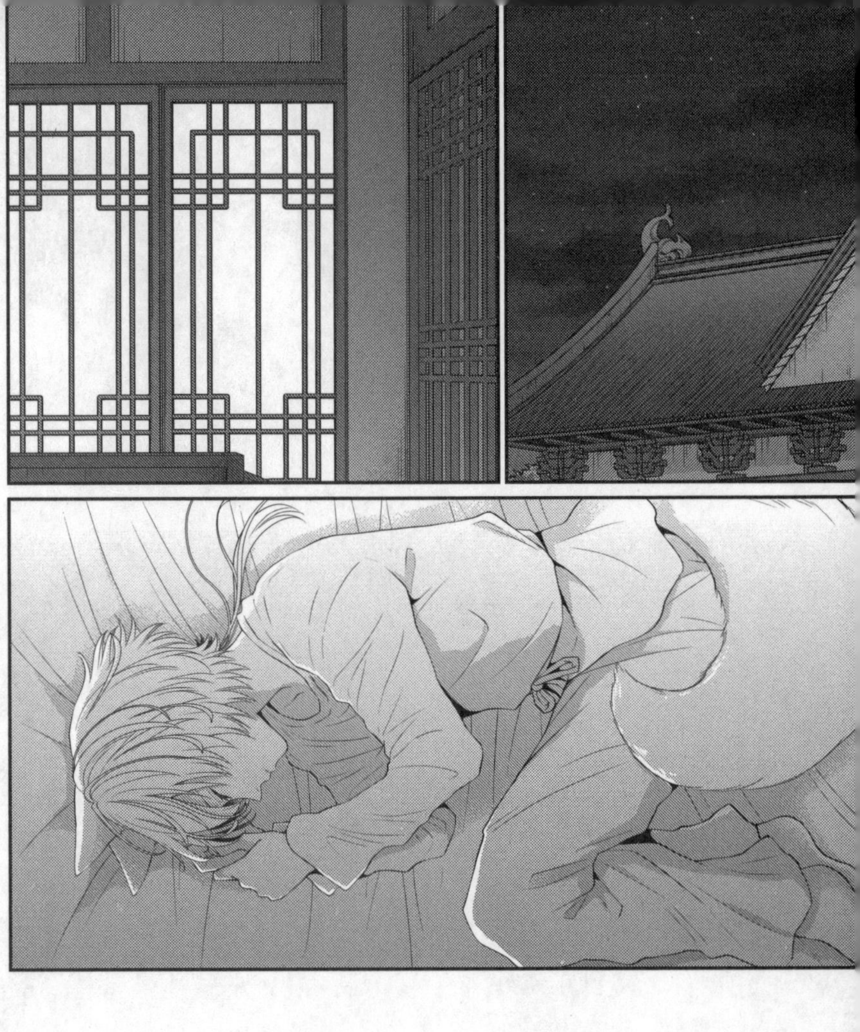

THE KING'S Beast

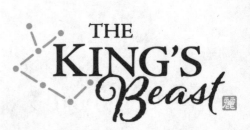

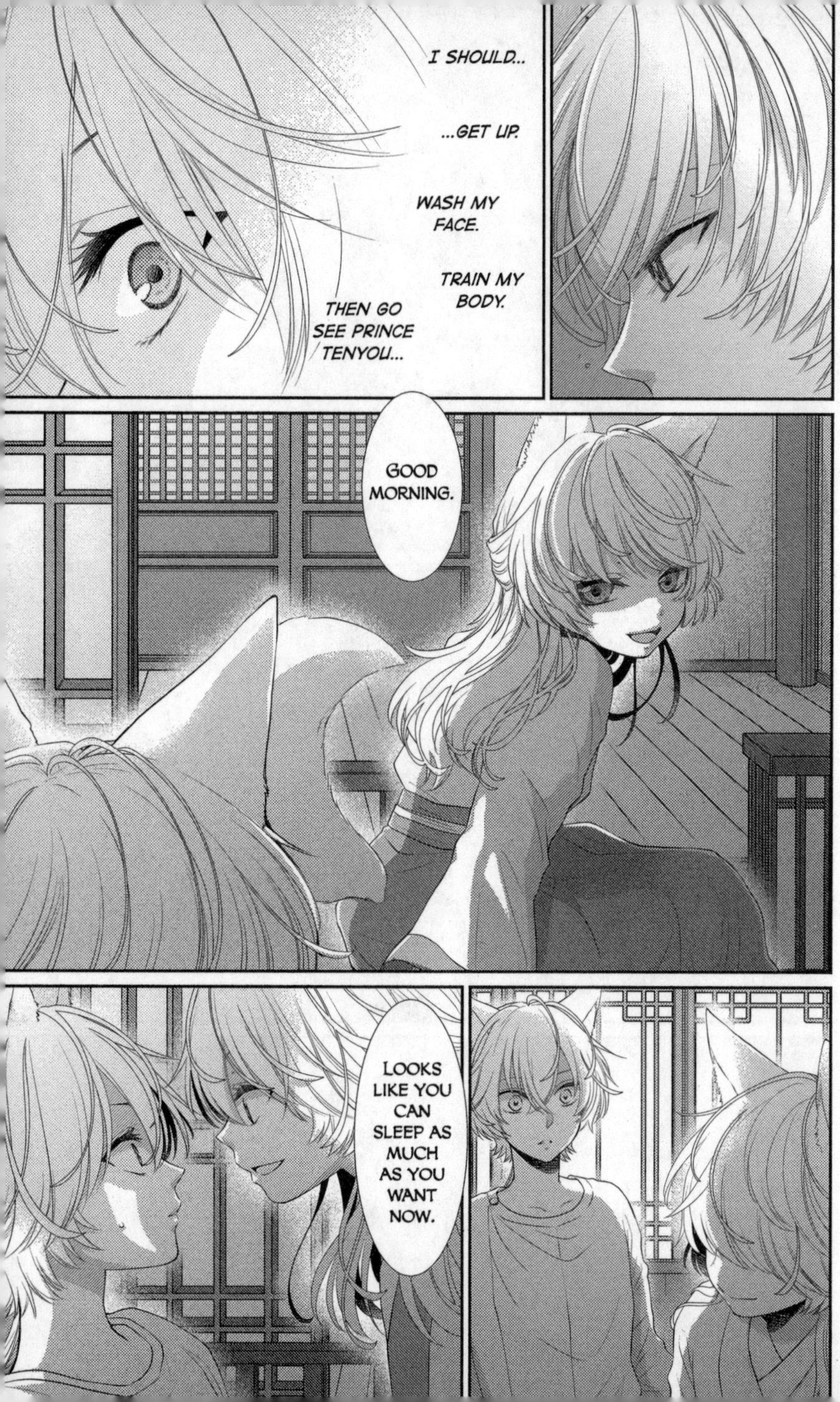
I SHOULD...
...GET UP.
WASH MY FACE.
TRAIN MY BODY.
THEN GO SEE PRINCE TENYOU...
GOOD MORNING.
LOOKS LIKE YOU CAN SLEEP AS MUCH AS YOU WANT NOW.

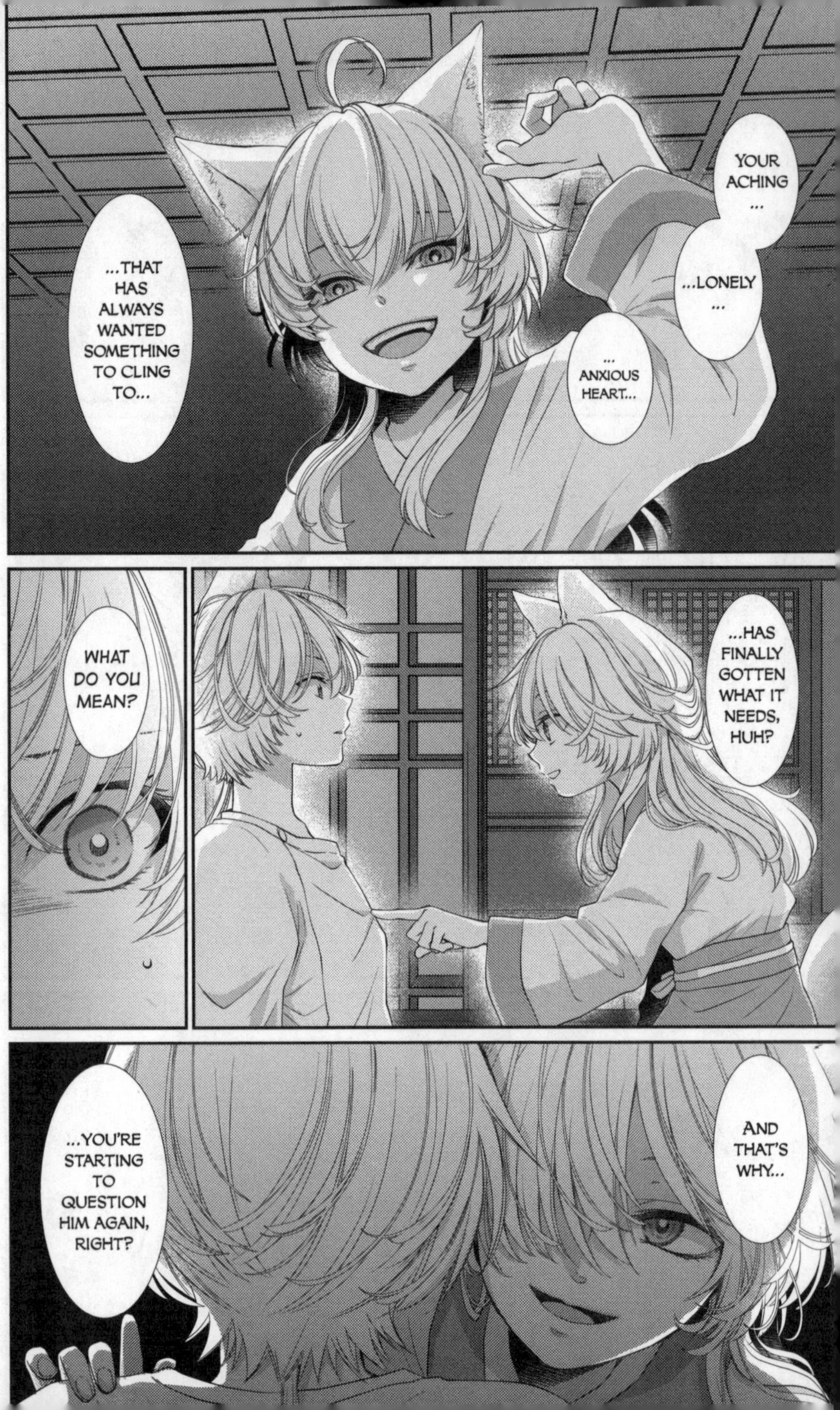
YOUR ACHING...
...LONELY...
...ANXIOUS HEART...
...THAT HAS ALWAYS WANTED SOMETHING TO CLING TO...
...HAS FINALLY GOTTEN WHAT IT NEEDS, HUH?
WHAT DO YOU MEAN?
AND THAT'S WHY...
...YOU'RE STARTING TO QUESTION HIM AGAIN, RIGHT?

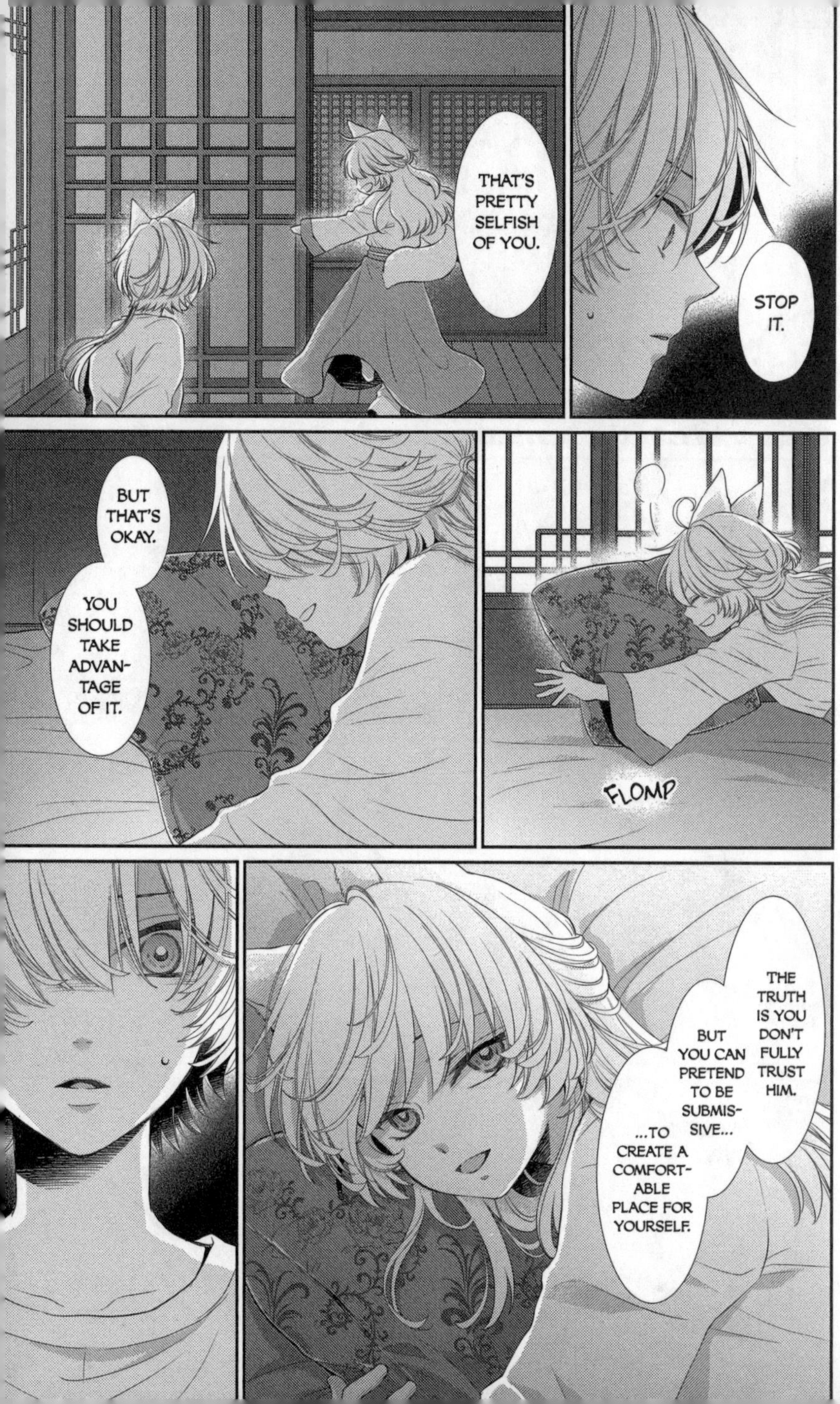
STOP IT.
THAT'S PRETTY SELFISH OF YOU.
FLOMP
BUT THAT'S OKAY.
YOU SHOULD TAKE ADVAN-TAGE OF IT.
THE TRUTH IS YOU DON'T FULLY TRUST HIM.
BUT YOU CAN PRETEND TO BE SUBMIS-SIVE...
...TO CREATE A COMFORT-ABLE PLACE FOR YOURSELF.

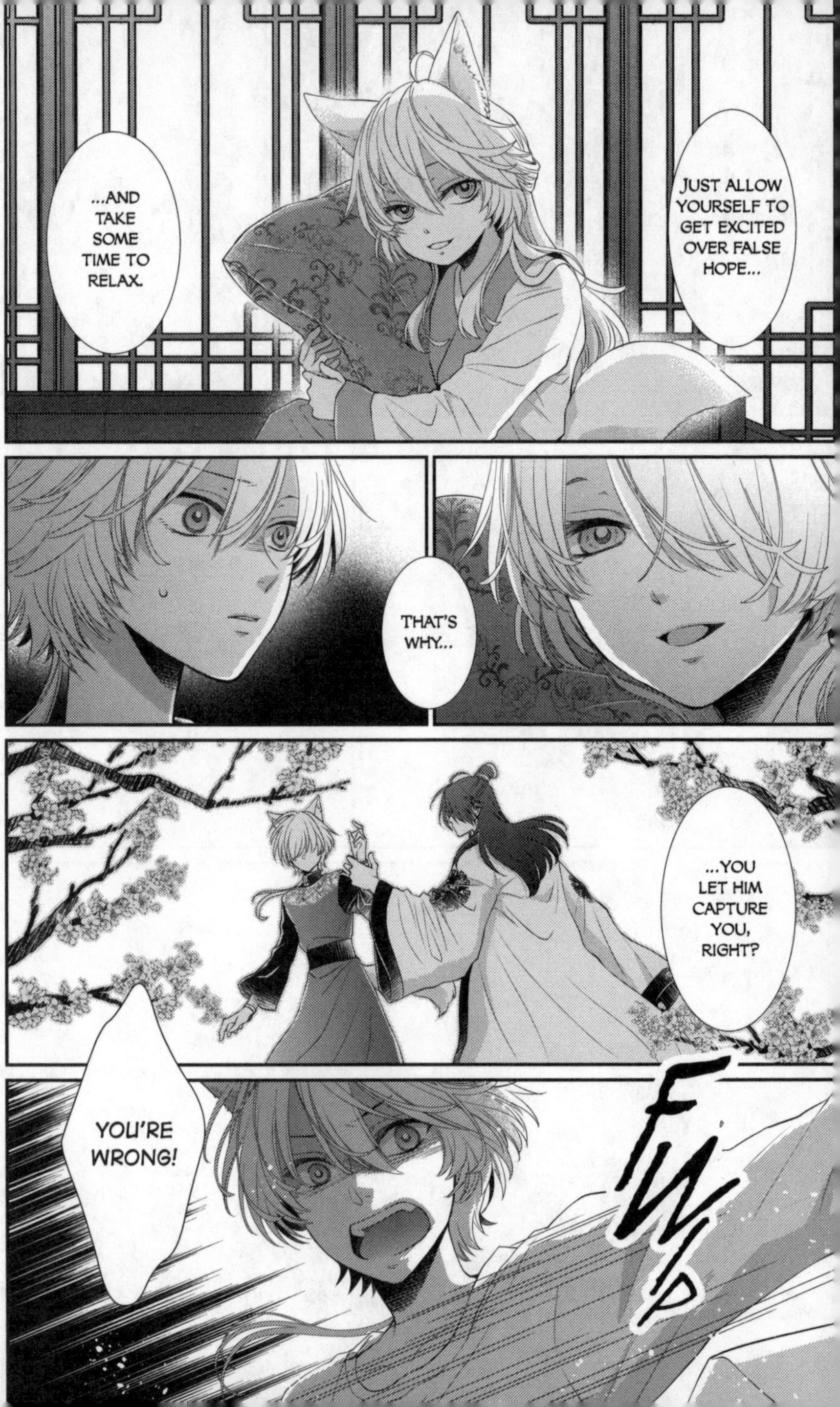
JUST ALLOW YOURSELF TO GET EXCITED OVER FALSE HOPE...
...AND TAKE SOME TIME TO RELAX.
THAT'S WHY...
...YOU LET HIM CAPTURE YOU, RIGHT?
FWIP
YOU'RE WRONG!

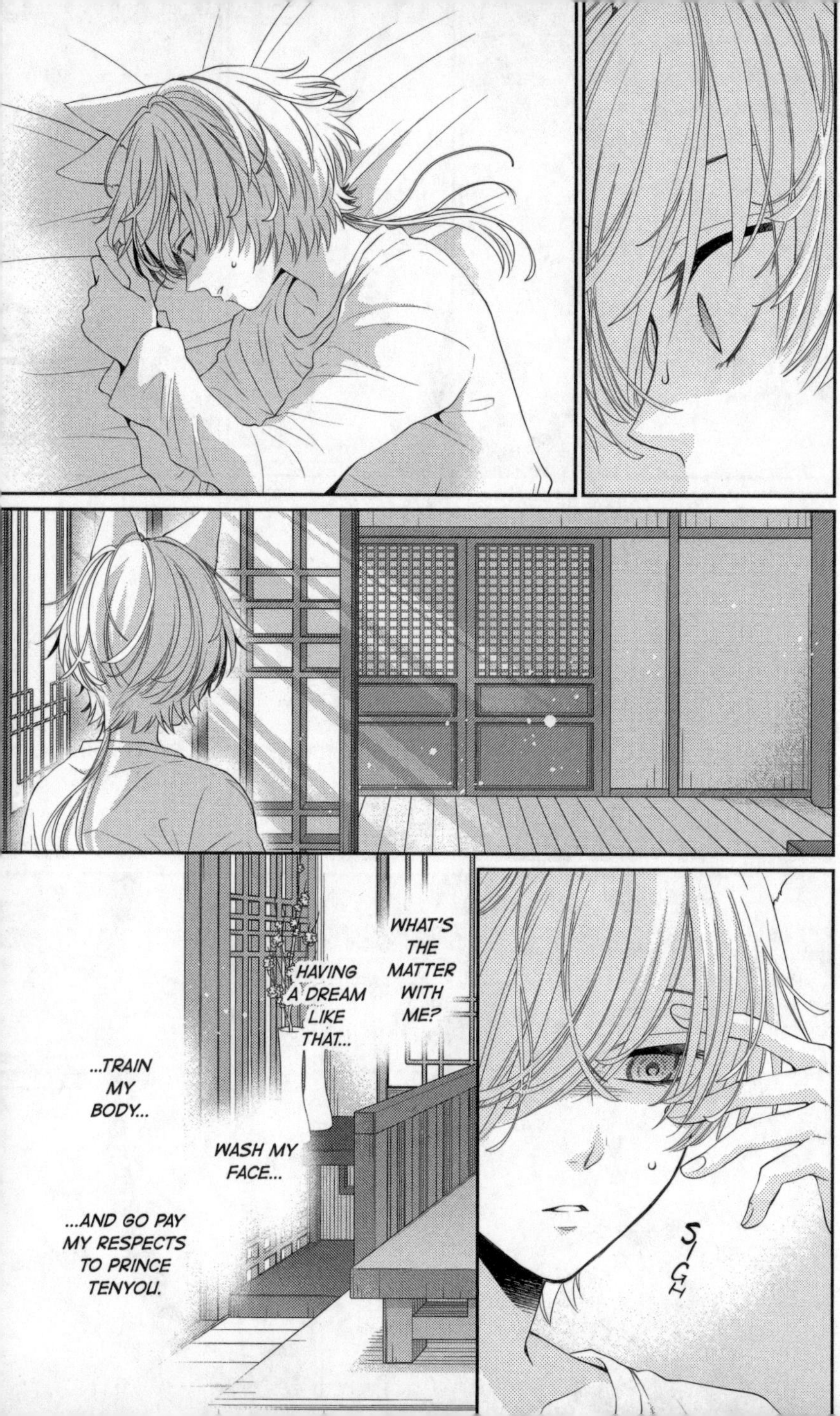
SIGH
WHAT'S THE MATTER WITH ME?
HAVING A DREAM LIKE THAT...
...TRAIN MY BODY...
WASH MY FACE...
...AND GO PAY MY RESPECTS TO PRINCE TENYOU.

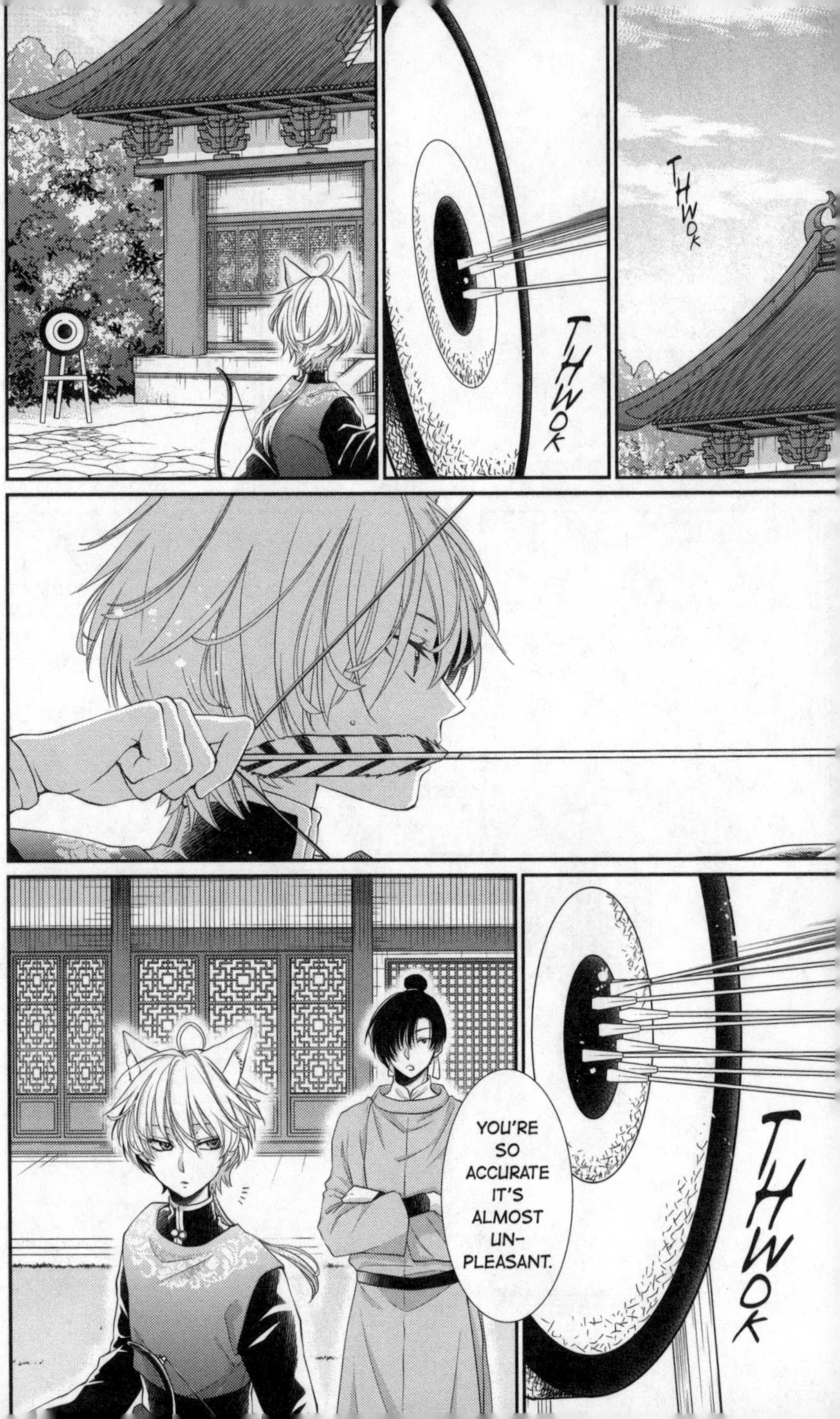
THWOK
THWOK
THWOK
YOU'RE SO ACCURATE IT'S ALMOST UN- PLEASANT.

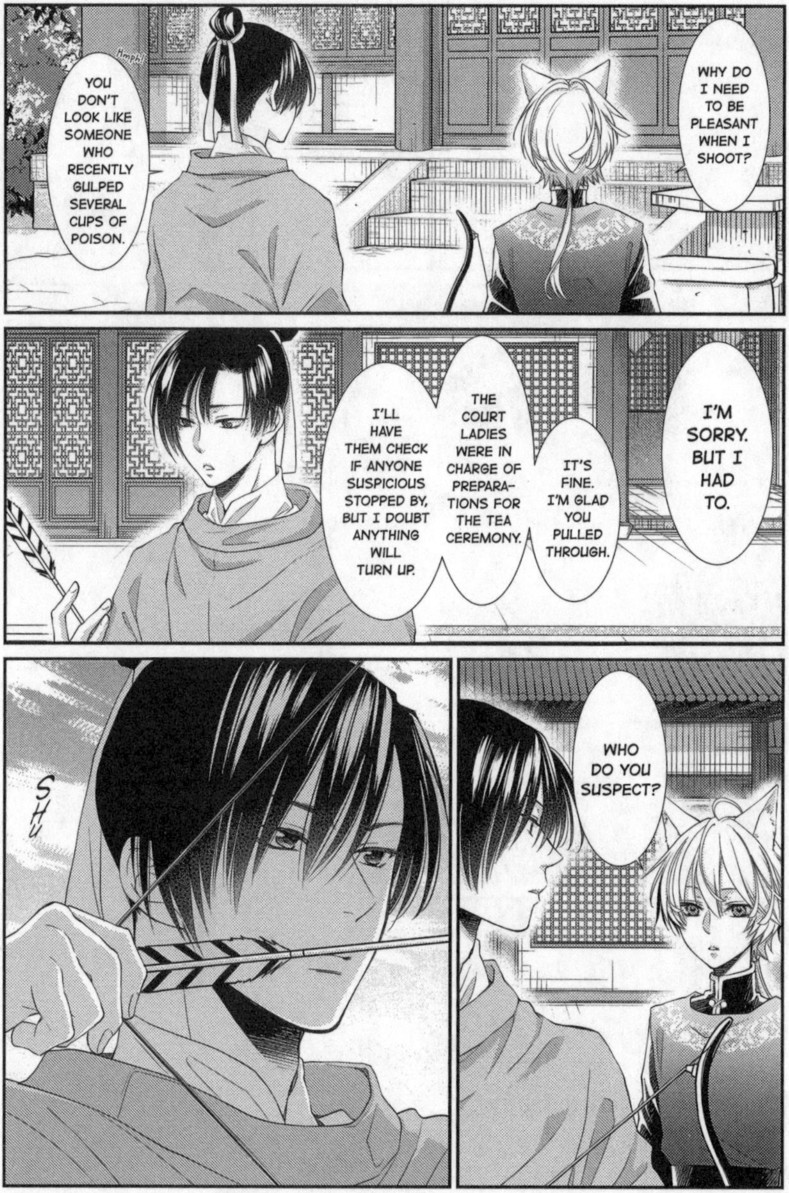
WHY DO I NEED TO BE PLEASANT WHEN I SHOOT?
Hmph!
YOU DON'T LOOK LIKE SOMEONE WHO RECENTLY GULPED SEVERAL CUPS OF POISON.
I'M SORRY. BUT I HAD TO.
IT'S FINE. I'M GLAD YOU PULLED THROUGH.
THE COURT LADIES WERE IN CHARGE OF PREPARA-TIONS FOR THE TEA CEREMONY.
I'LL HAVE THEM CHECK IF ANYONE SUSPICIOUS STOPPED BY, BUT I DOUBT ANYTHING WILL TURN UP.
WHO DO YOU SUSPECT?
SHU

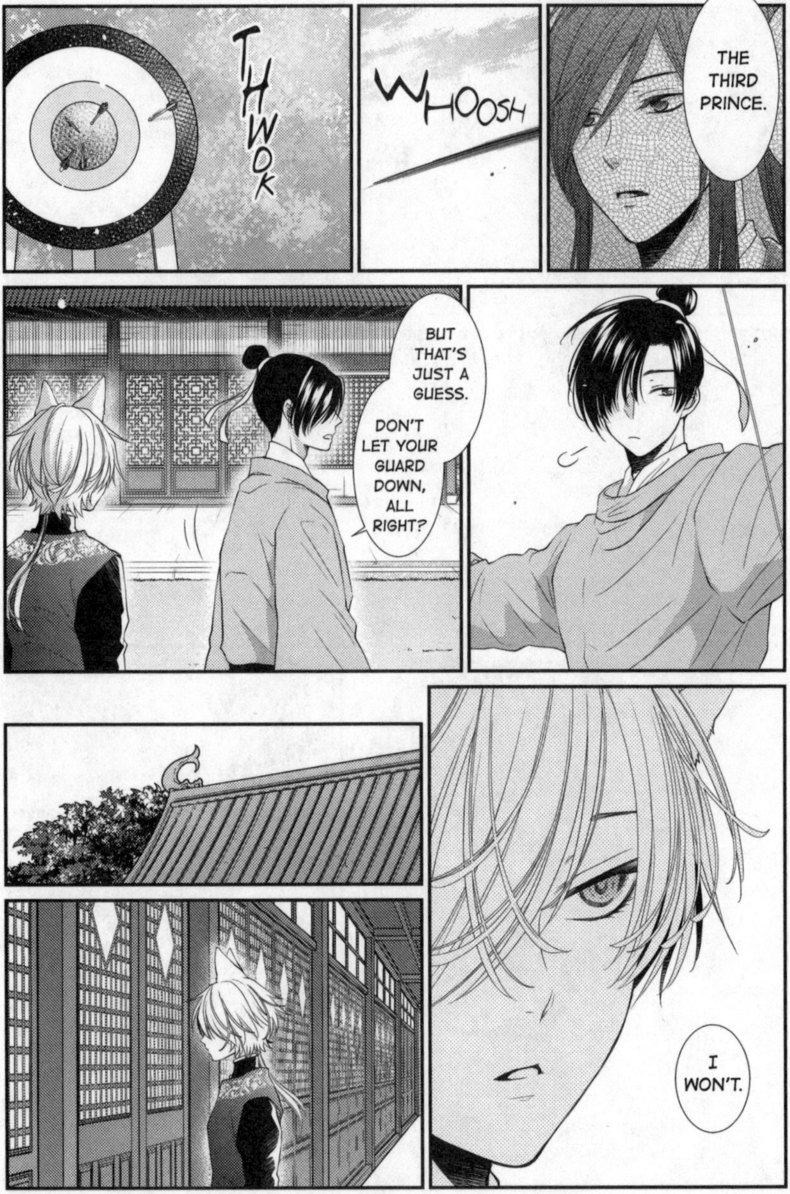
THE THIRD PRINCE.
WHOOSH
THWOK
BUT THAT'S JUST A GUESS.
DON'T LET YOUR GUARD DOWN, ALL RIGHT?
I WON'T.

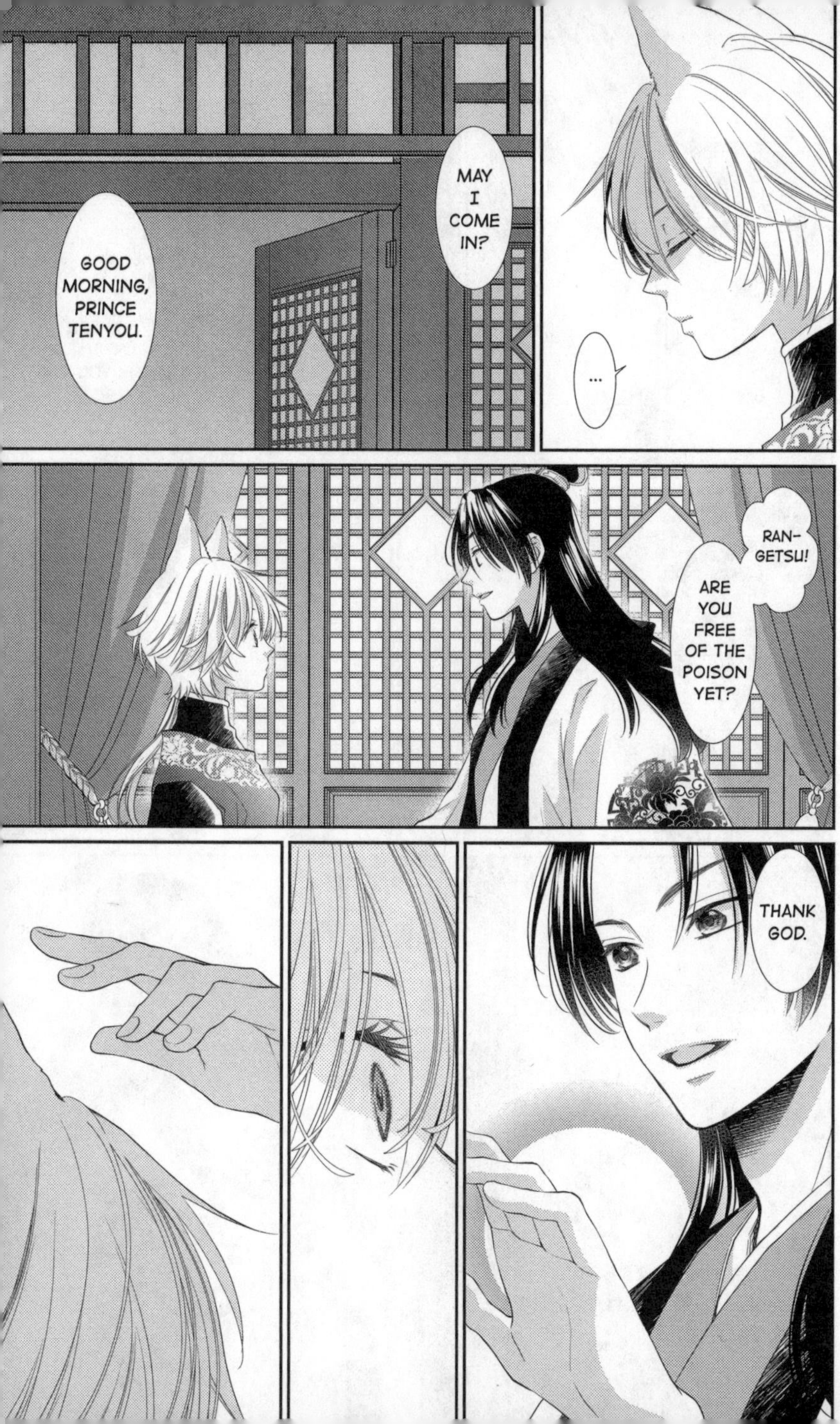
...
MAY I COME IN?
GOOD MORNING, PRINCE TENYOU.
RAN-GETSU!
ARE YOU FREE OF THE POISON YET?
THANK GOD.

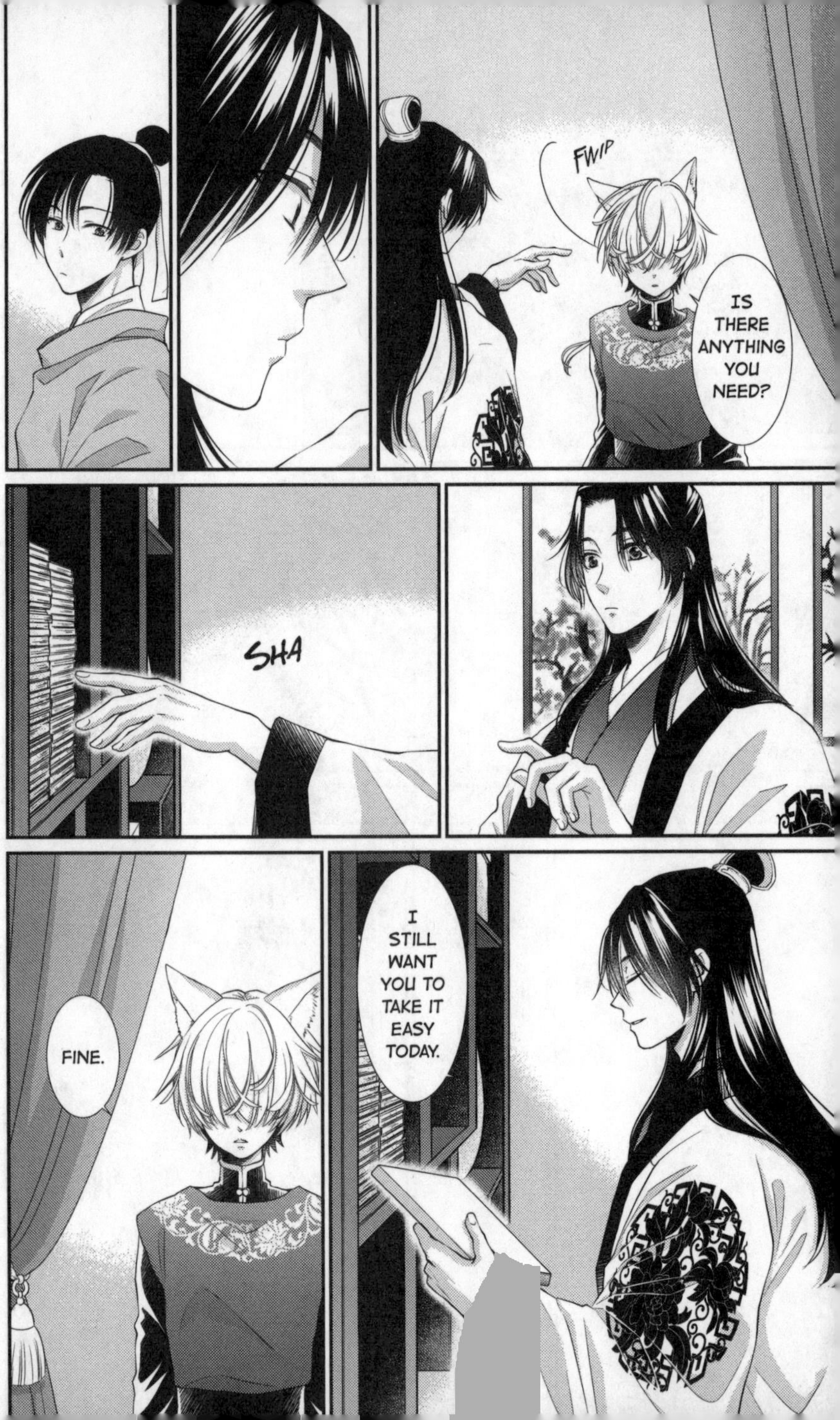
FWIP
IS THERE ANYTHING YOU NEED?
SHA
I STILL WANT YOU TO TAKE IT EASY TODAY.
FINE.

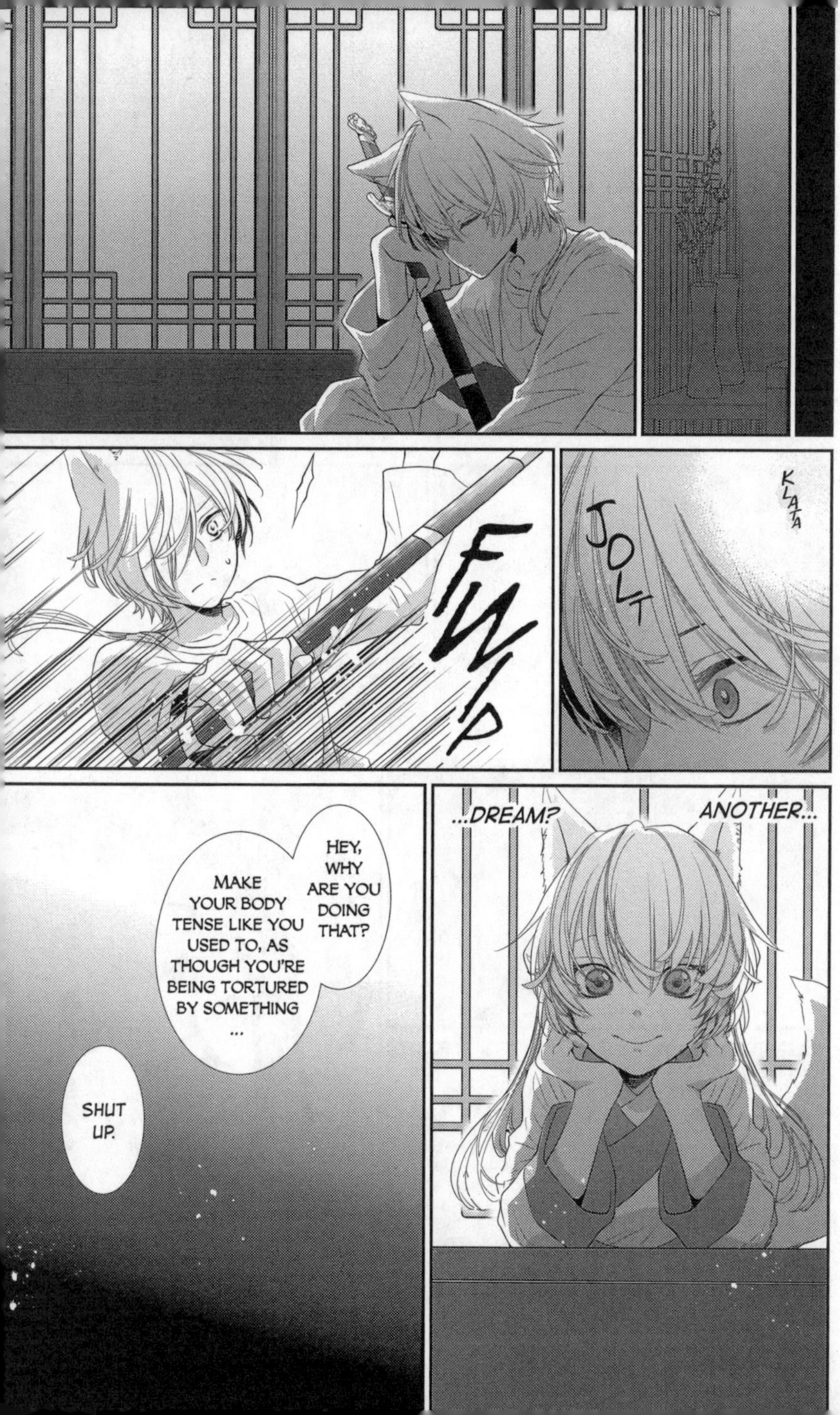
KLATA
JOLT
FWIP
ANOTHER...
...DREAM?
HEY, WHY ARE YOU DOING THAT?
MAKE YOUR BODY TENSE LIKE YOU USED TO, AS THOUGH YOU'RE BEING TORTURED BY SOMETHING...
SHUT UP.

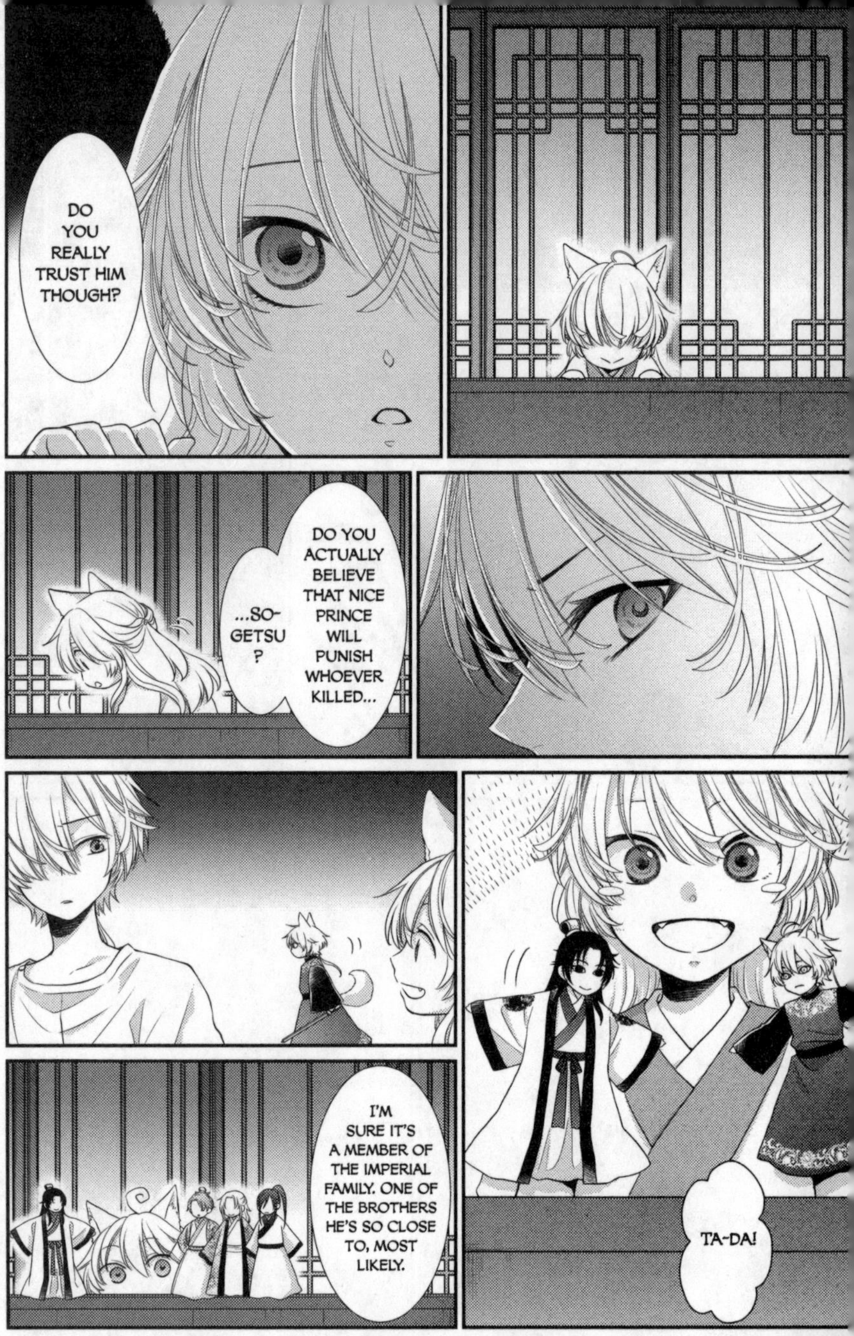
DO YOU REALLY TRUST HIM THOUGH?
DO YOU ACTUALLY BELIEVE THAT NICE PRINCE WILL PUNISH WHOEVER KILLED...
...SO-GETSU?
TA-DA!
I'M SURE IT'S A MEMBER OF THE IMPERIAL FAMILY. ONE OF THE BROTHERS HE'S SO CLOSE TO, MOST LIKELY.

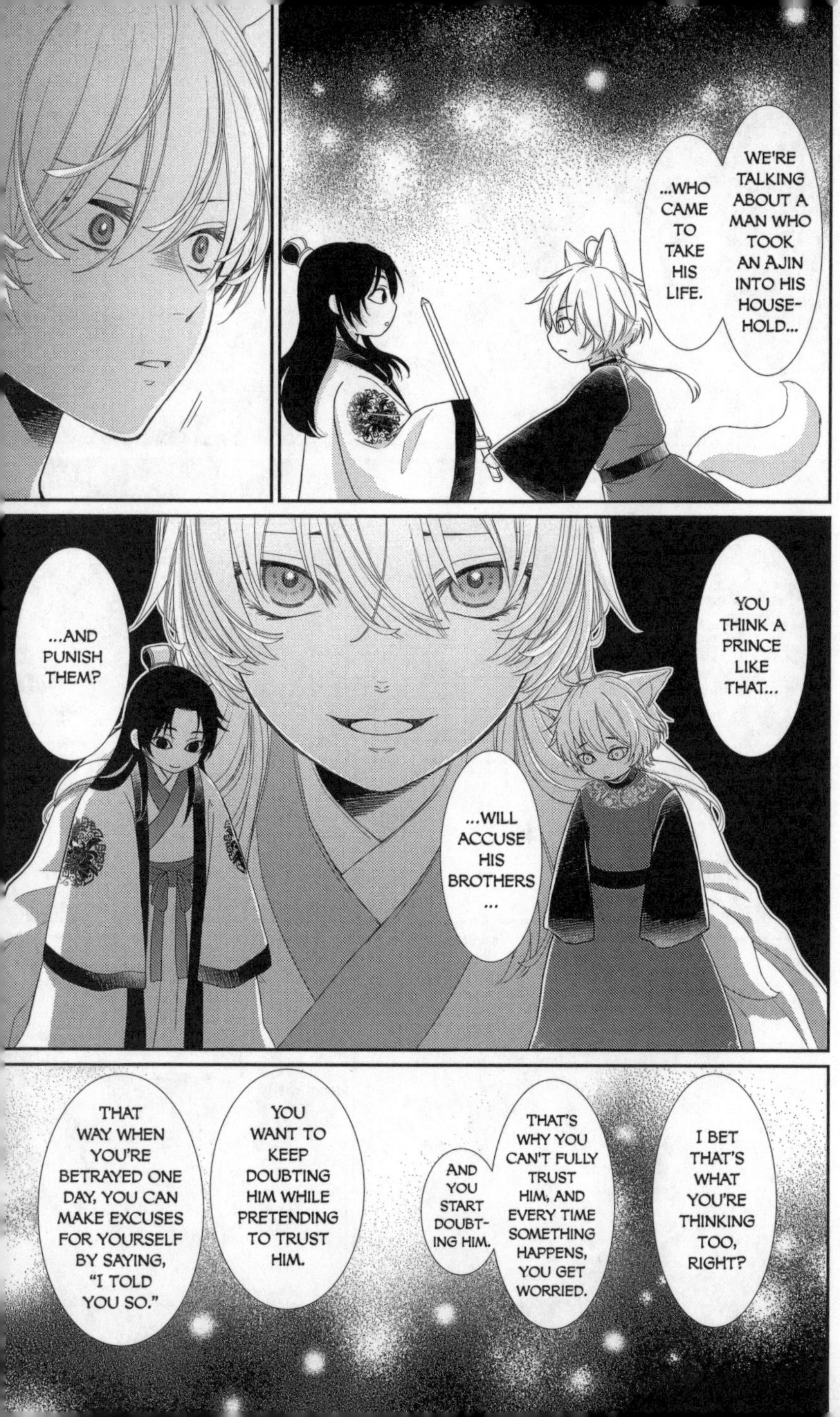
WE'RE TALKING ABOUT A MAN WHO TOOK AN AJIN INTO HIS HOUSE-HOLD...
...WHO CAME TO TAKE HIS LIFE.
YOU THINK A PRINCE LIKE THAT...
...WILL ACCUSE HIS BROTHERS ...
...AND PUNISH THEM?
I BET THAT'S WHAT YOU'RE THINKING TOO, RIGHT?
THAT'S WHY YOU CAN'T FULLY TRUST HIM, AND EVERY TIME SOMETHING HAPPENS, YOU GET WORRIED.
AND YOU START DOUBT-ING HIM.
YOU WANT TO KEEP DOUBTING HIM WHILE PRETENDING TO TRUST HIM.
THAT WAY WHEN YOU'RE BETRAYED ONE DAY, YOU CAN MAKE EXCUSES FOR YOURSELF BY SAYING, "I TOLD YOU SO."

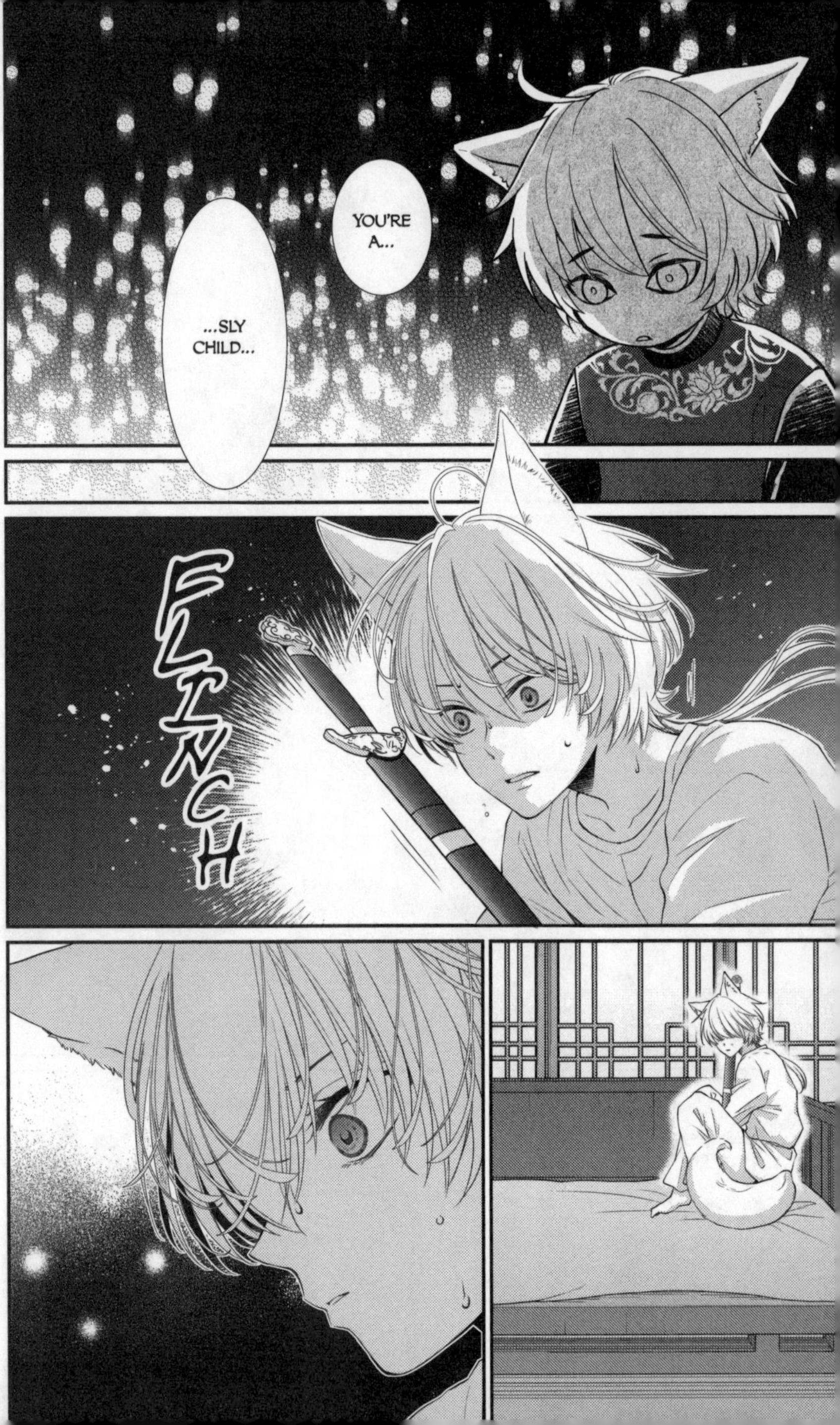
YOU'RE A...
...SLY CHILD...
FLINCH

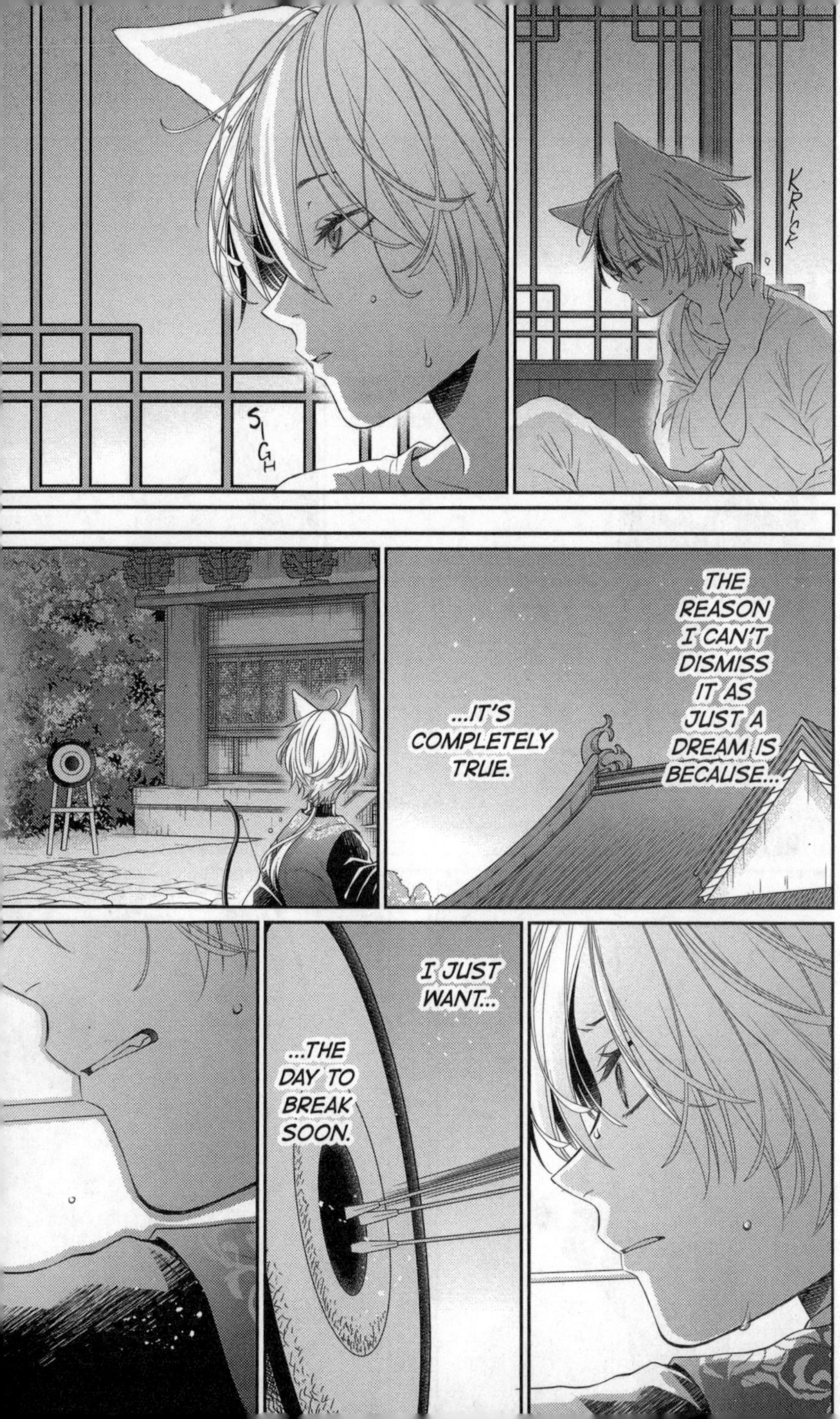
KRICK
SIGH
THE REASON I CAN'T DISMISS IT AS JUST A DREAM IS BECAUSE...
...IT'S COMPLETELY TRUE.
I JUST WANT...
...THE DAY TO BREAK SOON.

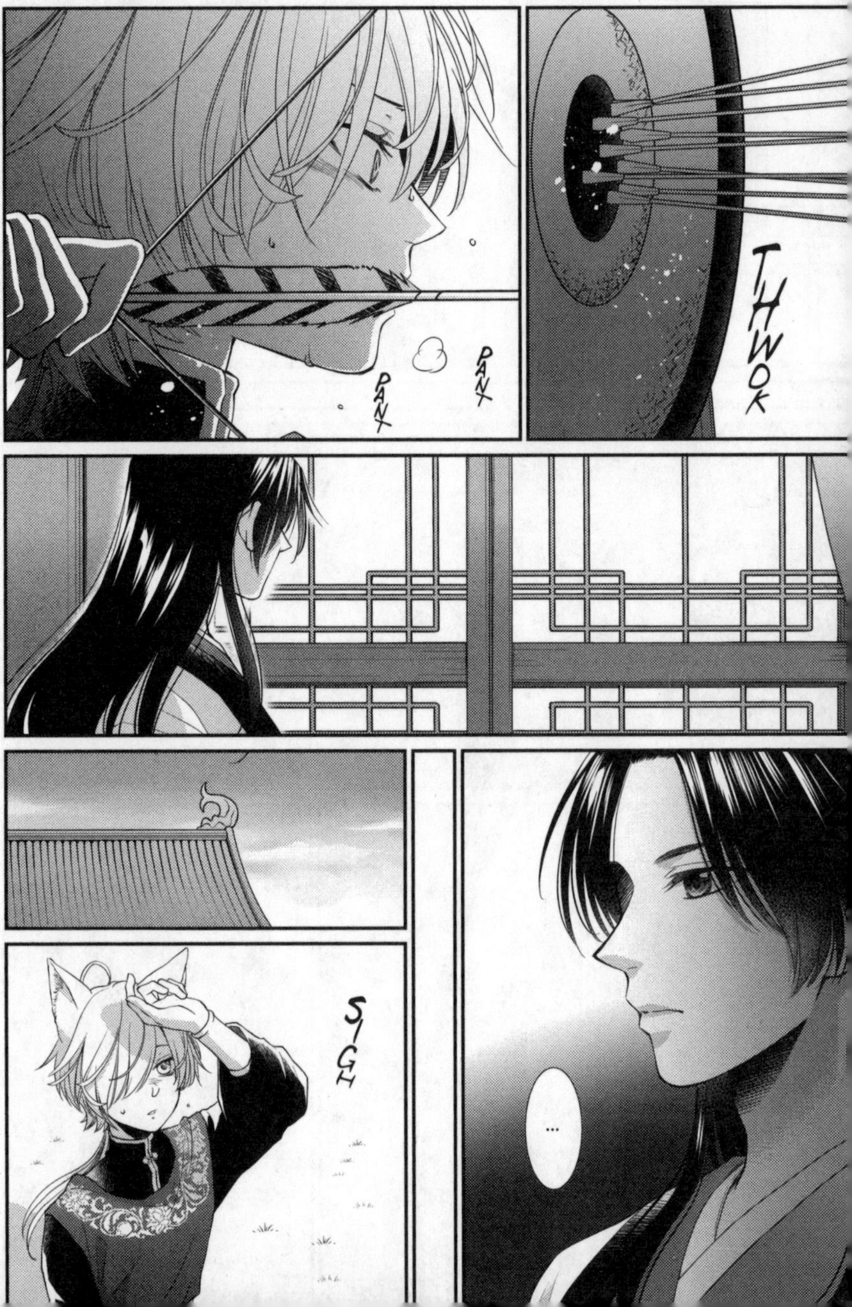
THWOK
PANT
PANT
...
SIGH

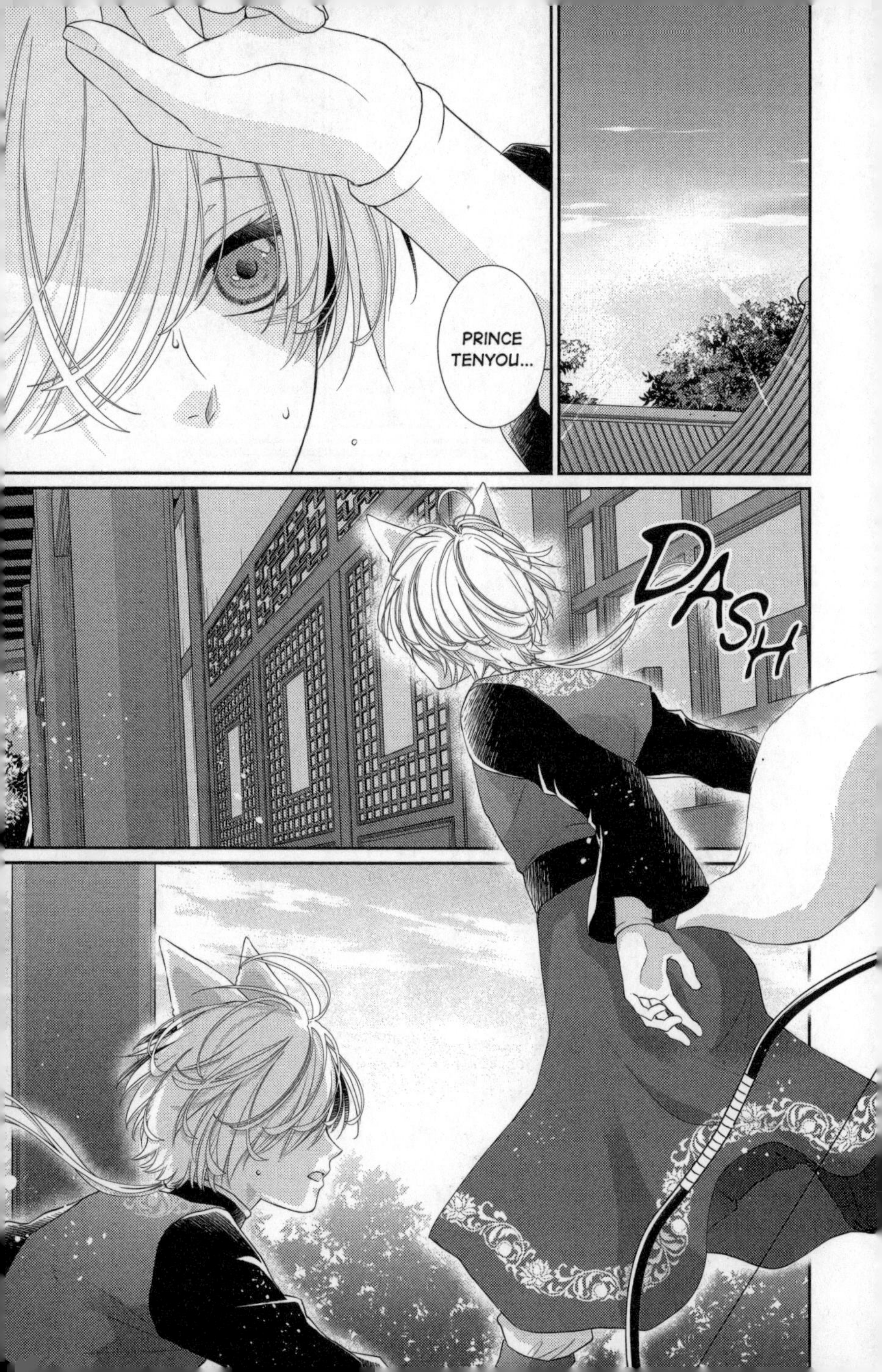
PRINCE TENYOU...
DASH

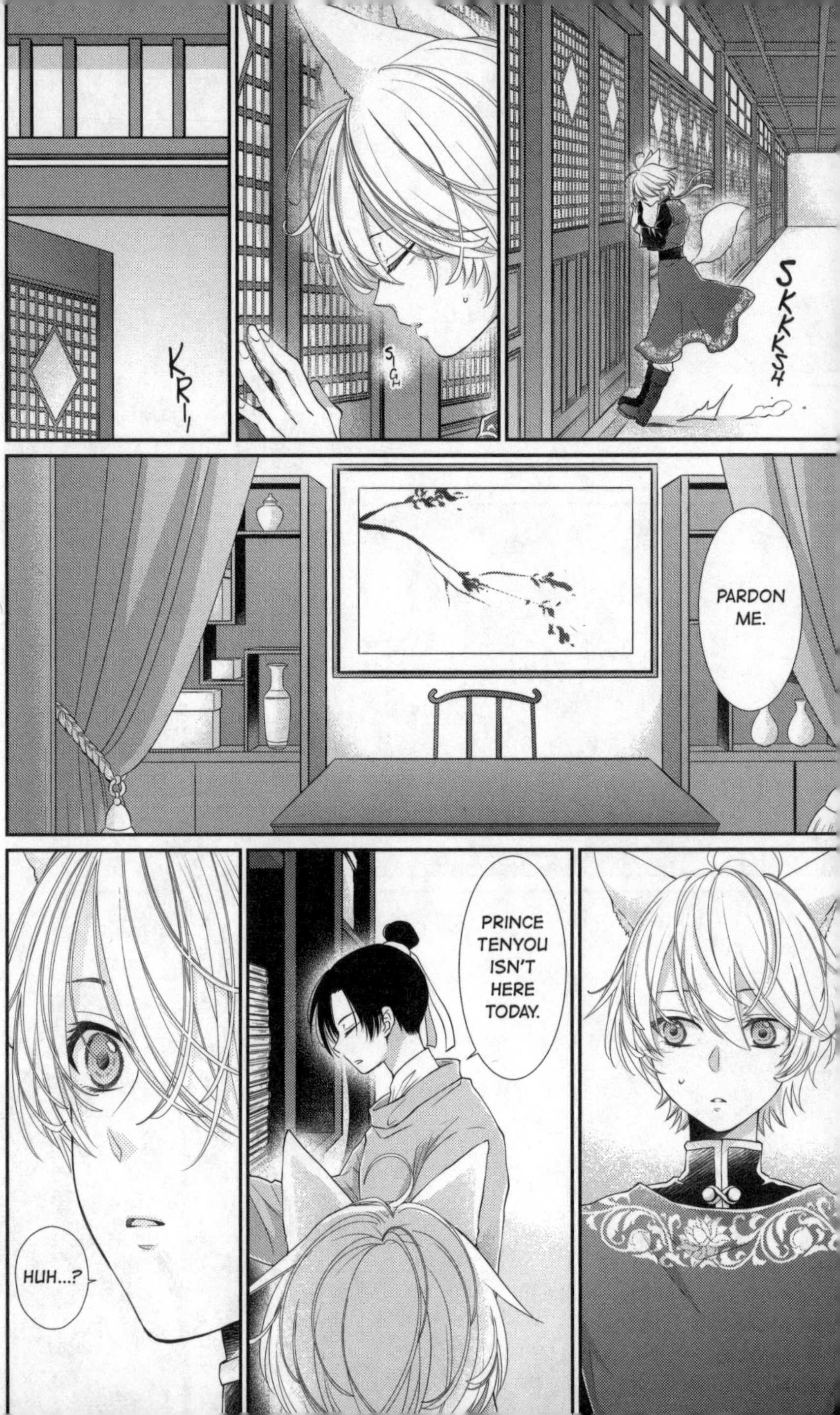
SKKKSH
SIGH
KRII
PARDON ME.
PRINCE TENYOU ISN'T HERE TODAY.
HUH...?

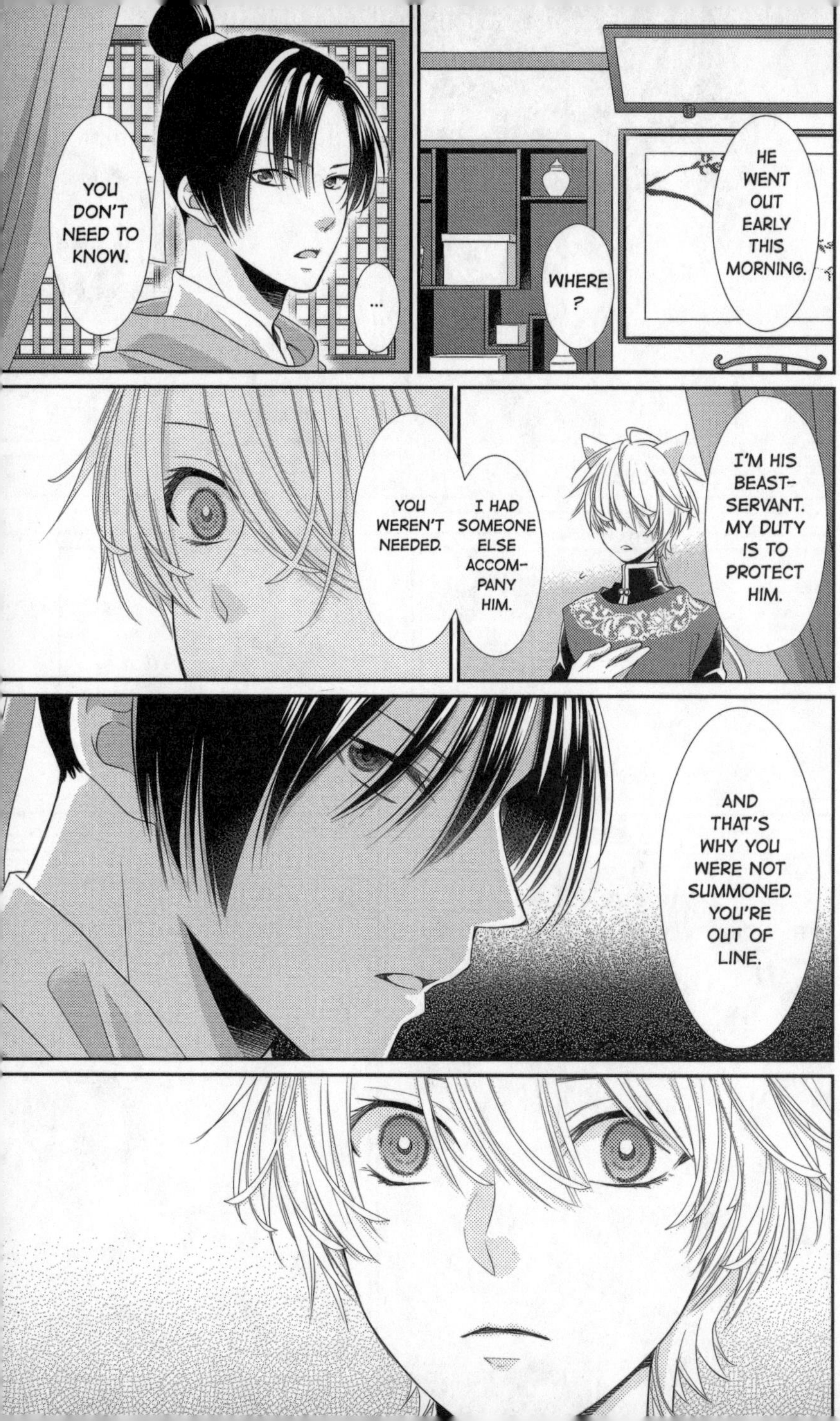
HE WENT OUT EARLY THIS MORNING.
WHERE?
YOU DON'T NEED TO KNOW.
...
I'M HIS BEAST-SERVANT. MY DUTY IS TO PROTECT HIM.
I HAD SOMEONE ELSE ACCOMPANY HIM.
YOU WEREN'T NEEDED.
AND THAT'S WHY YOU WERE NOT SUMMONED. YOU'RE OUT OF LINE.

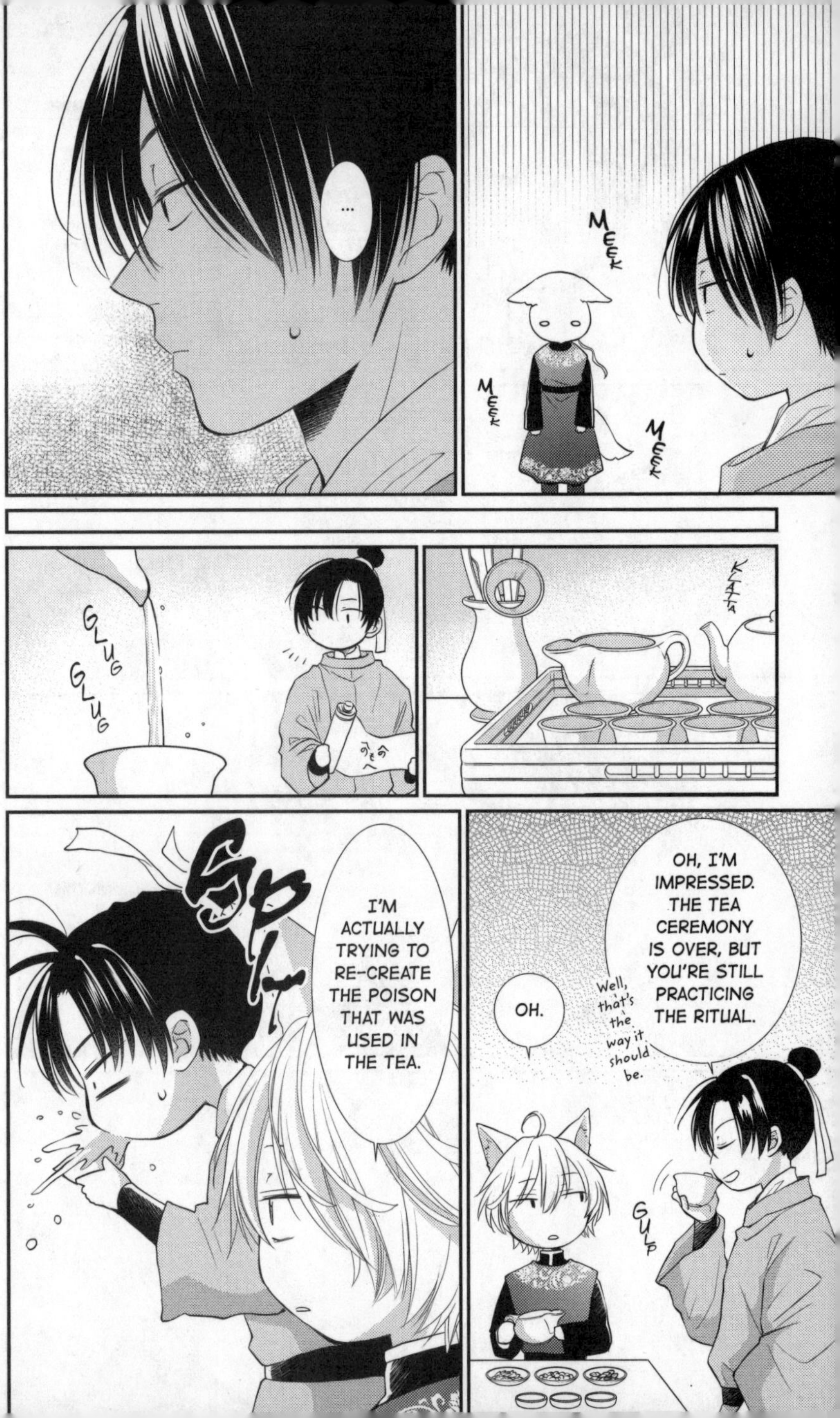
MEEK
MEEK
MEEK
...
KLATTA
GLUG
GLUG
OH, I'M IMPRESSED. THE TEA CEREMONY IS OVER, BUT YOU'RE STILL PRACTICING THE RITUAL.
Well, that's the way it should be.
OH.
GULP
I'M ACTUALLY TRYING TO RE-CREATE THE POISON THAT WAS USED IN THE TEA.
SPIT

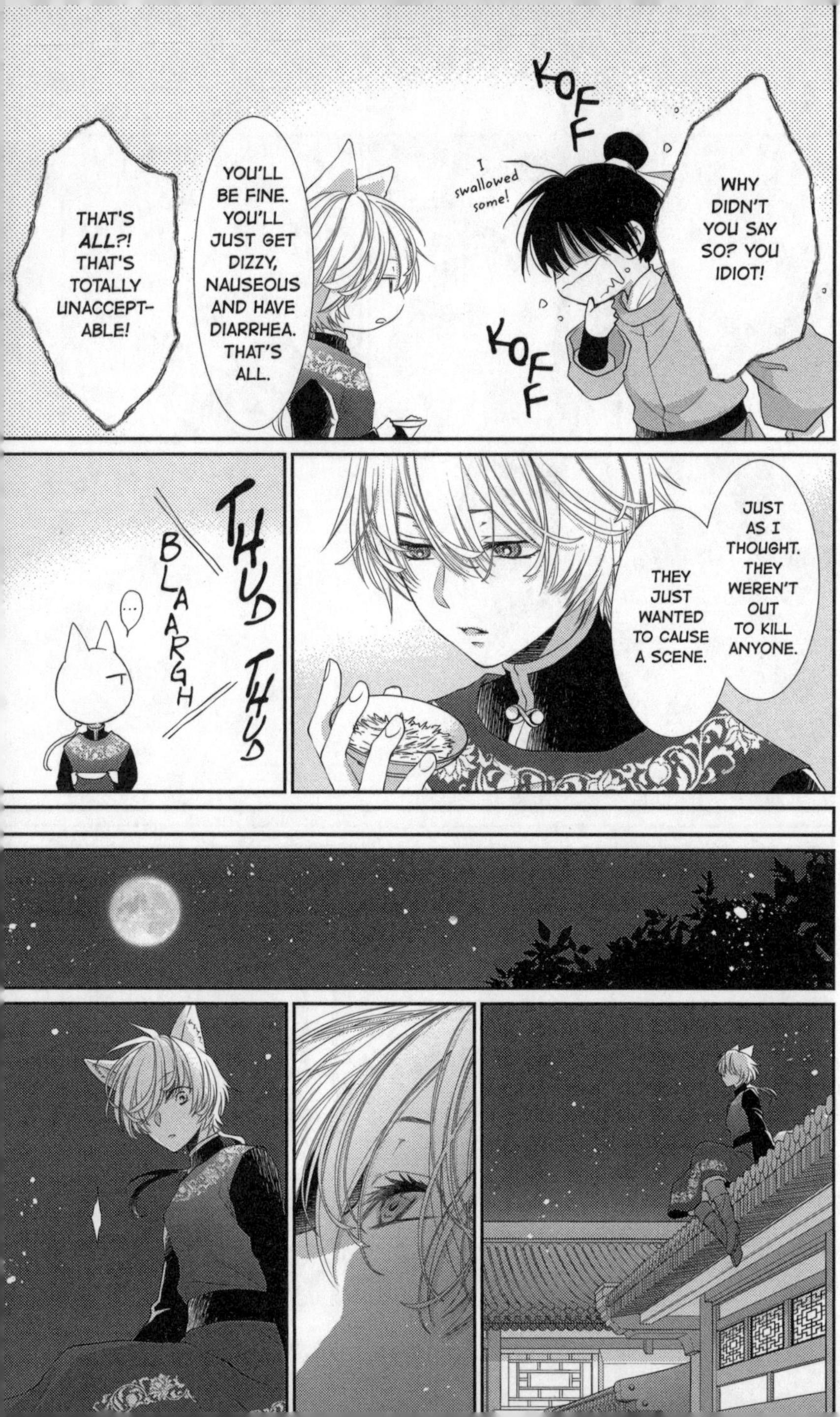
KOFF KOFF
WHY DIDN'T YOU SAY SO? YOU IDIOT!
I swallowed some!
KOFF KOFF
YOU'LL BE FINE. YOU'LL JUST GET DIZZY, NAUSEOUS AND HAVE DIARRHEA. THAT'S ALL.
THAT'S *ALL*?! THAT'S TOTALLY UNACCEPT-ABLE!
JUST AS I THOUGHT. THEY WEREN'T OUT TO KILL ANYONE.
THEY JUST WANTED TO CAUSE A SCENE.
THUD THUD
BLAARGH
...

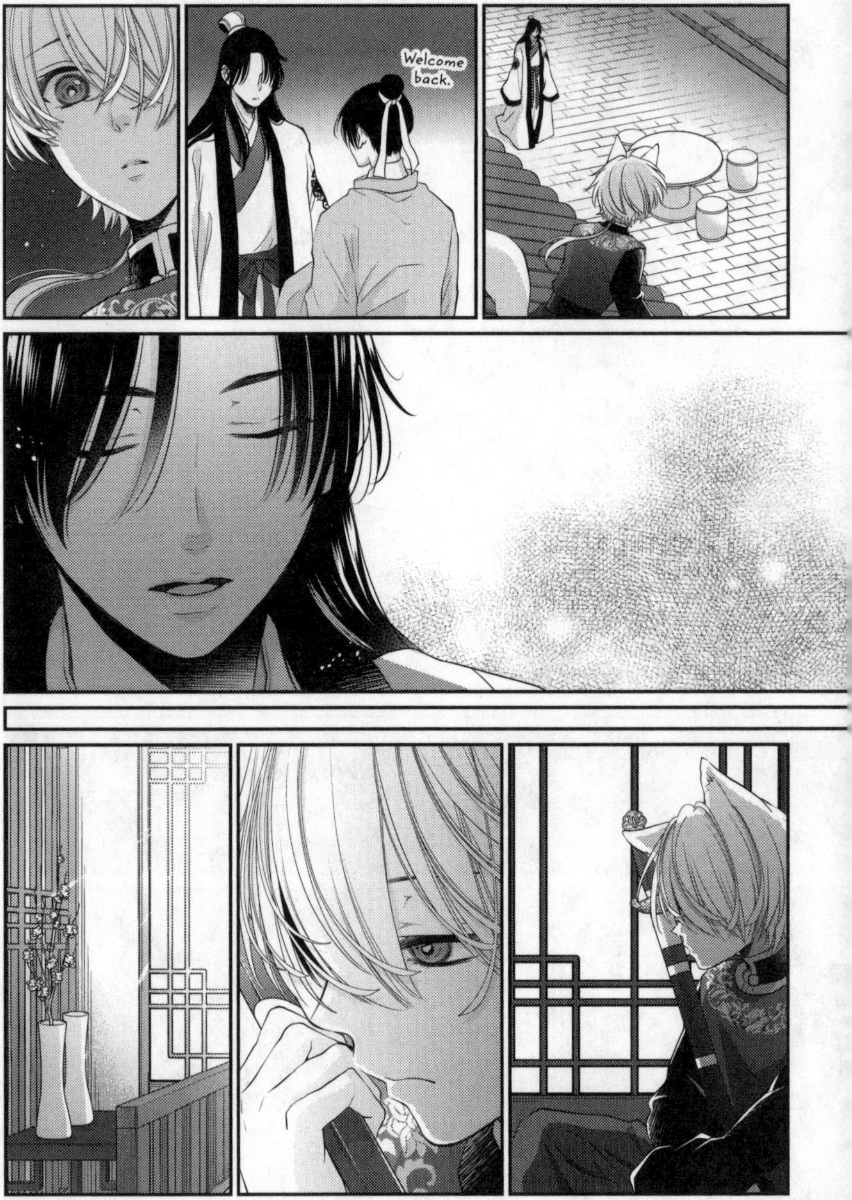
Welcome back.

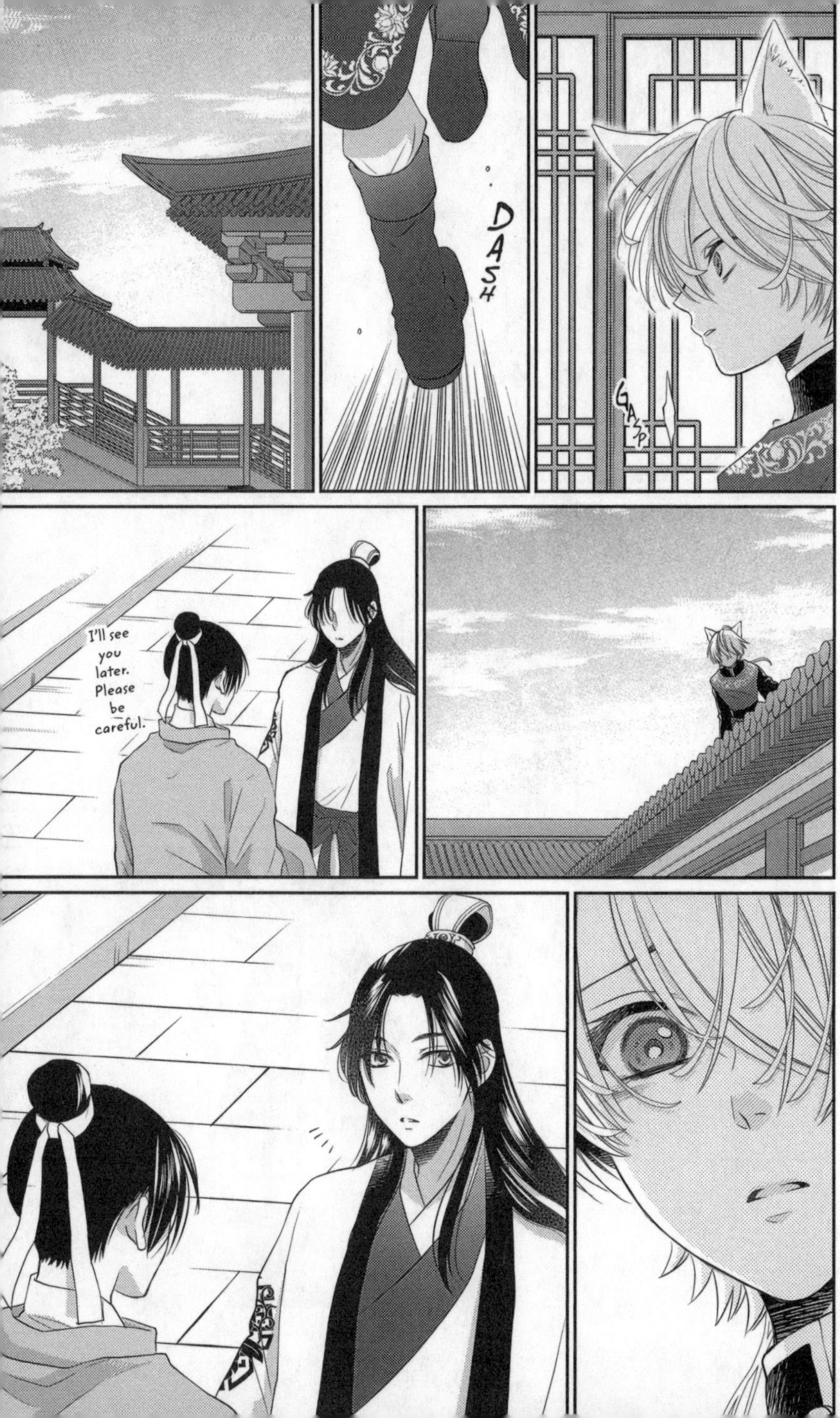
GASP
DASH
I'll see you later. Please be careful.

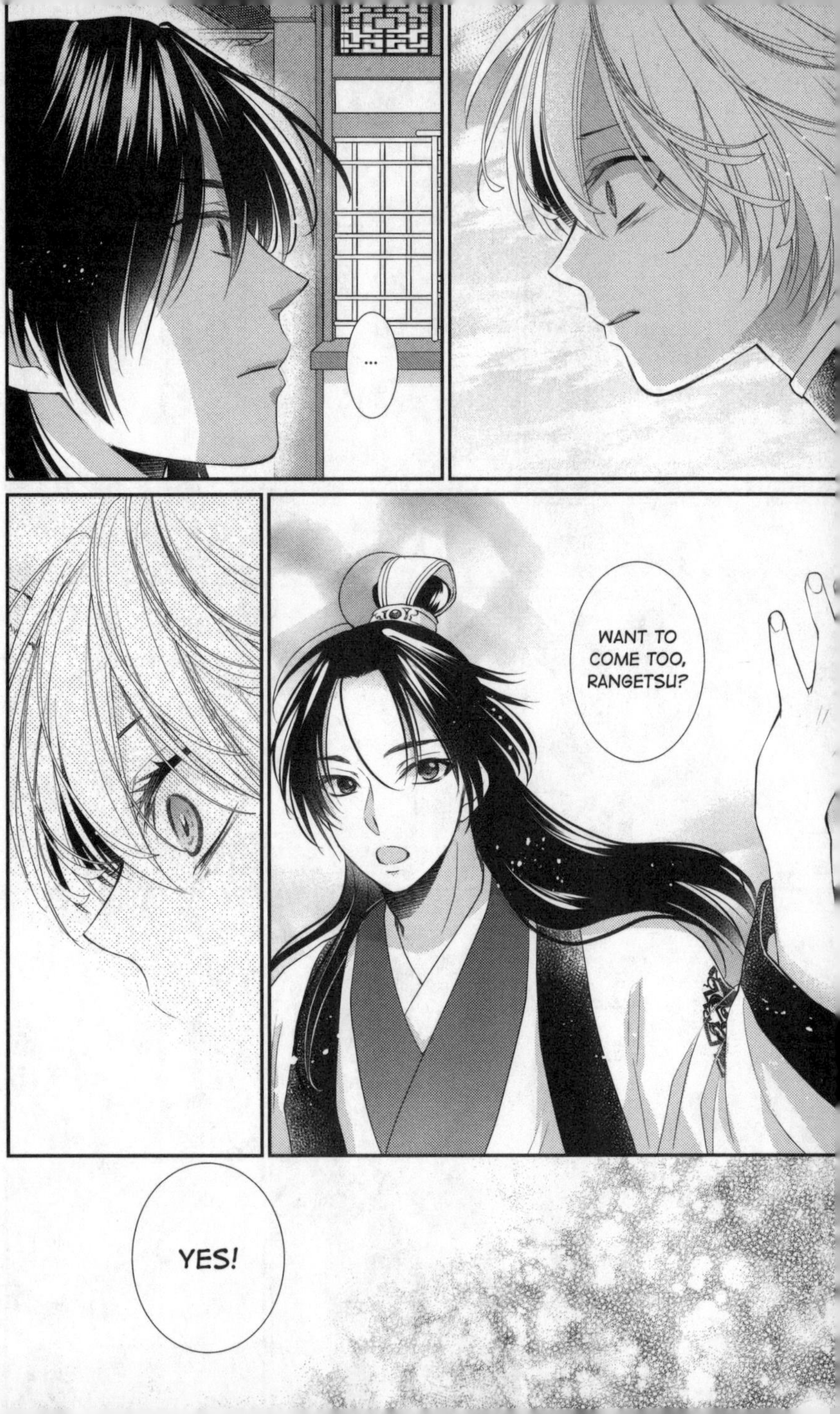
...
WANT TO COME TOO, RANGETSU?
YES!

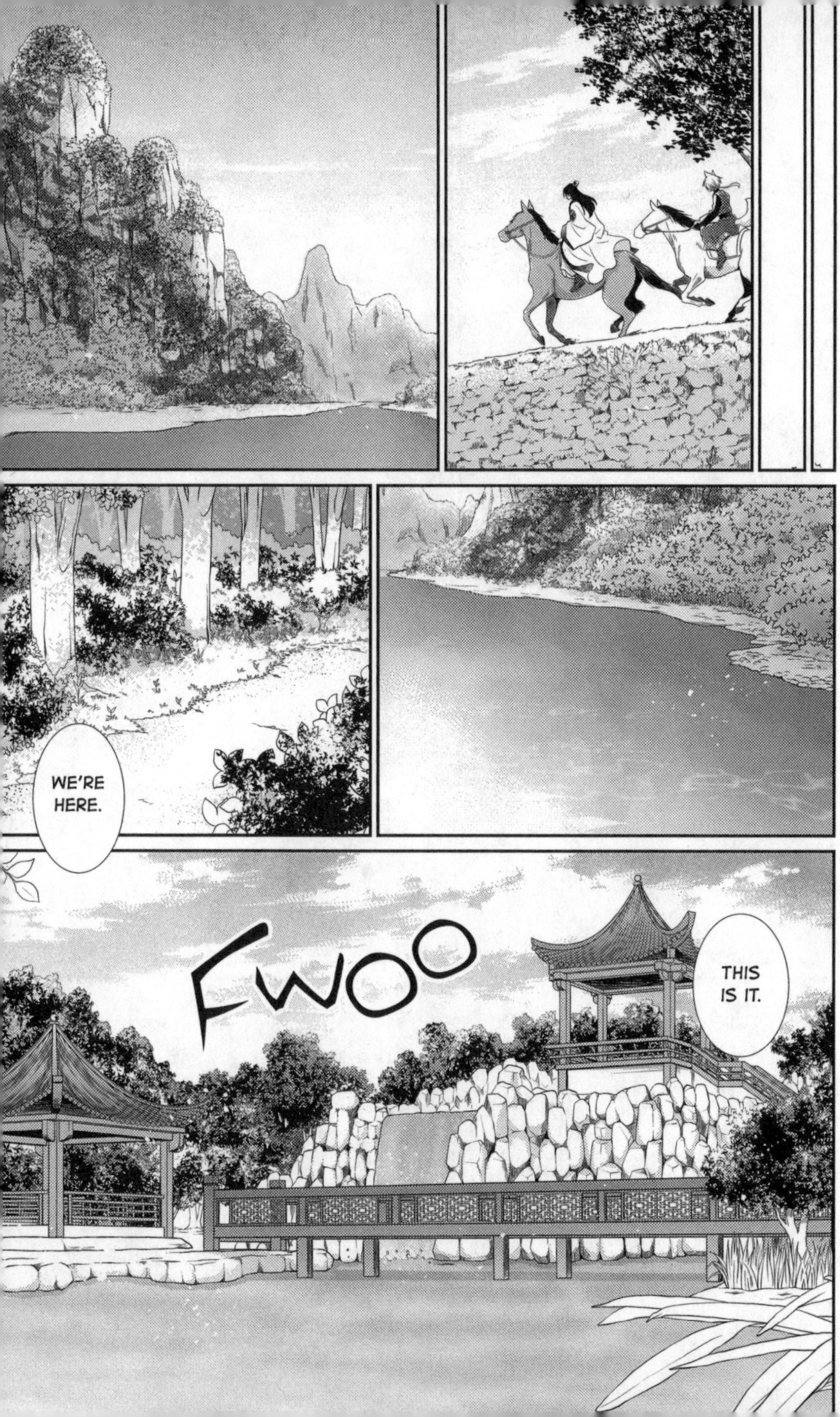
WE'RE HERE.
THIS IS IT.
FWOO

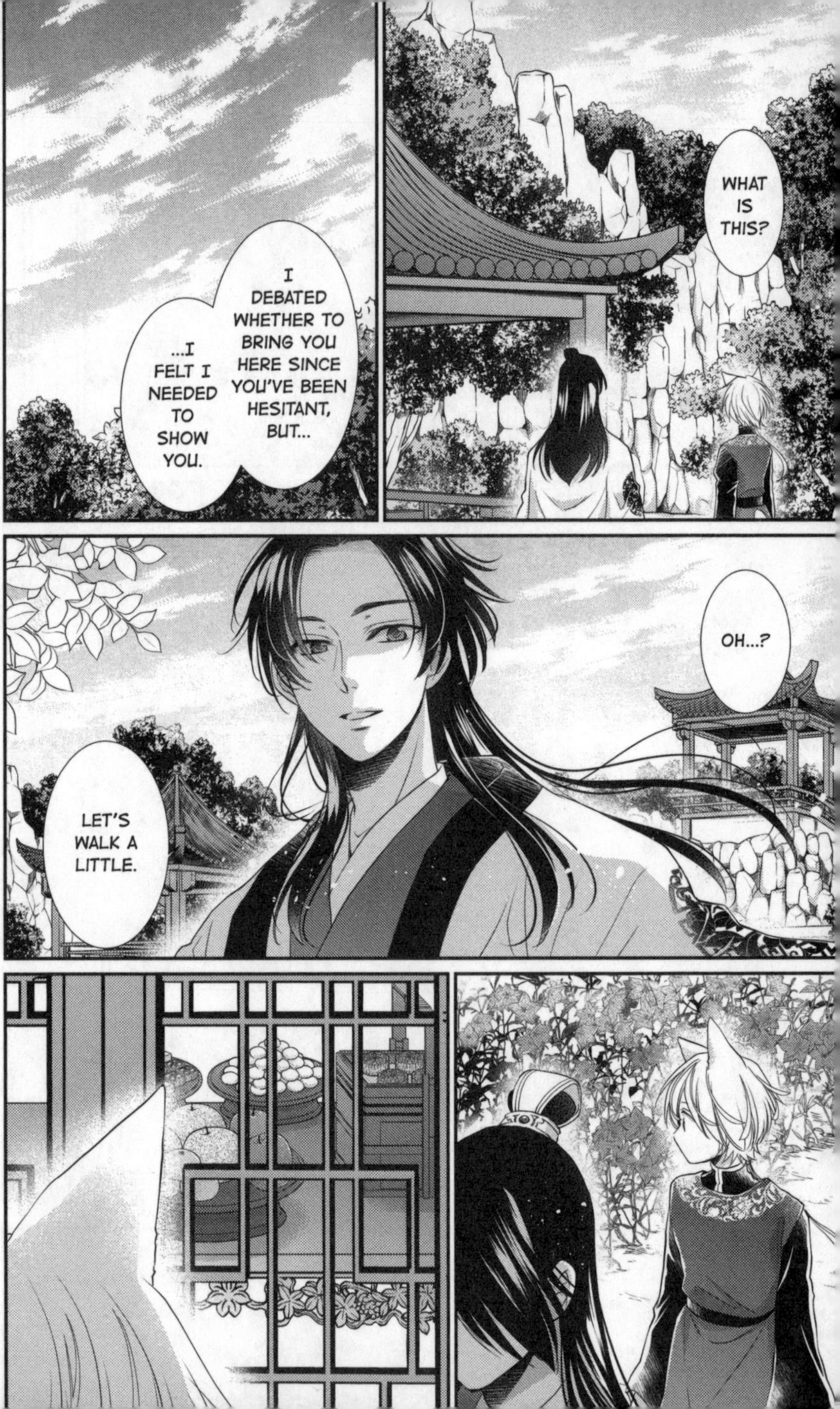
WHAT IS THIS?
I DEBATED WHETHER TO BRING YOU HERE SINCE YOU'VE BEEN HESITANT, BUT...
...I FELT I NEEDED TO SHOW YOU.
OH...?
LET'S WALK A LITTLE.

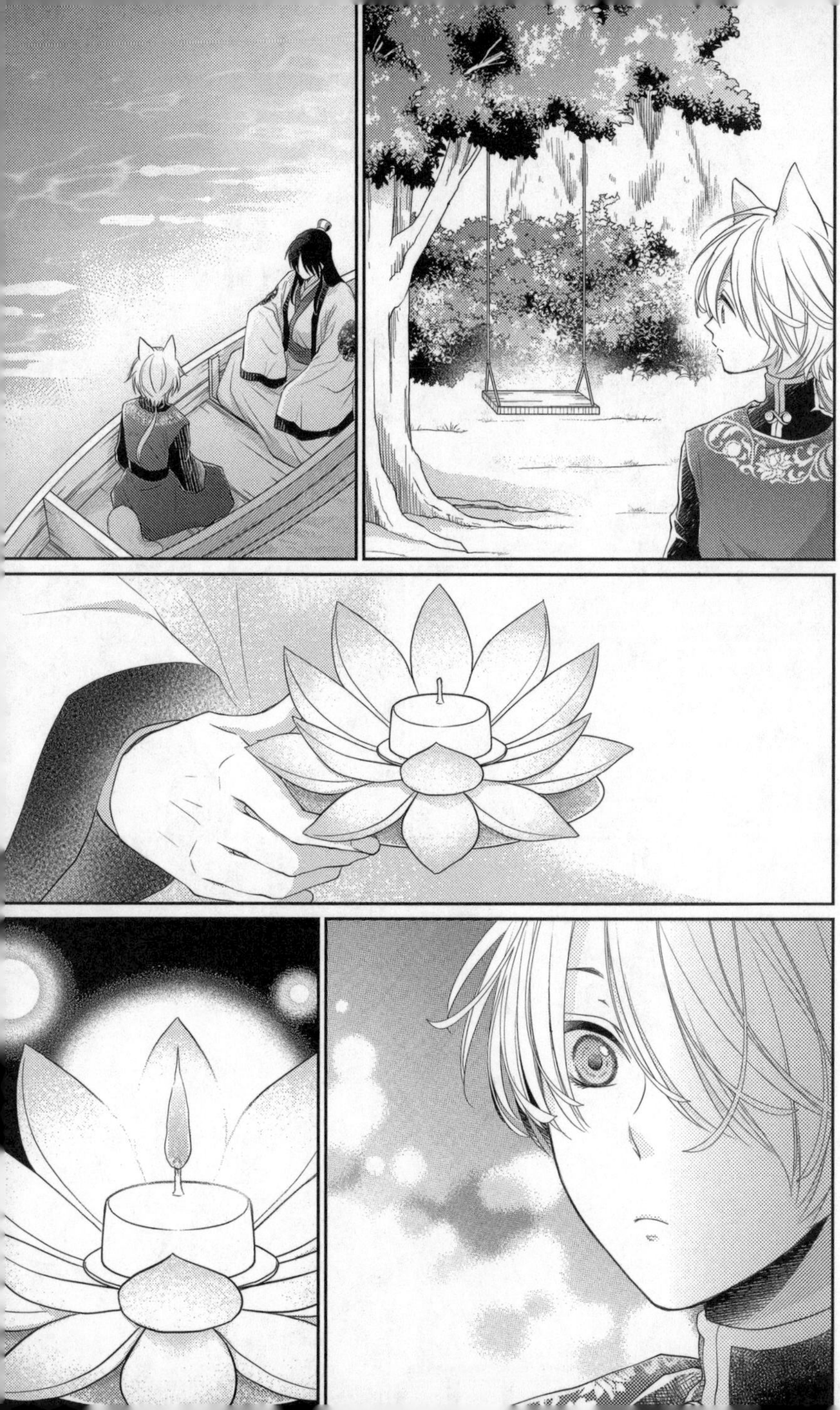

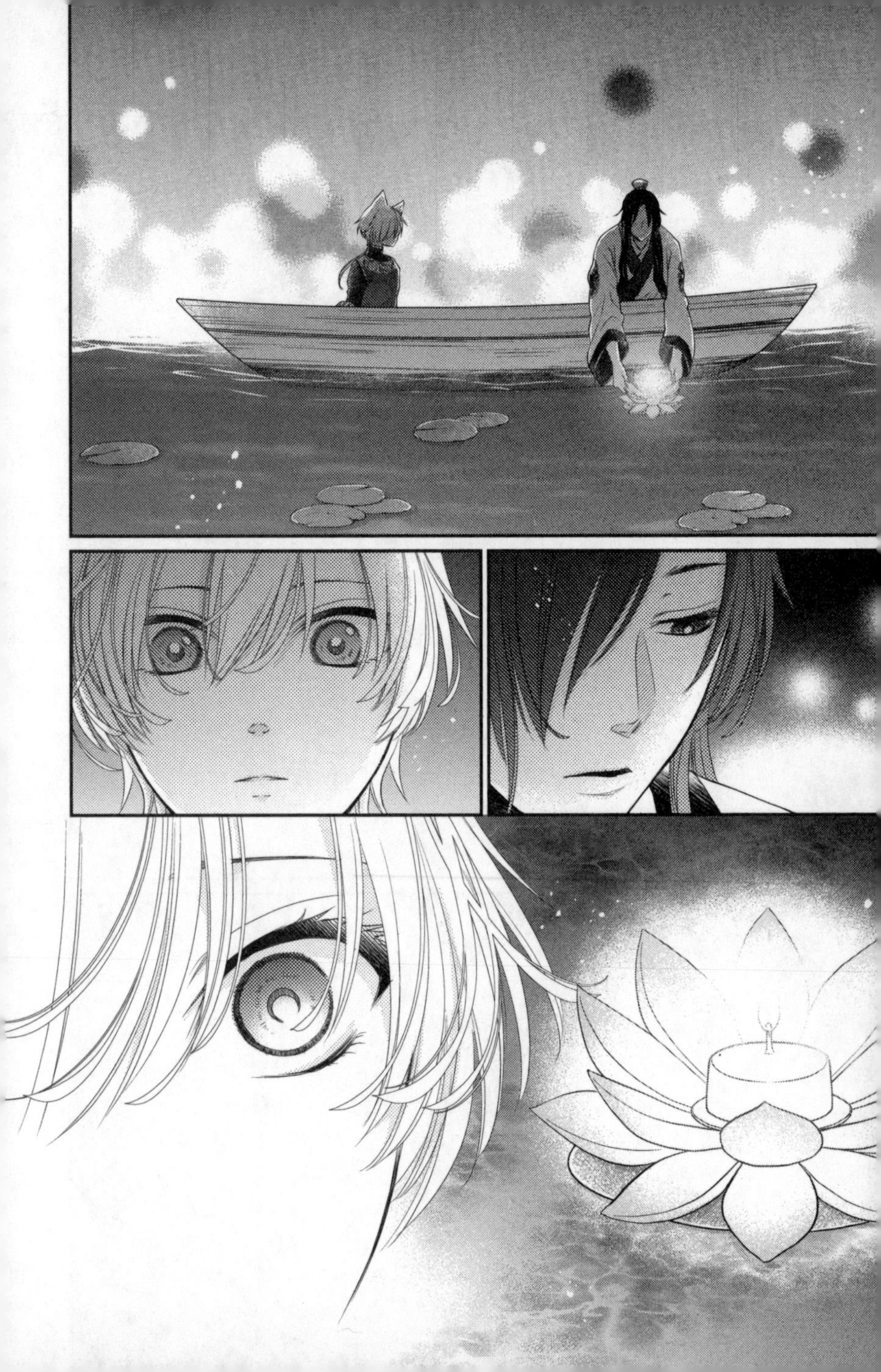

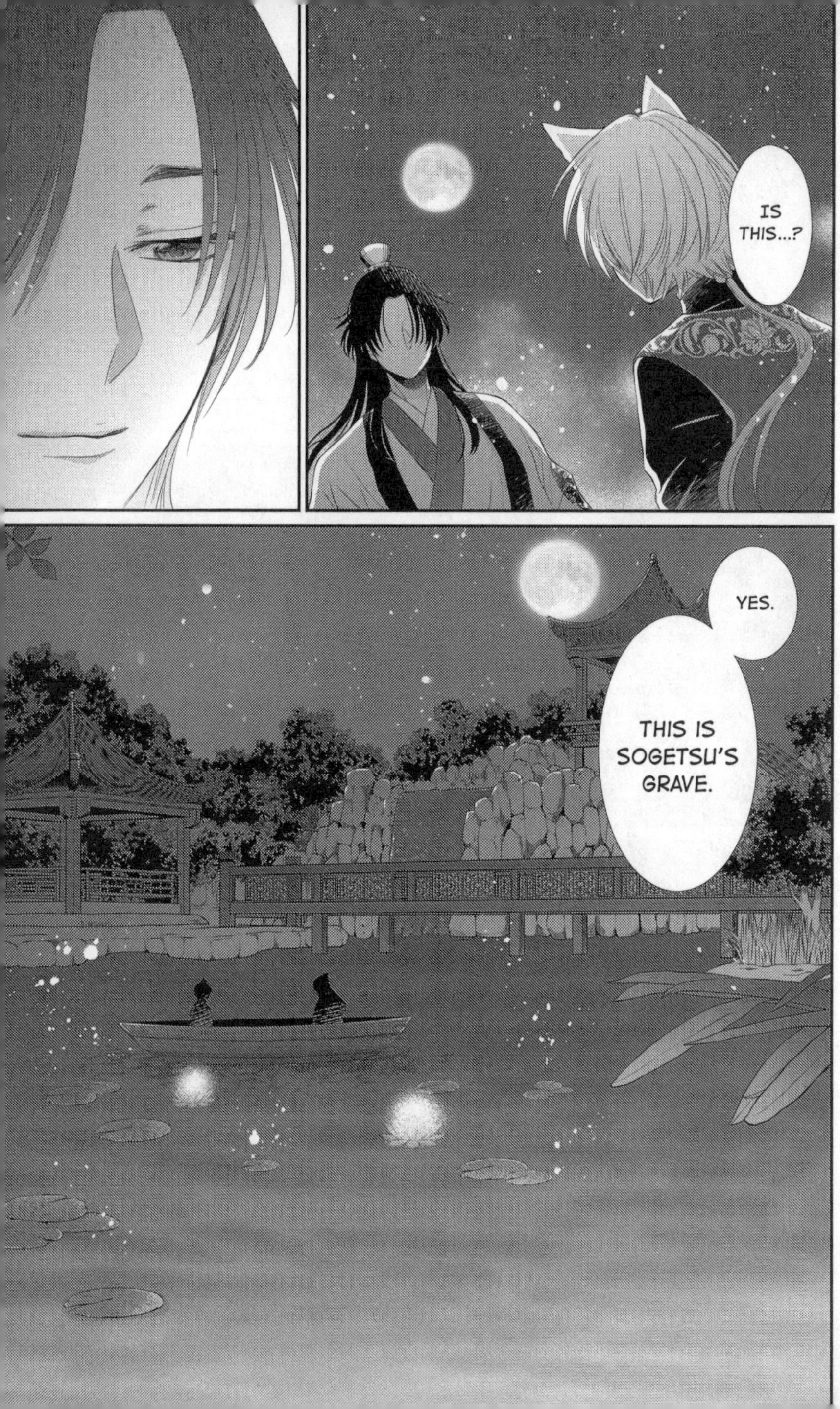
IS THIS...?
YES.
THIS IS SOGETSU'S GRAVE.

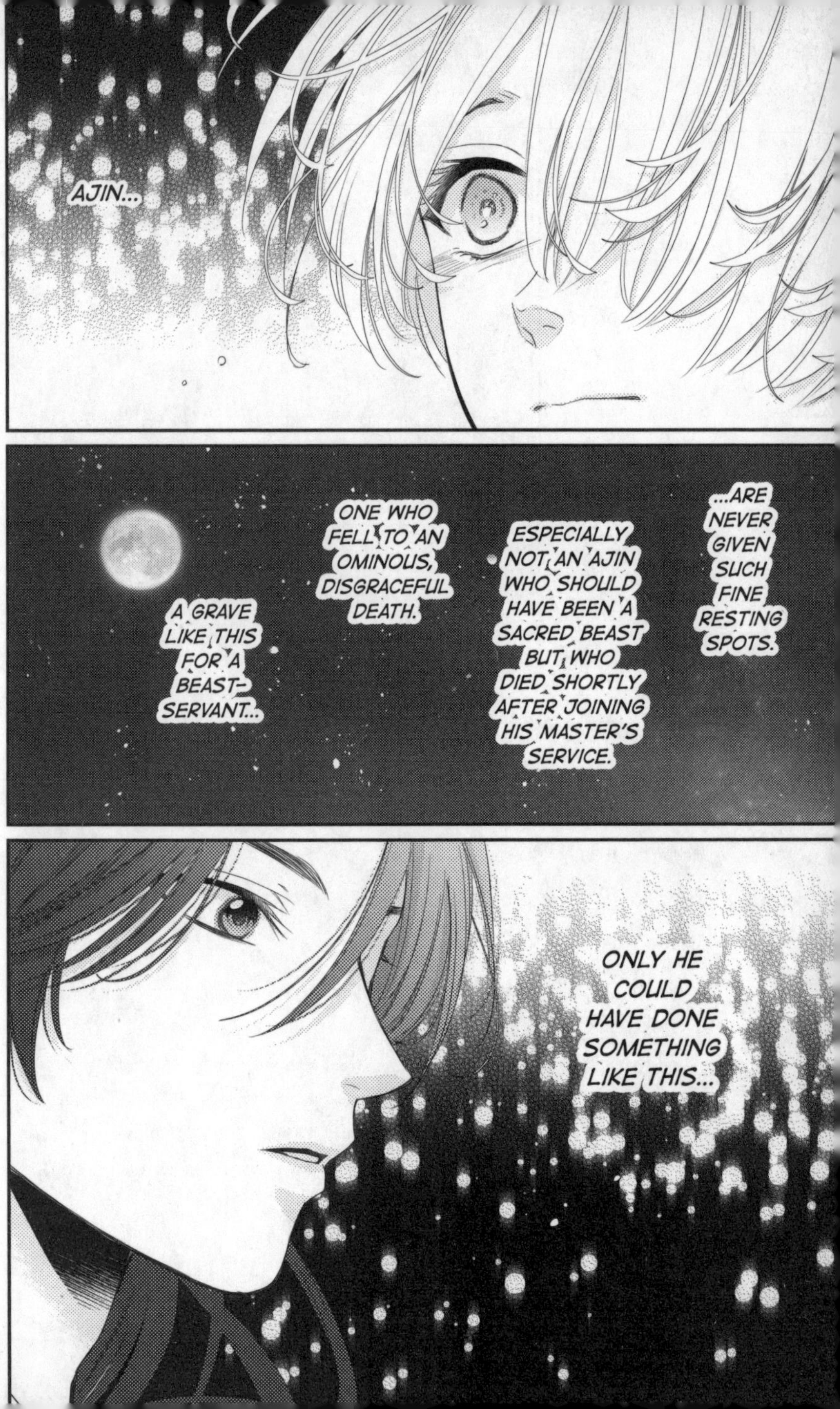
AJIN...
A GRAVE LIKE THIS FOR A BEAST-SERVANT...
ONE WHO FELL TO AN OMINOUS, DISGRACEFUL DEATH.
ESPECIALLY NOT AN AJIN WHO SHOULD HAVE BEEN A SACRED BEAST BUT WHO DIED SHORTLY AFTER JOINING HIS MASTER'S SERVICE.
...ARE NEVER GIVEN SUCH FINE RESTING SPOTS.
ONLY HE COULD HAVE DONE SOMETHING LIKE THIS...

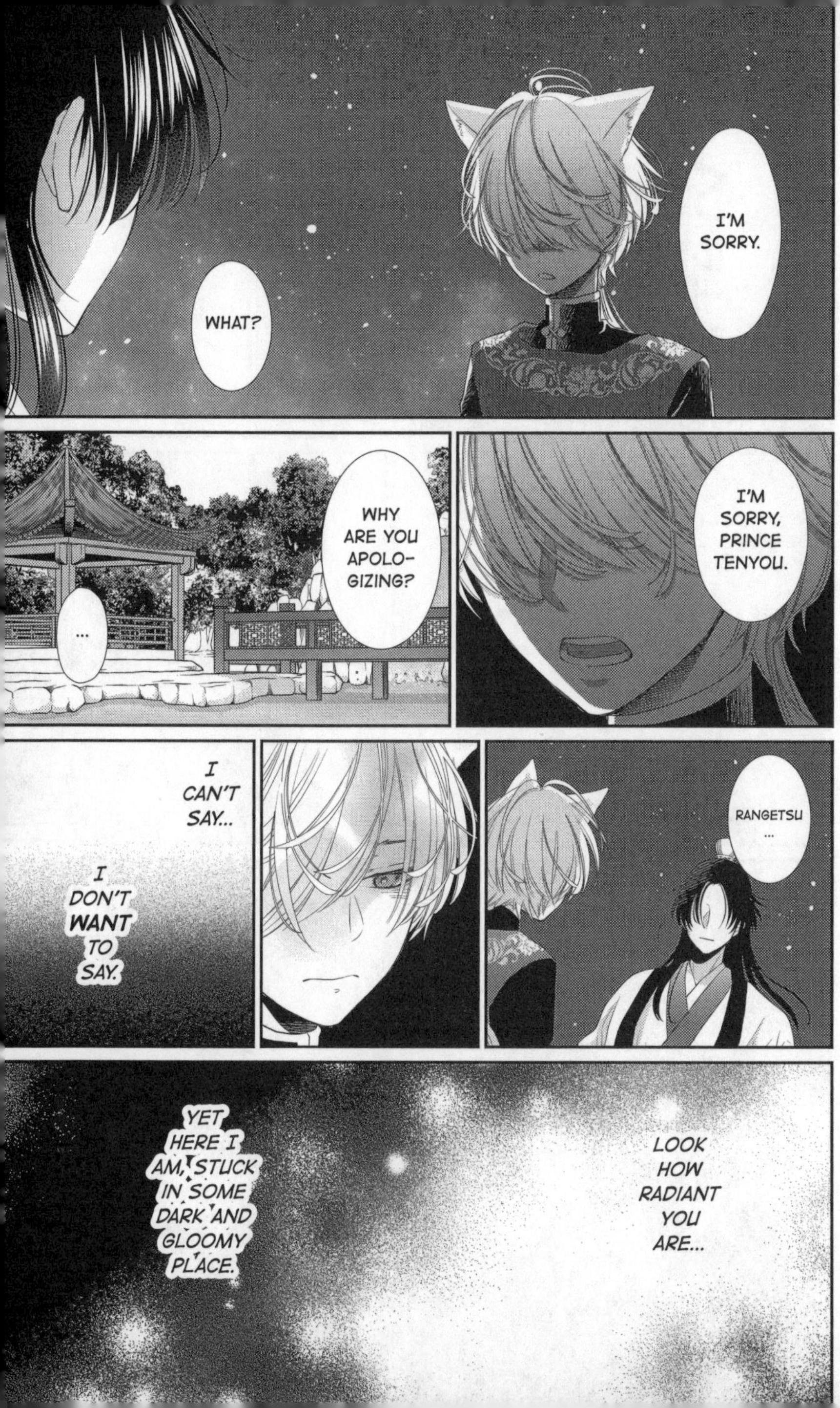
I'M SORRY.
WHAT?
I'M SORRY, PRINCE TENYOU.
WHY ARE YOU APOLOGIZING?
...
RANGETSU ...
I CAN'T SAY...
I DON'T WANT TO SAY.
LOOK HOW RADIANT YOU ARE...
YET HERE I AM, STUCK IN SOME DARK AND GLOOMY PLACE.

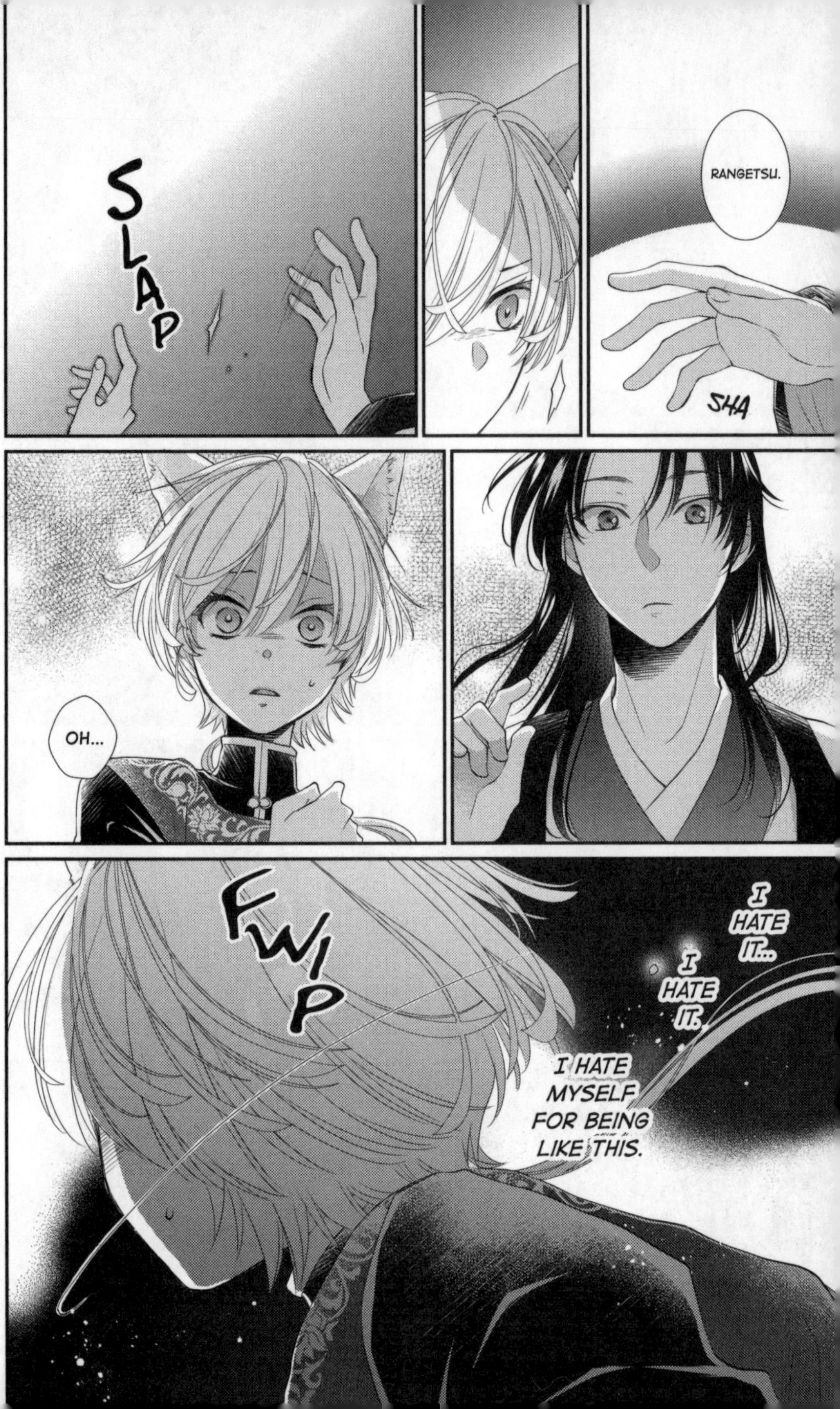
RANGETSU.
SHA
SLAP
OH...
I HATE IT...
I HATE IT.
FWIP
I HATE MYSELF FOR BEING LIKE THIS.

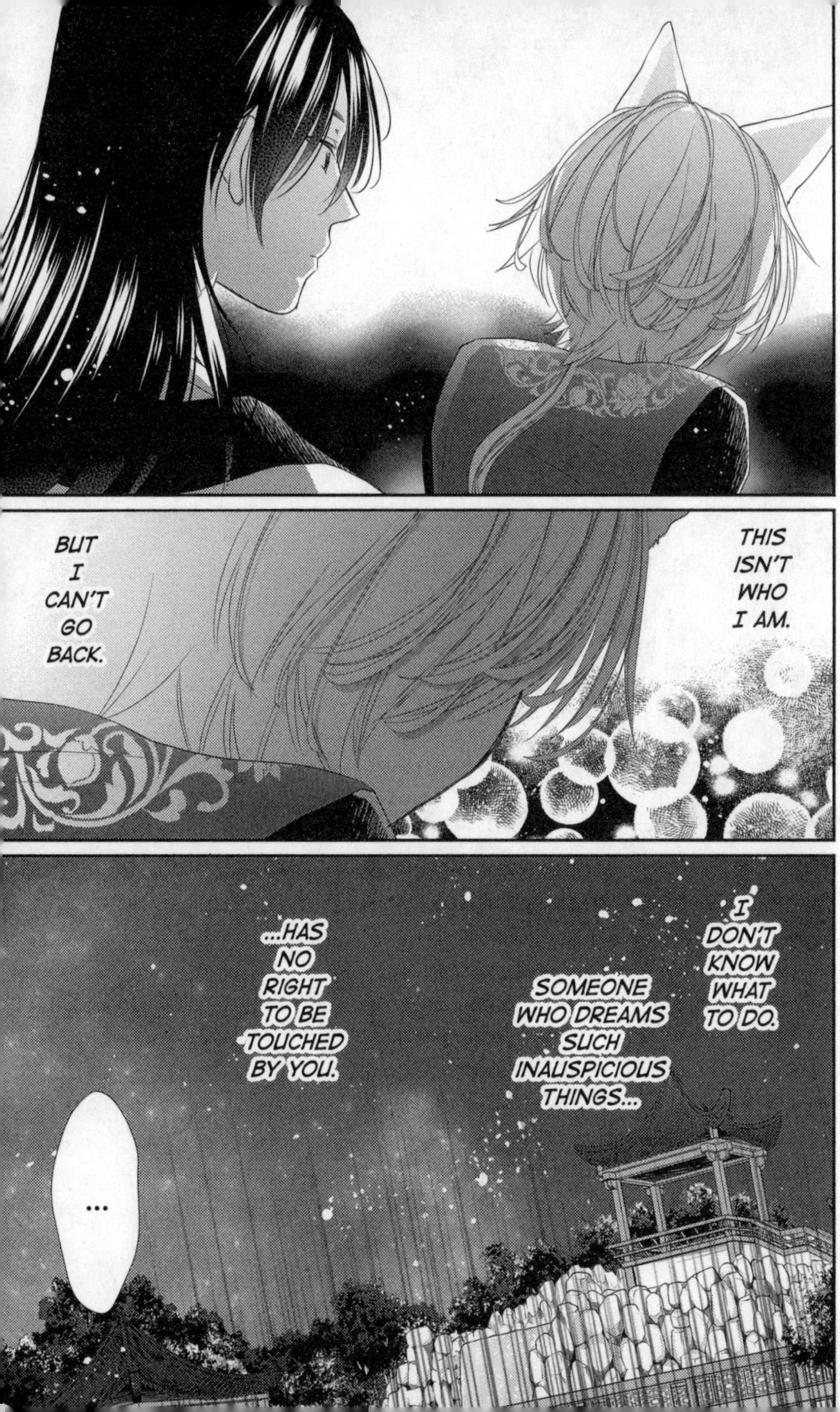
THIS ISN'T WHO I AM.
BUT I CAN'T GO BACK.
I DON'T KNOW WHAT TO DO.
SOMEONE WHO DREAMS SUCH INAUSPICIOUS THINGS...
...HAS NO RIGHT TO BE TOUCHED BY YOU.
...

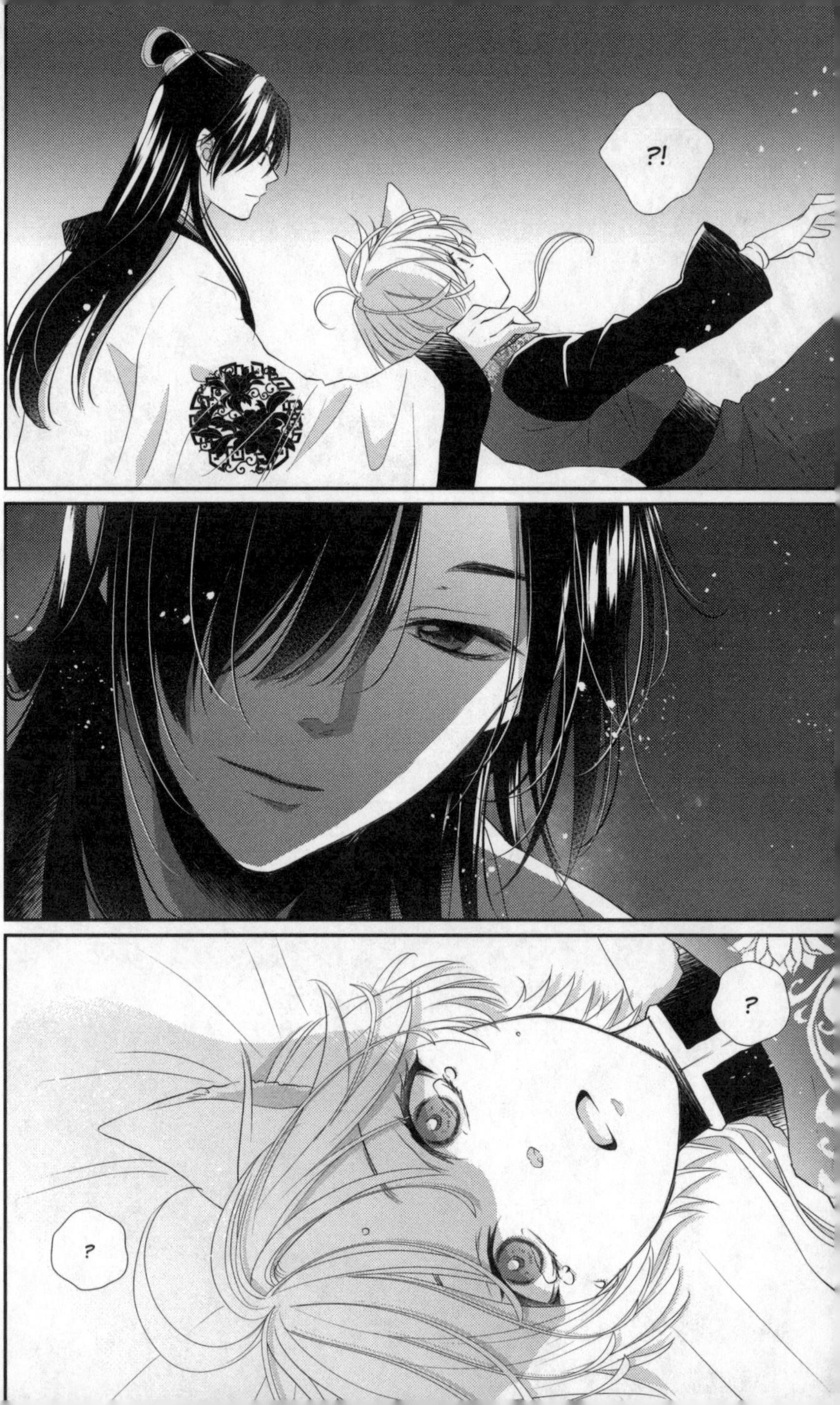
?!
?
?

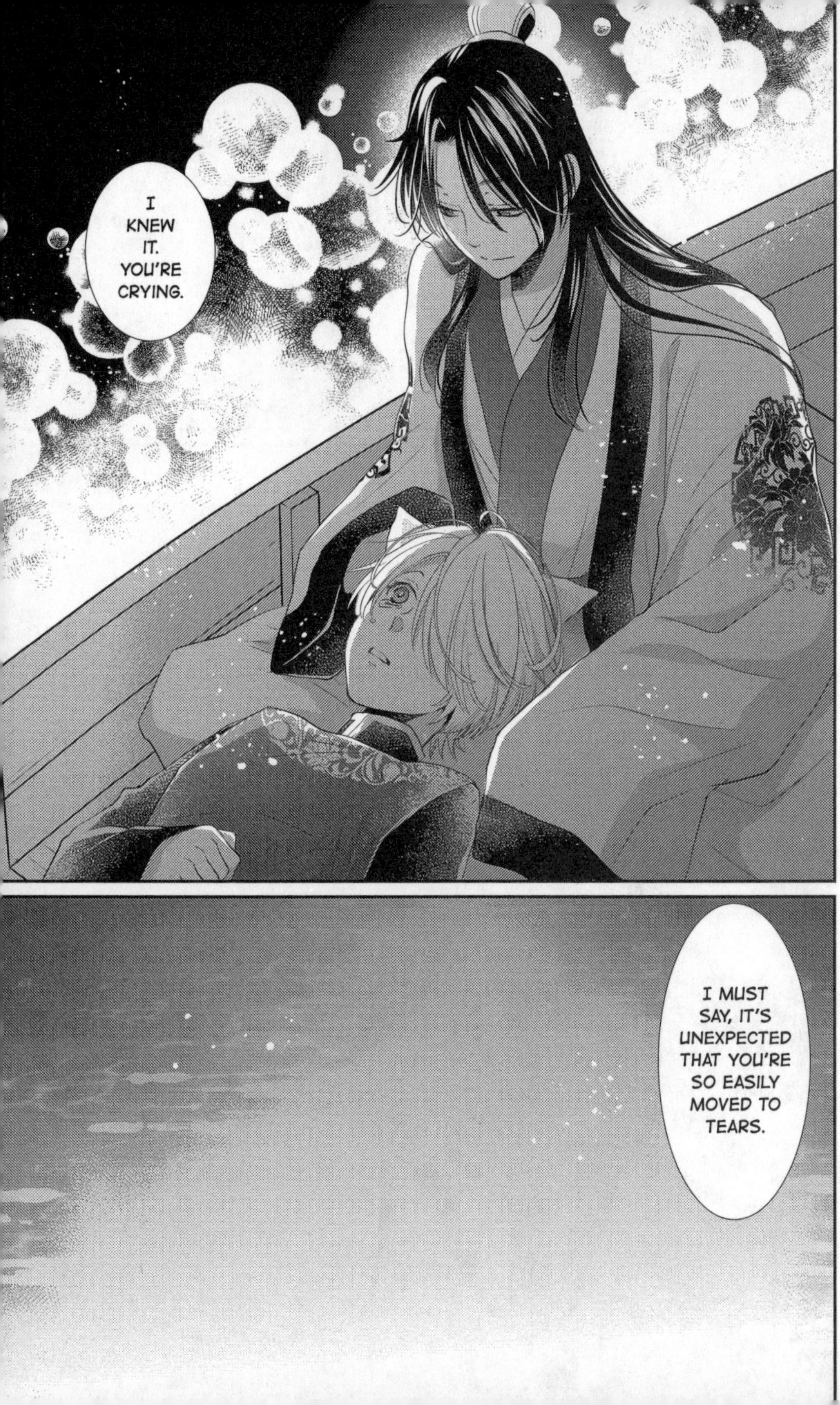
I KNEW IT. YOU'RE CRYING.
I MUST SAY, IT'S UNEXPECTED THAT YOU'RE SO EASILY MOVED TO TEARS.

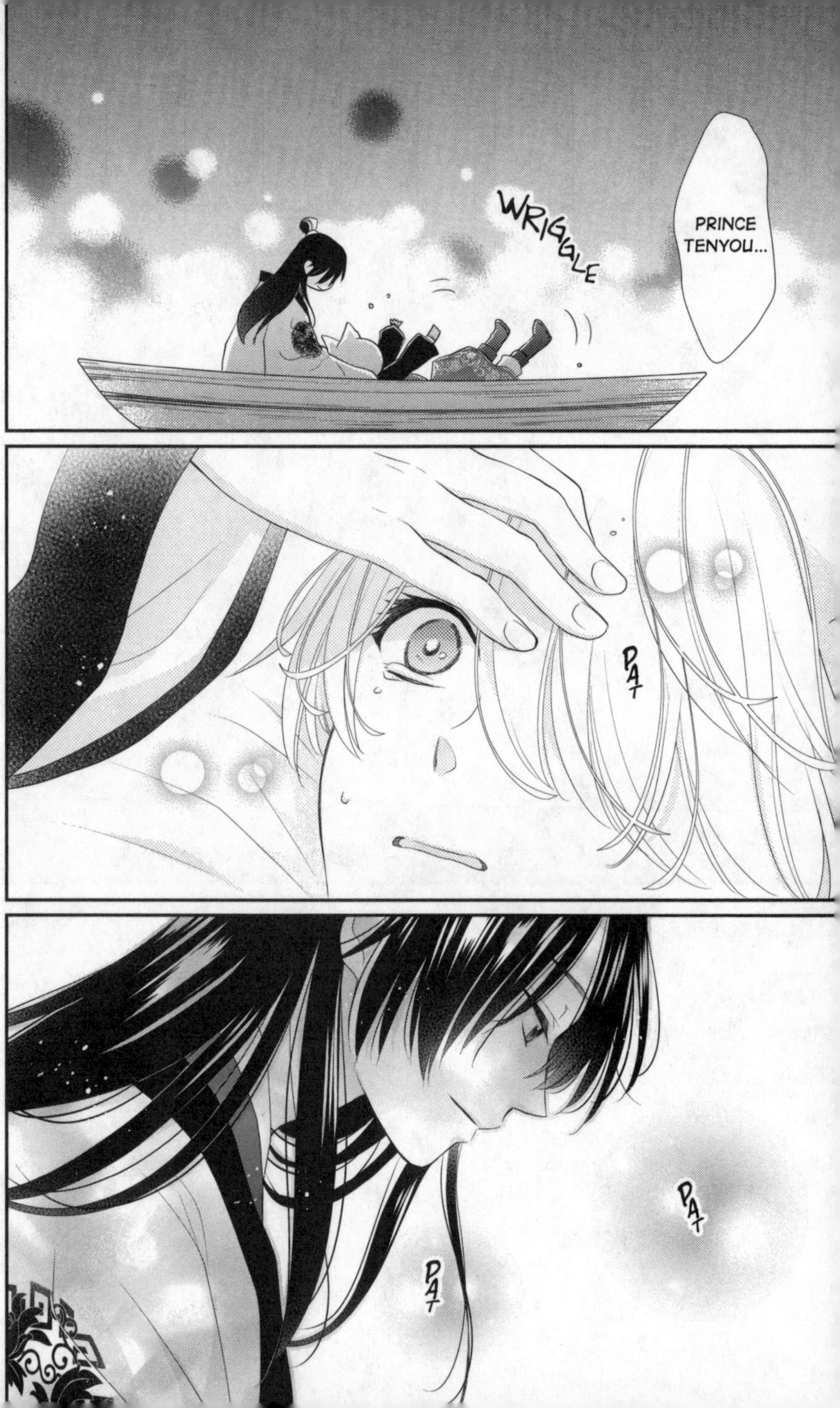
PRINCE TENYOU...
WRIGGLE
PAT
PAT
PAT

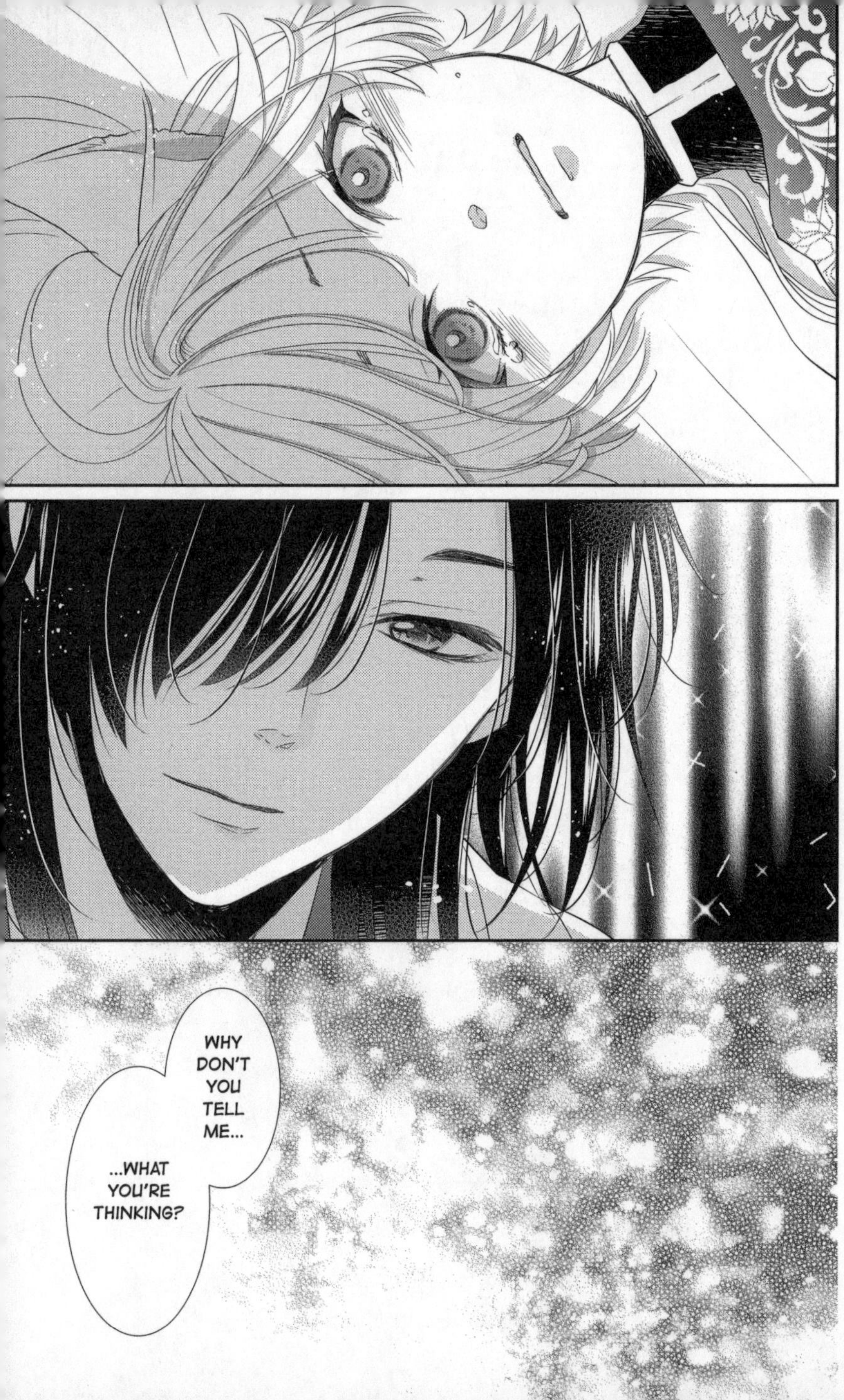
WHY DON'T YOU TELL ME...
...WHAT YOU'RE THINKING?

THE KING'S Beast

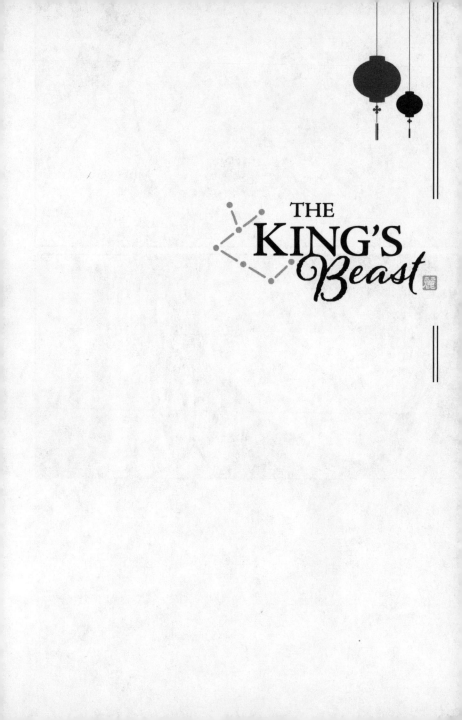

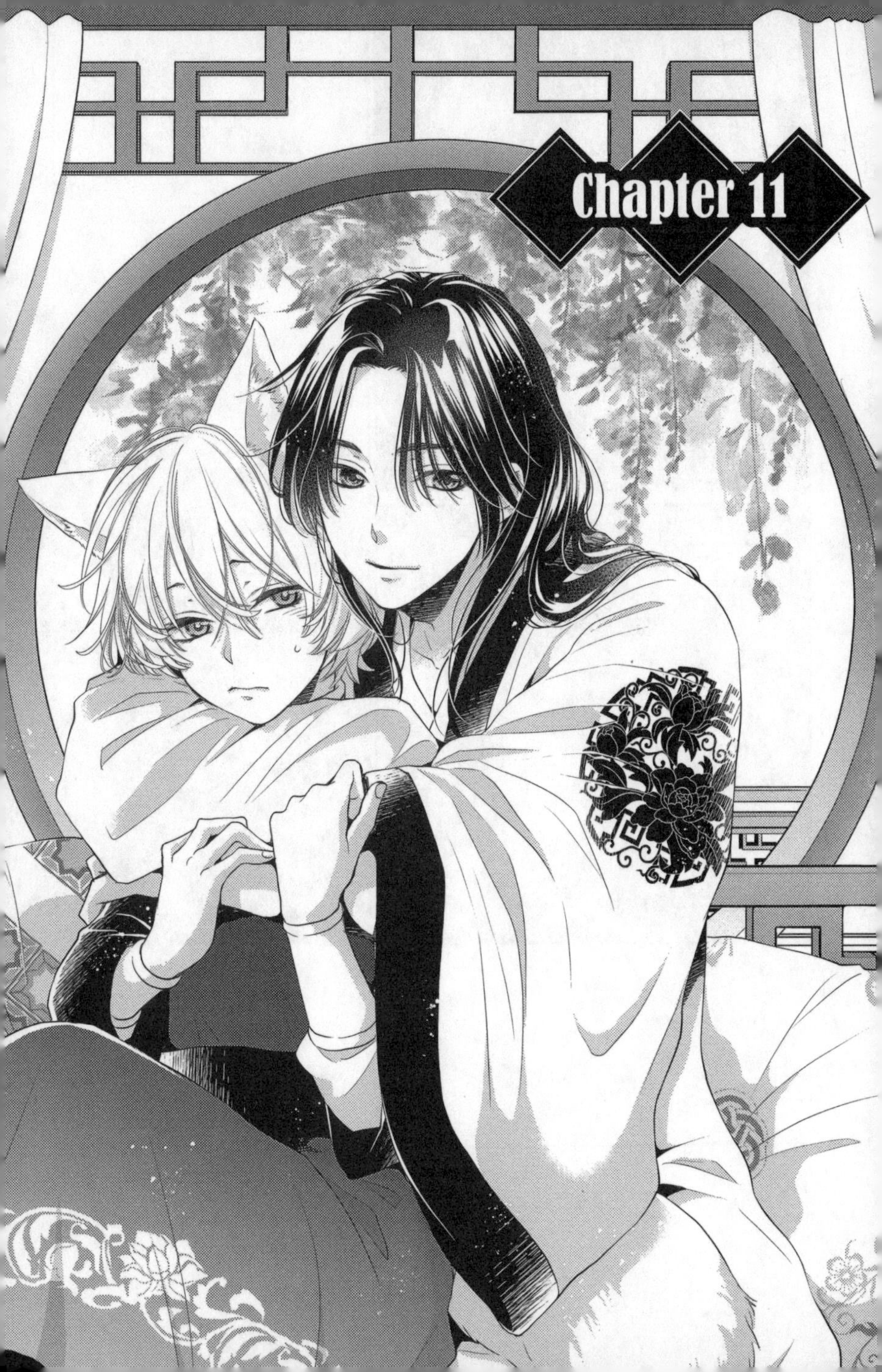
Chapter 11

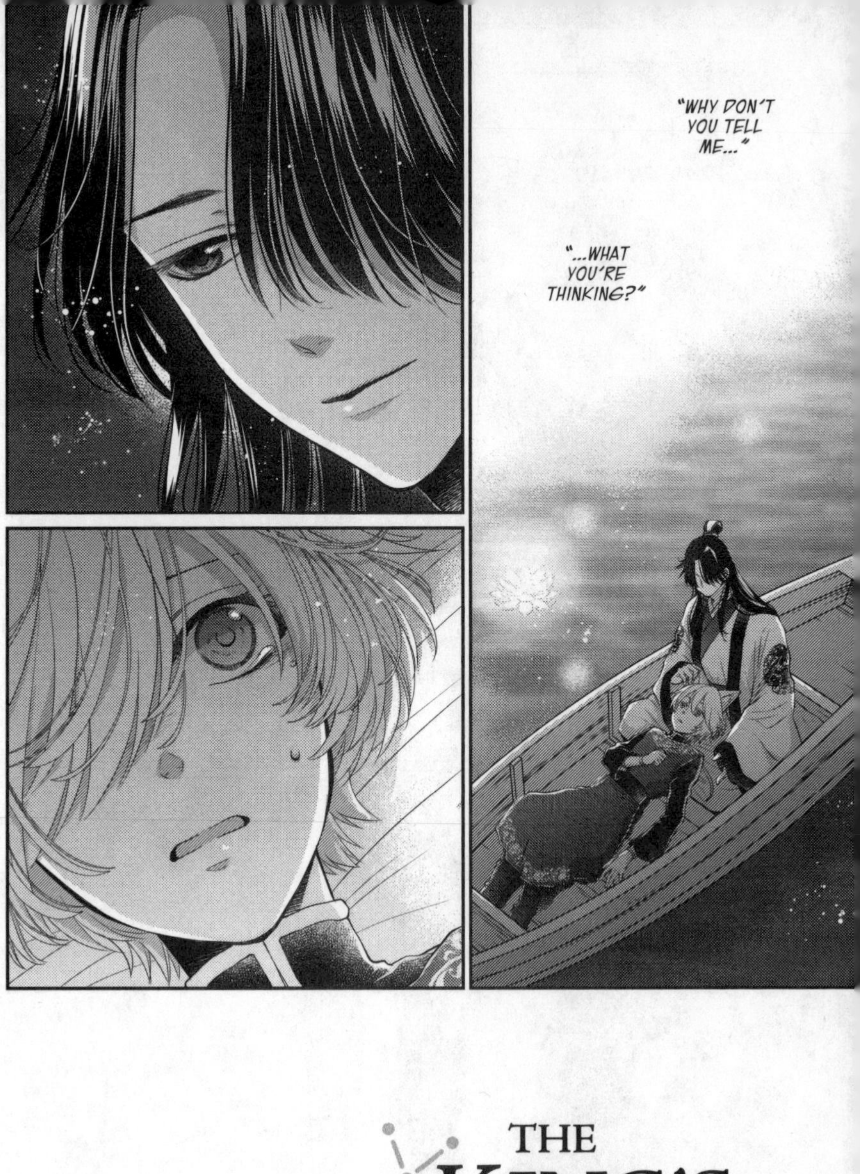
"WHY DON'T YOU TELL ME..."
"...WHAT YOU'RE THINKING?"

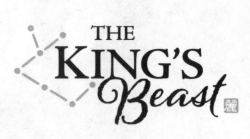

THE KING'S Beast

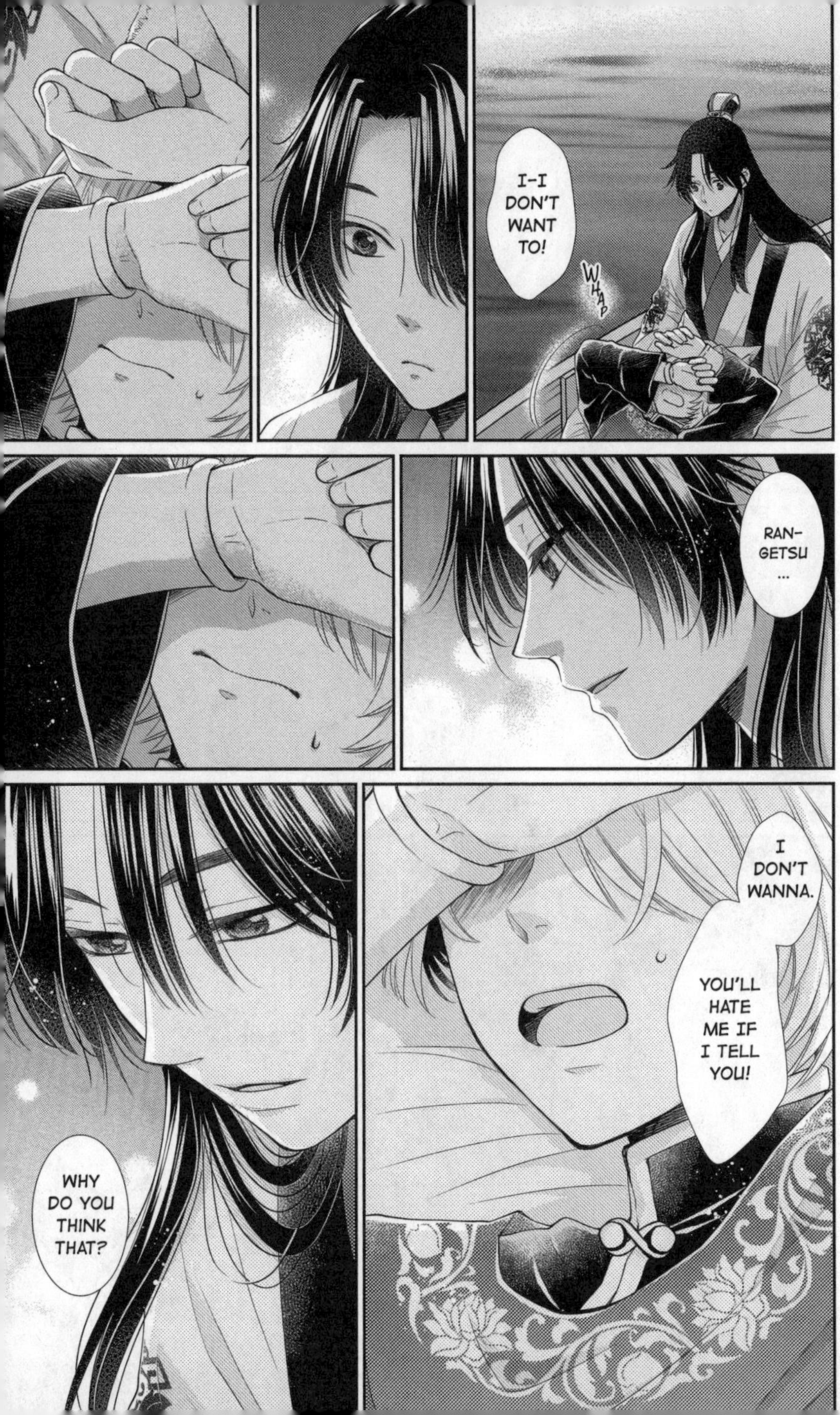
I-I DON'T WANT TO!
WHAP
RAN-GETSU...
I DON'T WANNA.
YOU'LL HATE ME IF I TELL YOU!
WHY DO YOU THINK THAT?

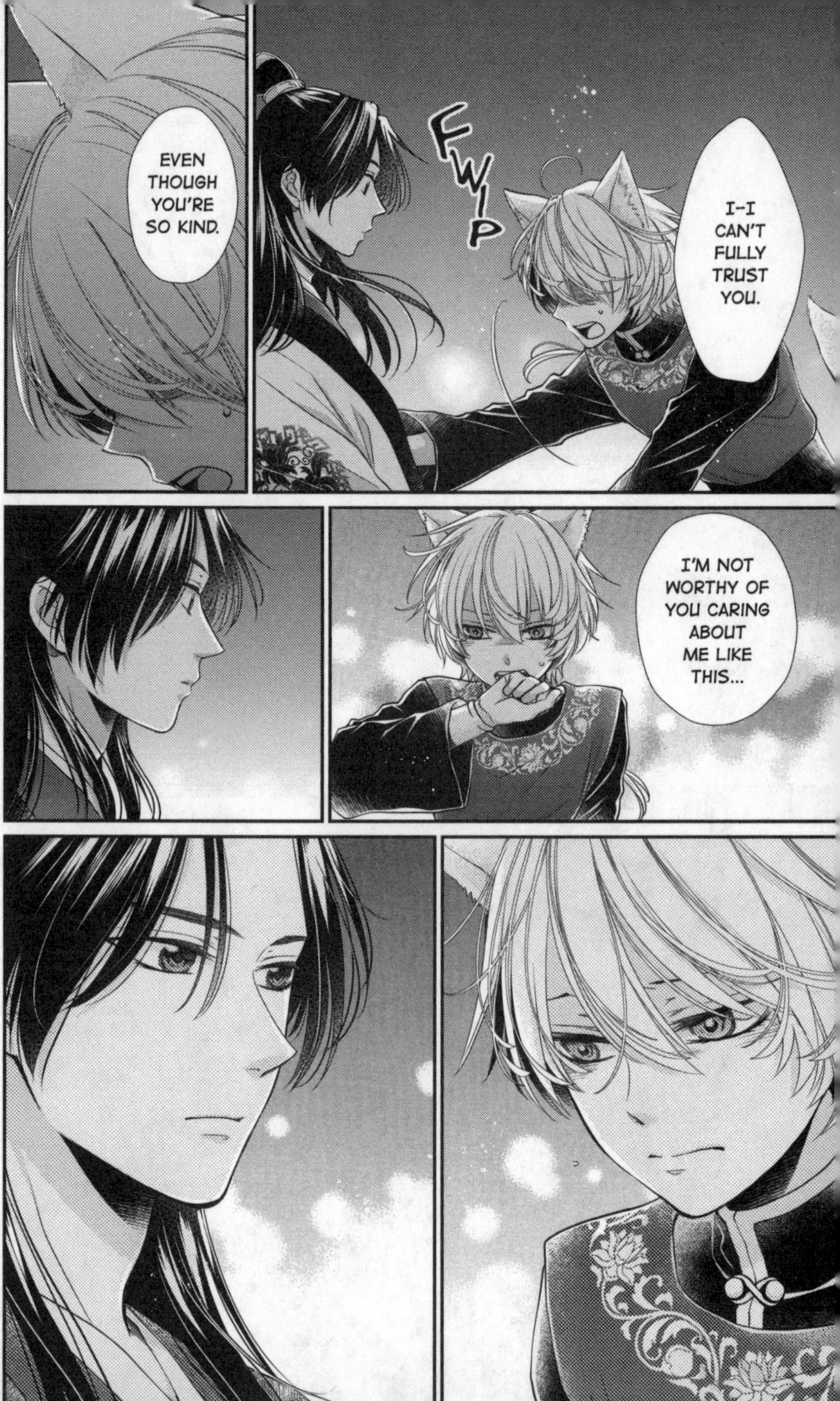
I-I CAN'T FULLY TRUST YOU.
FWIP
EVEN THOUGH YOU'RE SO KIND.
I'M NOT WORTHY OF YOU CARING ABOUT ME LIKE THIS...

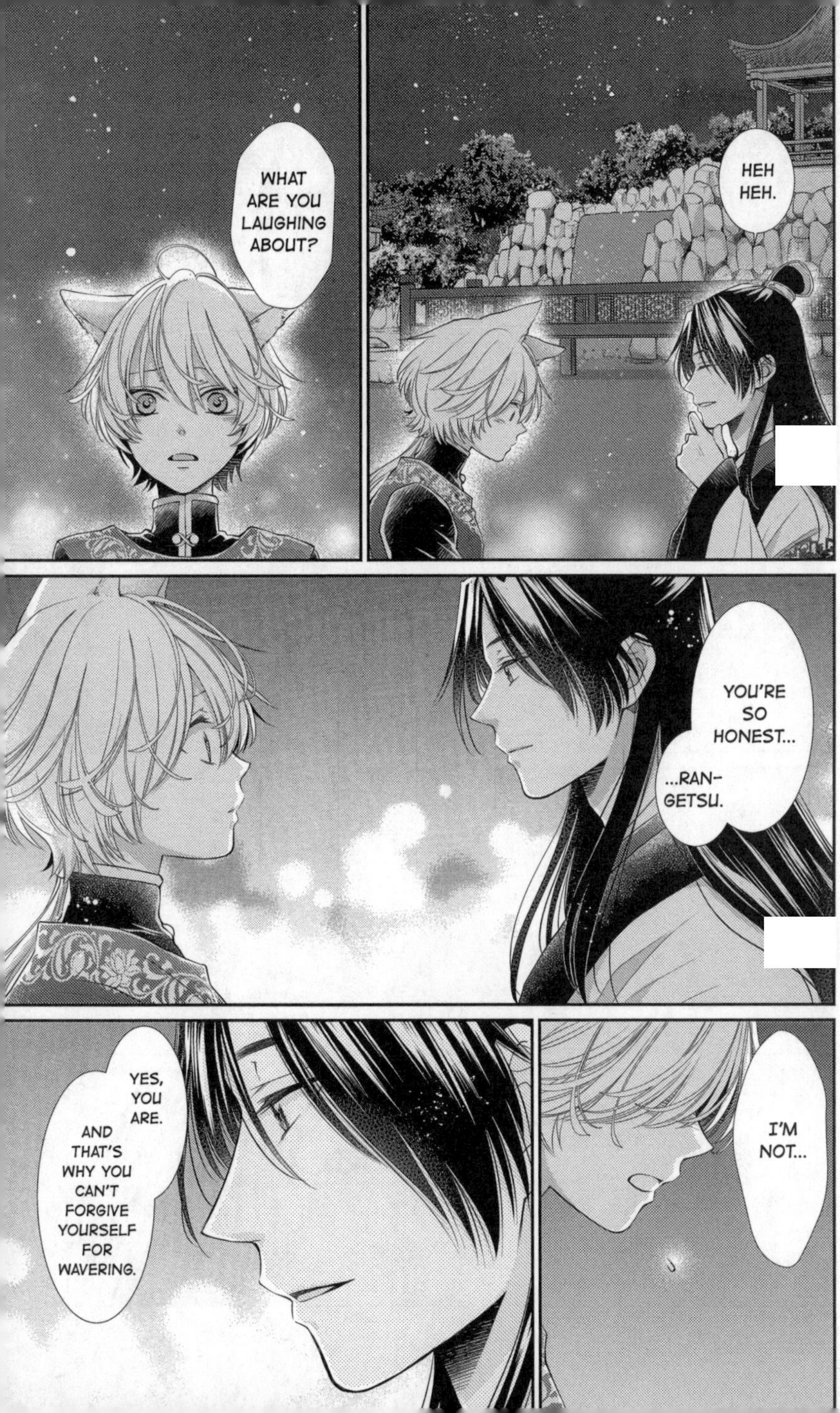
HEH HEH.
WHAT ARE YOU LAUGHING ABOUT?
YOU'RE SO HONEST...
...RAN-GETSU.
I'M NOT...
YES, YOU ARE.
AND THAT'S WHY YOU CAN'T FORGIVE YOURSELF FOR WAVERING.

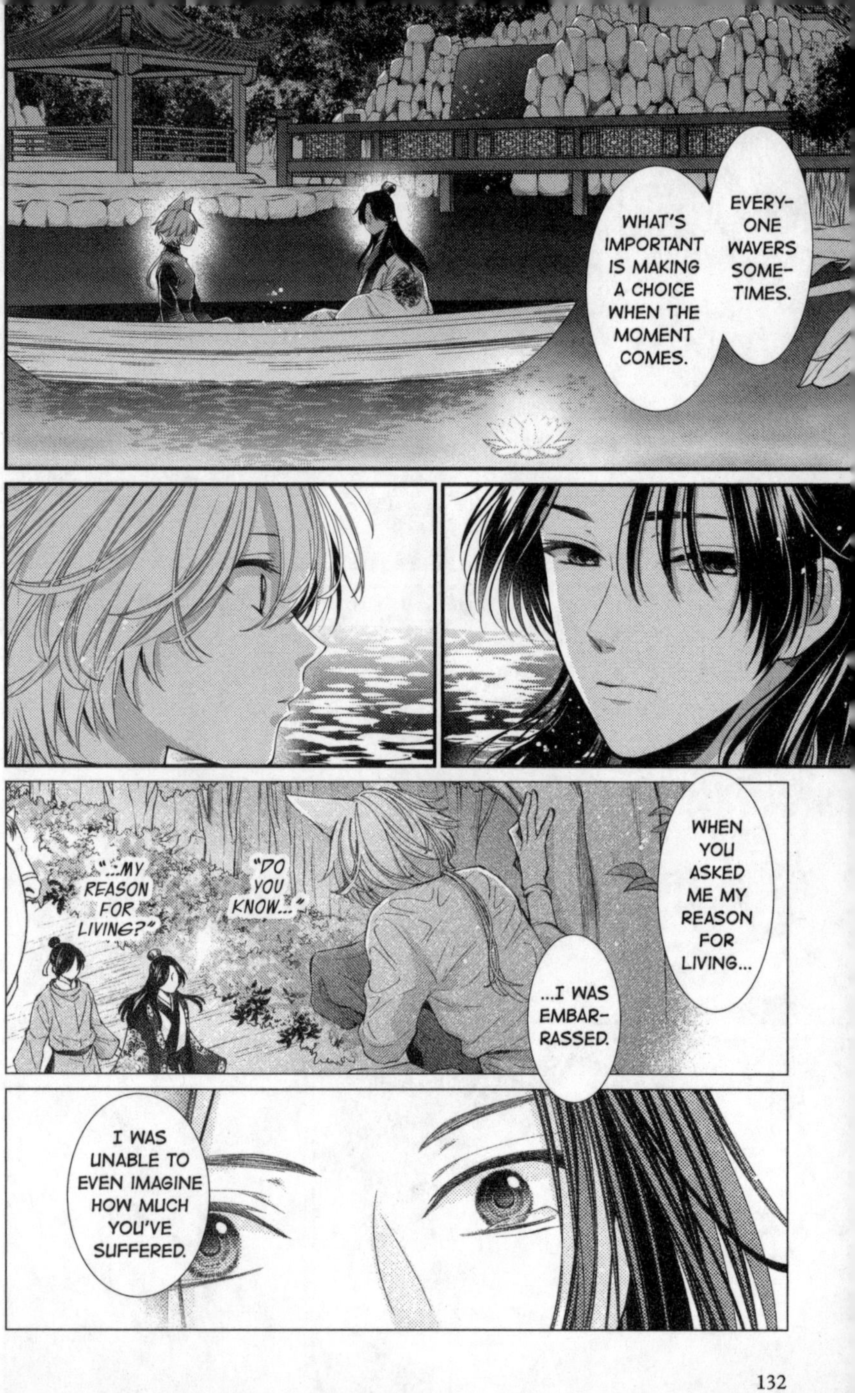
EVERY-ONE WAVERS SOME-TIMES.
WHAT'S IMPORTANT IS MAKING A CHOICE WHEN THE MOMENT COMES.
WHEN YOU ASKED ME MY REASON FOR LIVING...
...I WAS EMBAR-RASSED.
"DO YOU KNOW..."
"...MY REASON FOR LIVING?"
I WAS UNABLE TO EVEN IMAGINE HOW MUCH YOU'VE SUFFERED.

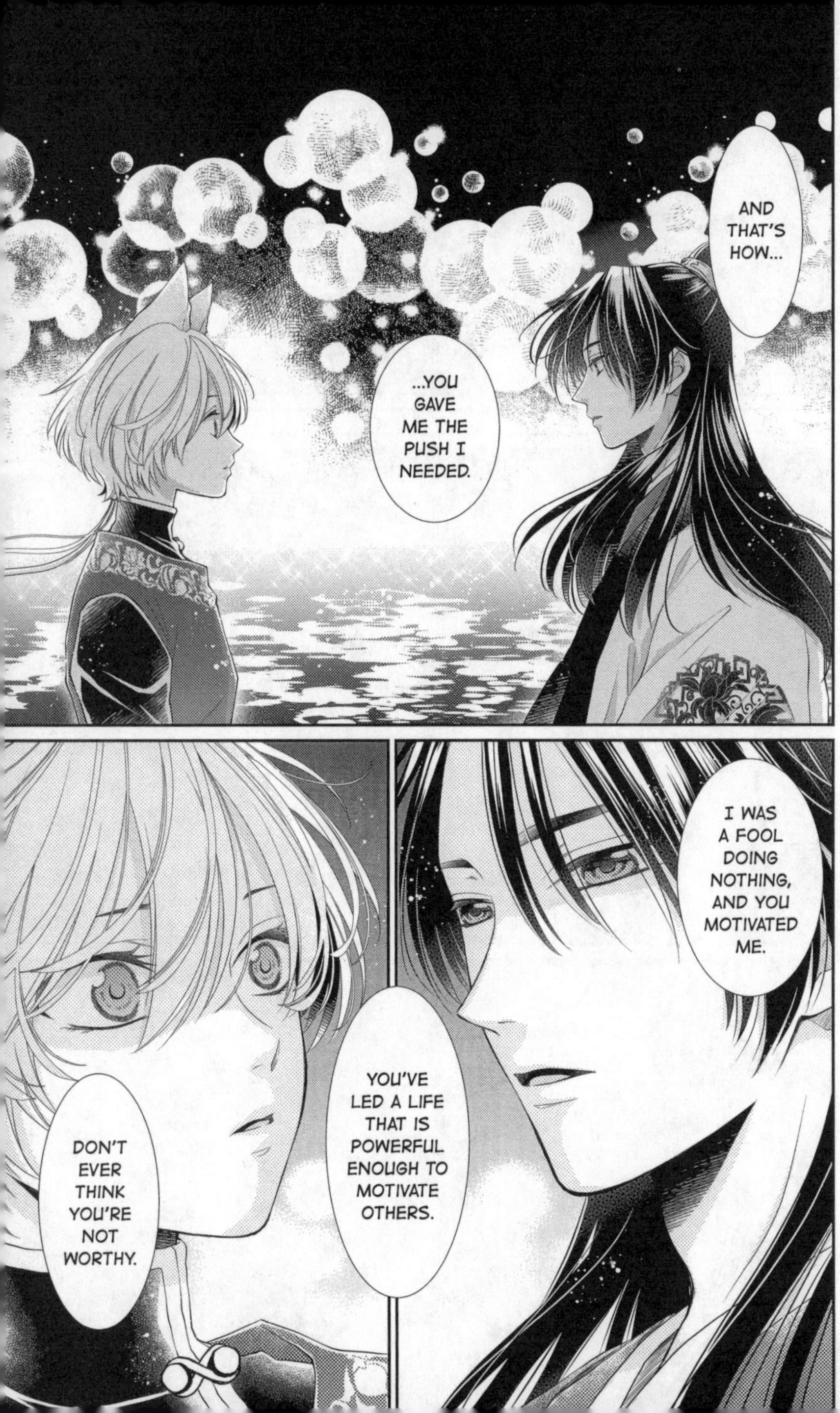
AND THAT'S HOW...
...YOU GAVE ME THE PUSH I NEEDED.
I WAS A FOOL DOING NOTHING, AND YOU MOTIVATED ME.
YOU'VE LED A LIFE THAT IS POWERFUL ENOUGH TO MOTIVATE OTHERS.
DON'T EVER THINK YOU'RE NOT WORTHY.

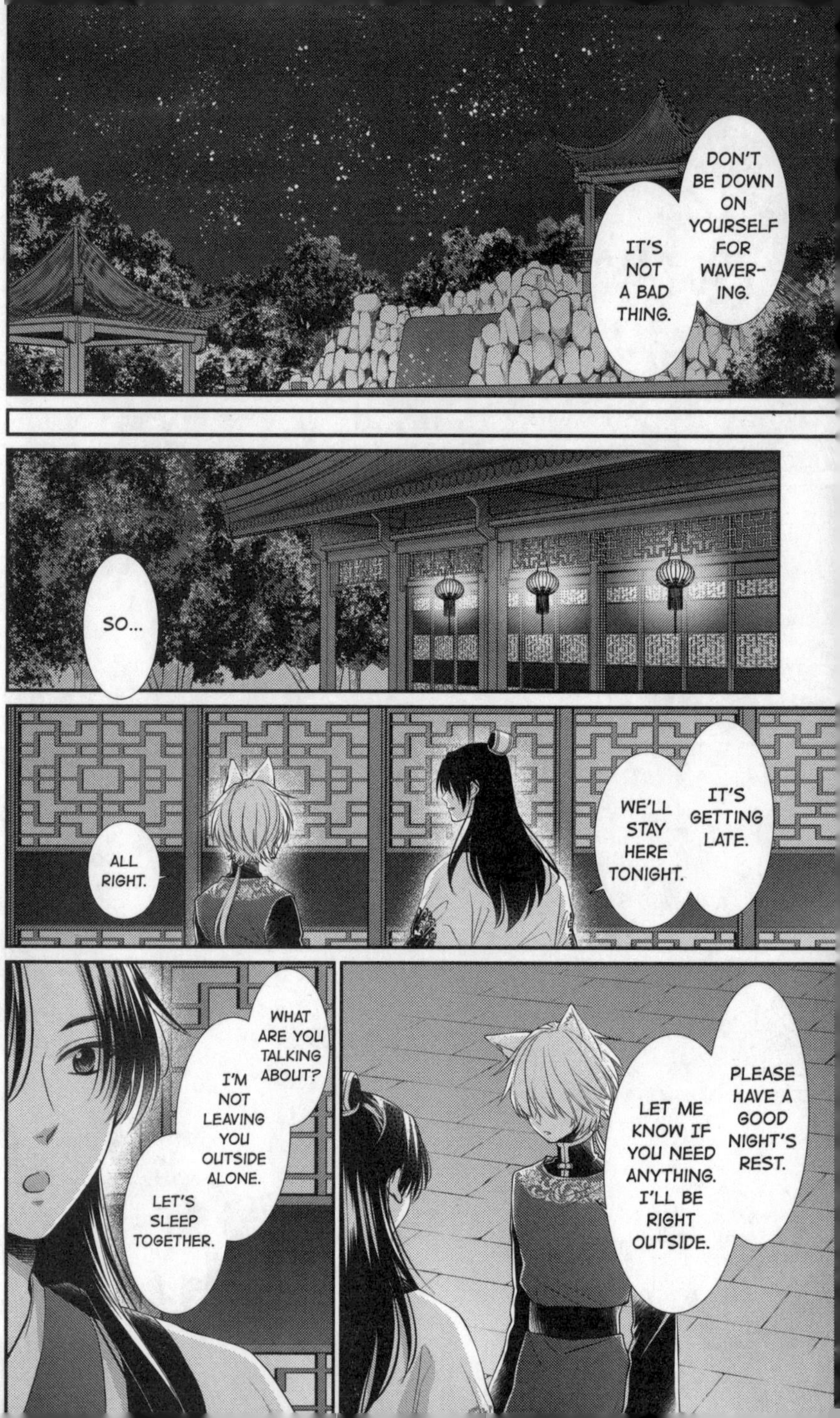
DON'T BE DOWN ON YOURSELF FOR WAVERING.
IT'S NOT A BAD THING.
SO...
IT'S GETTING LATE.
WE'LL STAY HERE TONIGHT.
ALL RIGHT.
PLEASE HAVE A GOOD NIGHT'S REST.
LET ME KNOW IF YOU NEED ANYTHING. I'LL BE RIGHT OUTSIDE.
WHAT ARE YOU TALKING ABOUT?
I'M NOT LEAVING YOU OUTSIDE ALONE.
LET'S SLEEP TOGETHER.

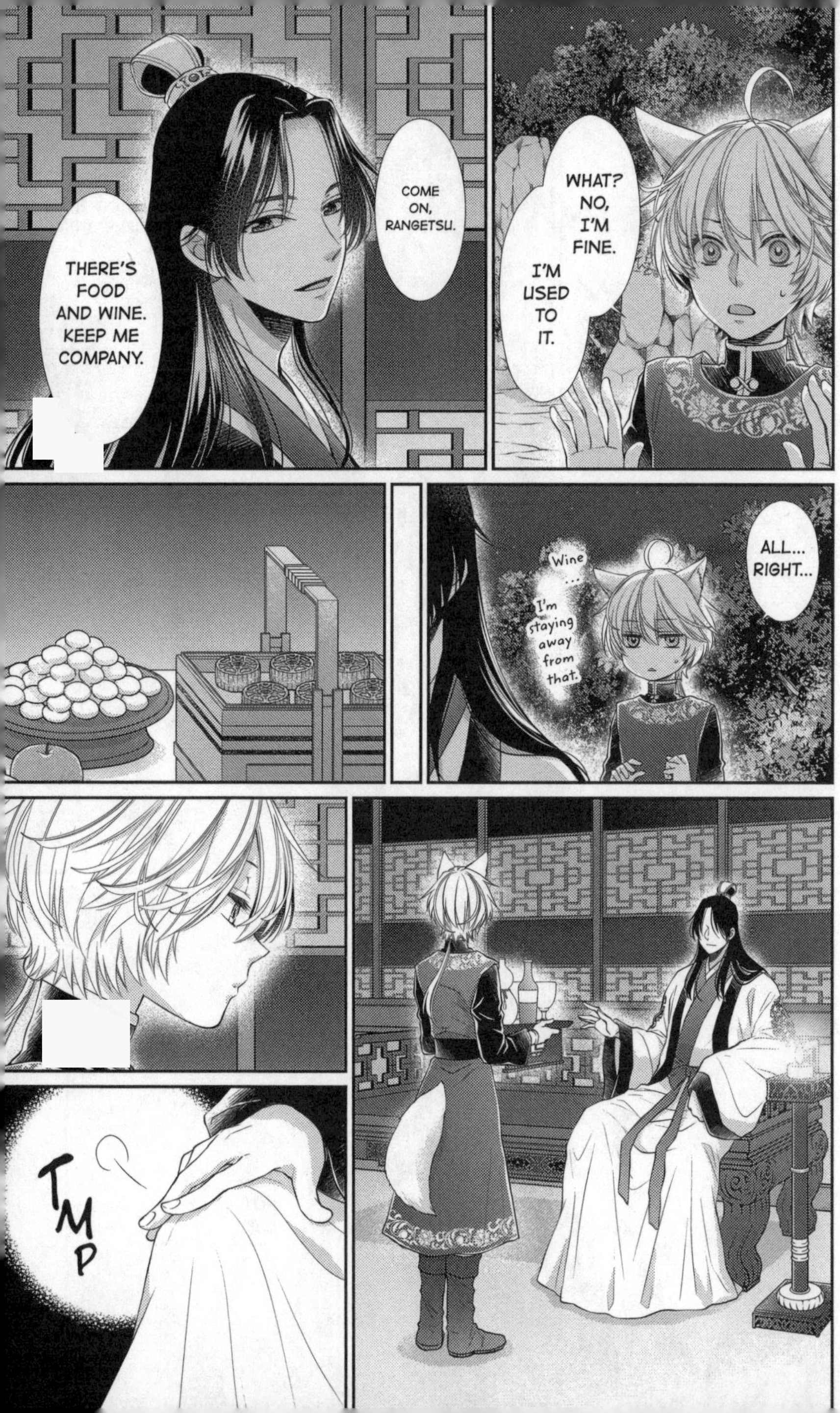
WHAT? NO, I'M FINE.
I'M USED TO IT.
COME ON, RANGETSU.
THERE'S FOOD AND WINE. KEEP ME COMPANY.
ALL... RIGHT...
Wine... I'm staying away from that.
TMP

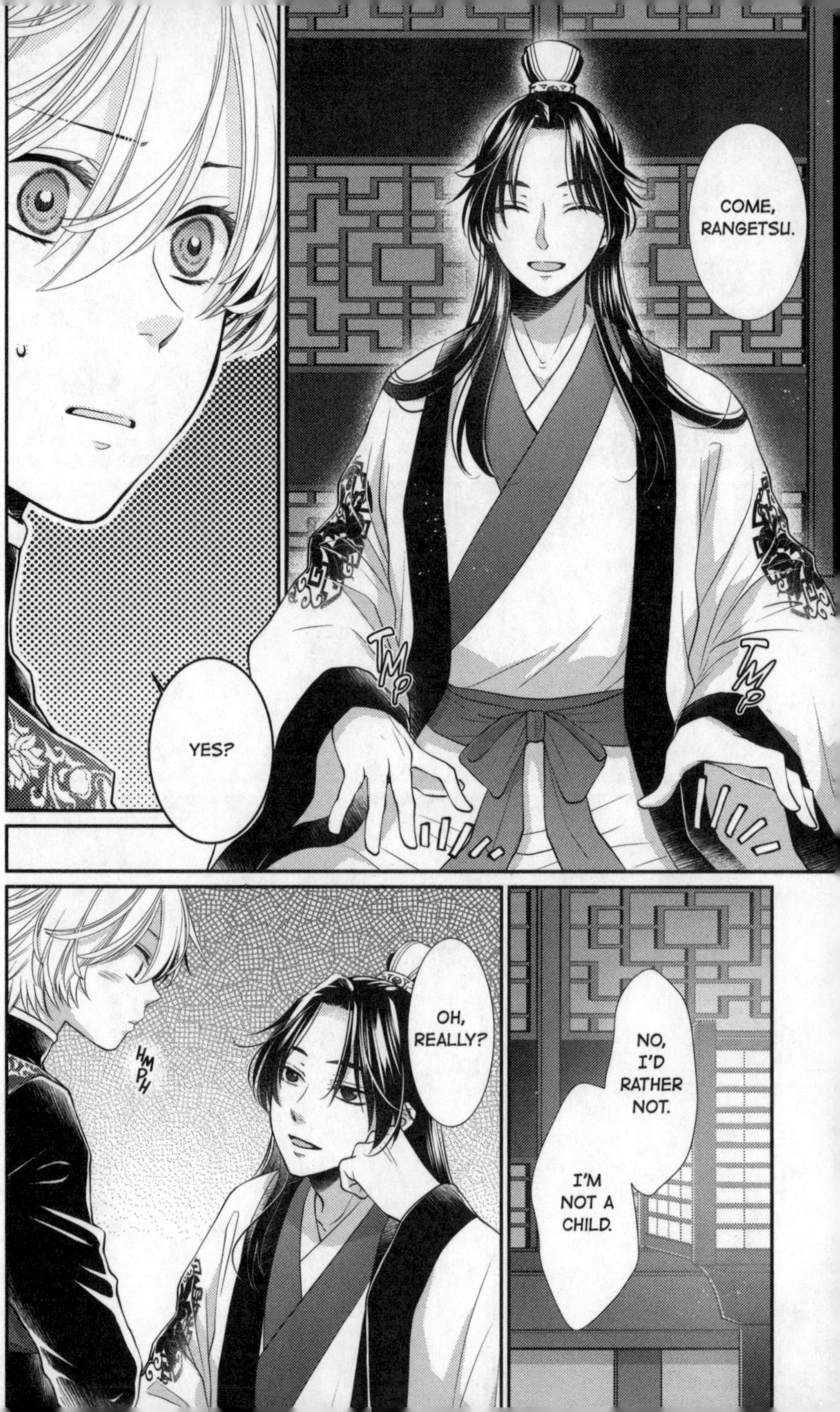
COME, RANGETSU.
TMP
TMP
YES?
NO, I'D RATHER NOT.
I'M NOT A CHILD.
OH, REALLY?
HMPH

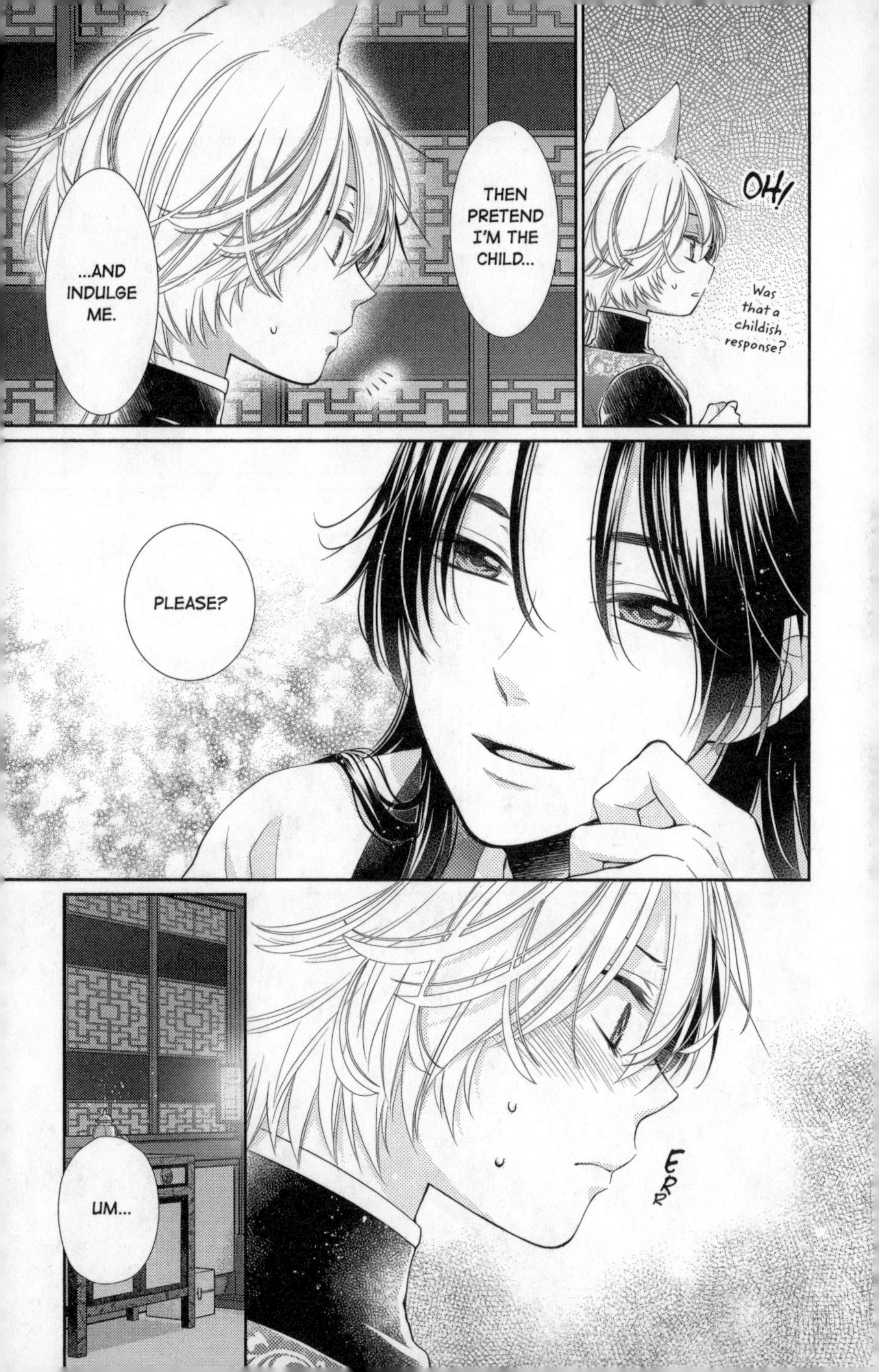
OH!
Was that a childish response?
THEN PRETEND I'M THE CHILD...
...AND INDULGE ME.
PLEASE?
ERR
UM...

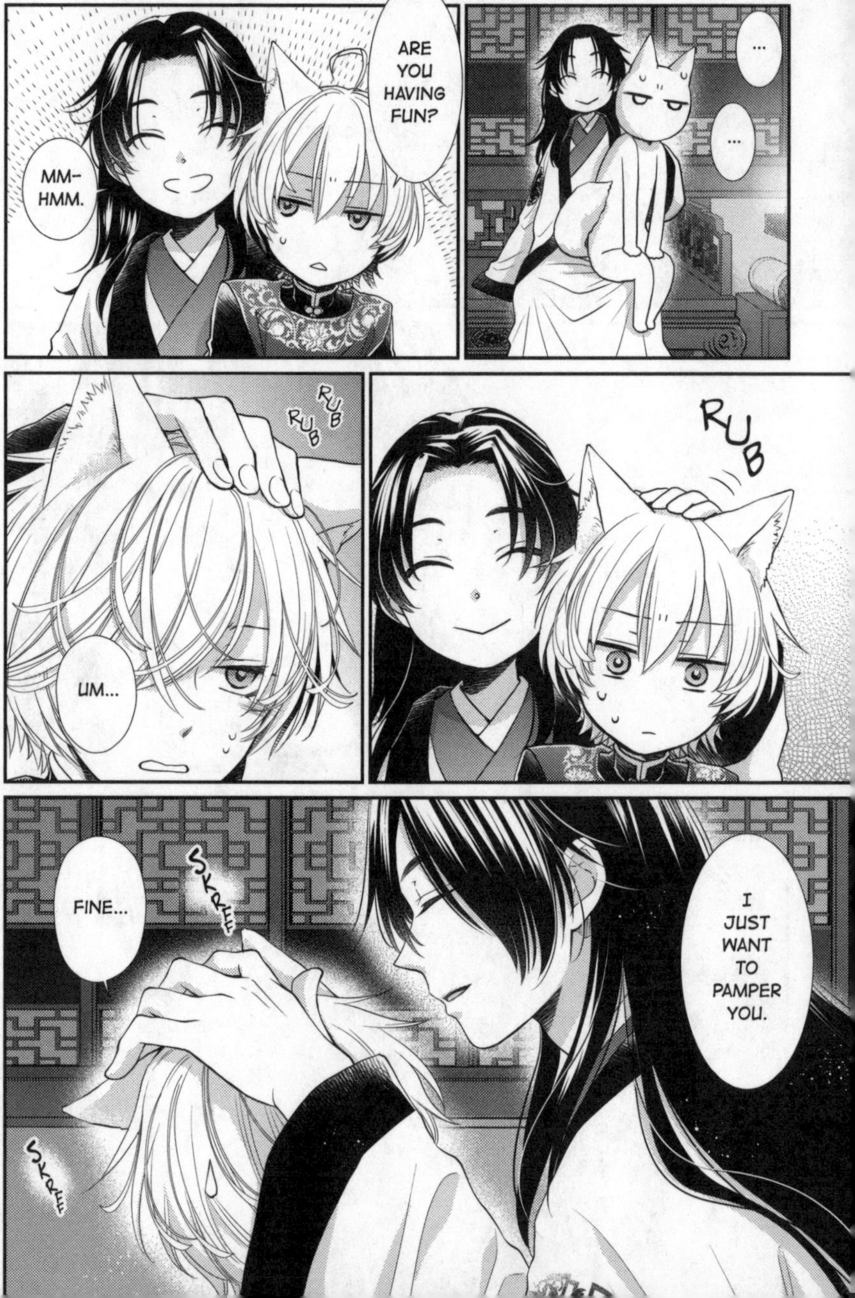
...
...
ARE YOU HAVING FUN?
MM-HMM.
RUB
RUB RUB
UM...
I JUST WANT TO PAMPER YOU.
SKREE
FINE...
SKREE

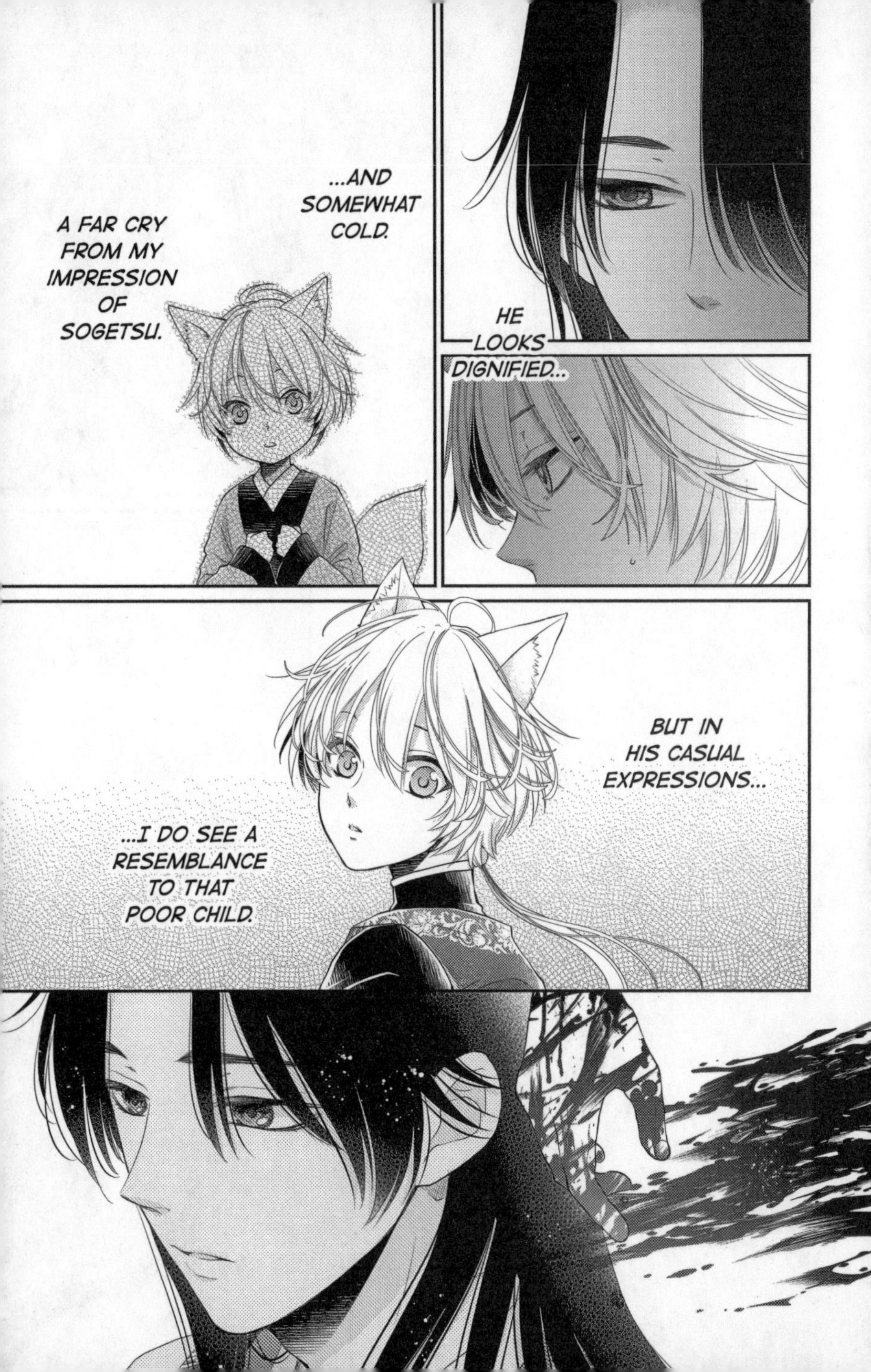
HE LOOKS DIGNIFIED...
...AND SOMEWHAT COLD.
A FAR CRY FROM MY IMPRESSION OF SOGETSU.
BUT IN HIS CASUAL EXPRESSIONS...
...I DO SEE A RESEMBLANCE TO THAT POOR CHILD.

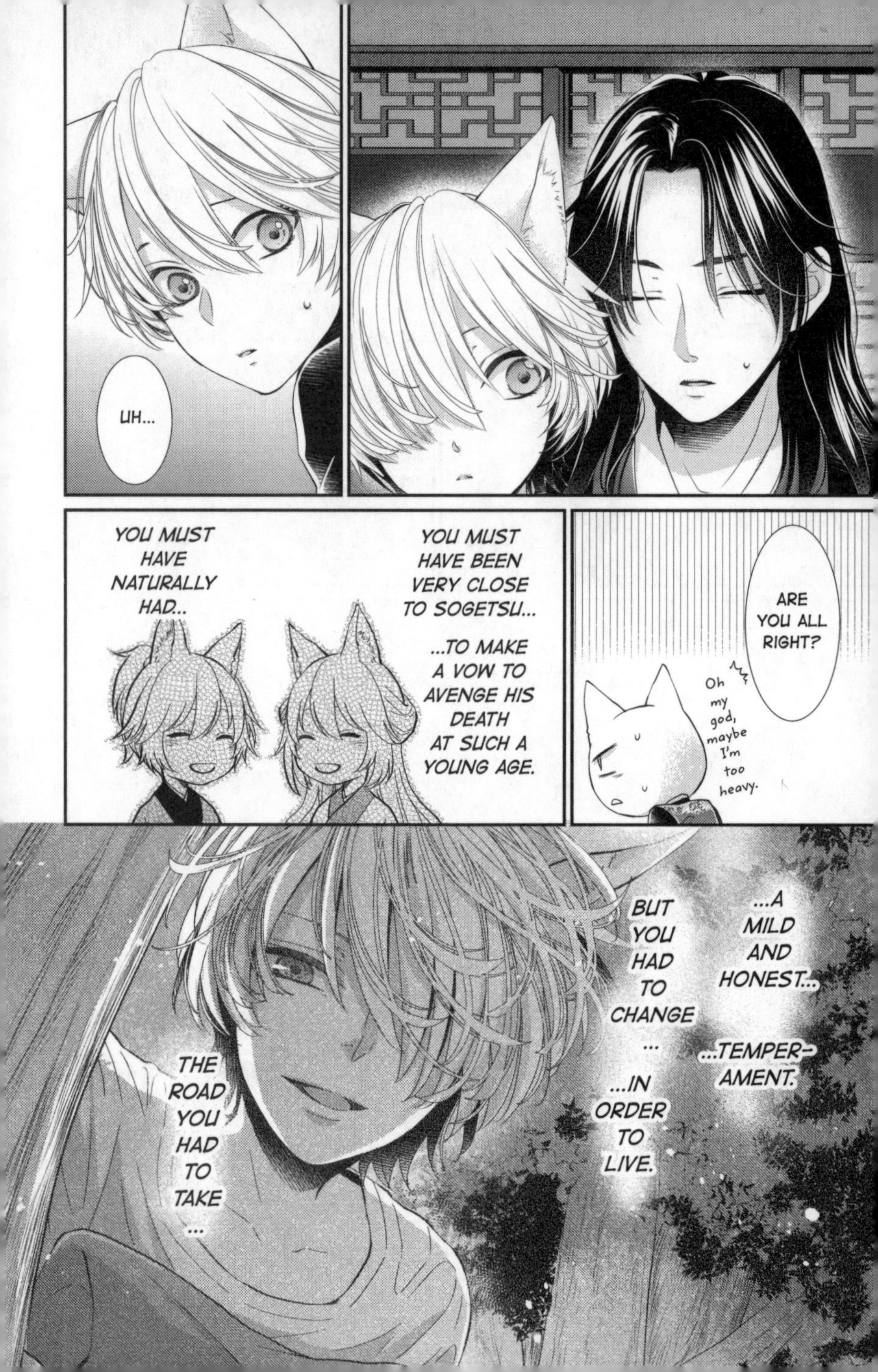
UH...
ARE YOU ALL RIGHT?
Oh my god, maybe I'm too heavy.
YOU MUST HAVE BEEN VERY CLOSE TO SOGETSU...
...TO MAKE A VOW TO AVENGE HIS DEATH AT SUCH A YOUNG AGE.
YOU MUST HAVE NATURALLY HAD...
...A MILD AND HONEST...
...TEMPER-AMENT.
BUT YOU HAD TO CHANGE...
...IN ORDER TO LIVE.
THE ROAD YOU HAD TO TAKE...

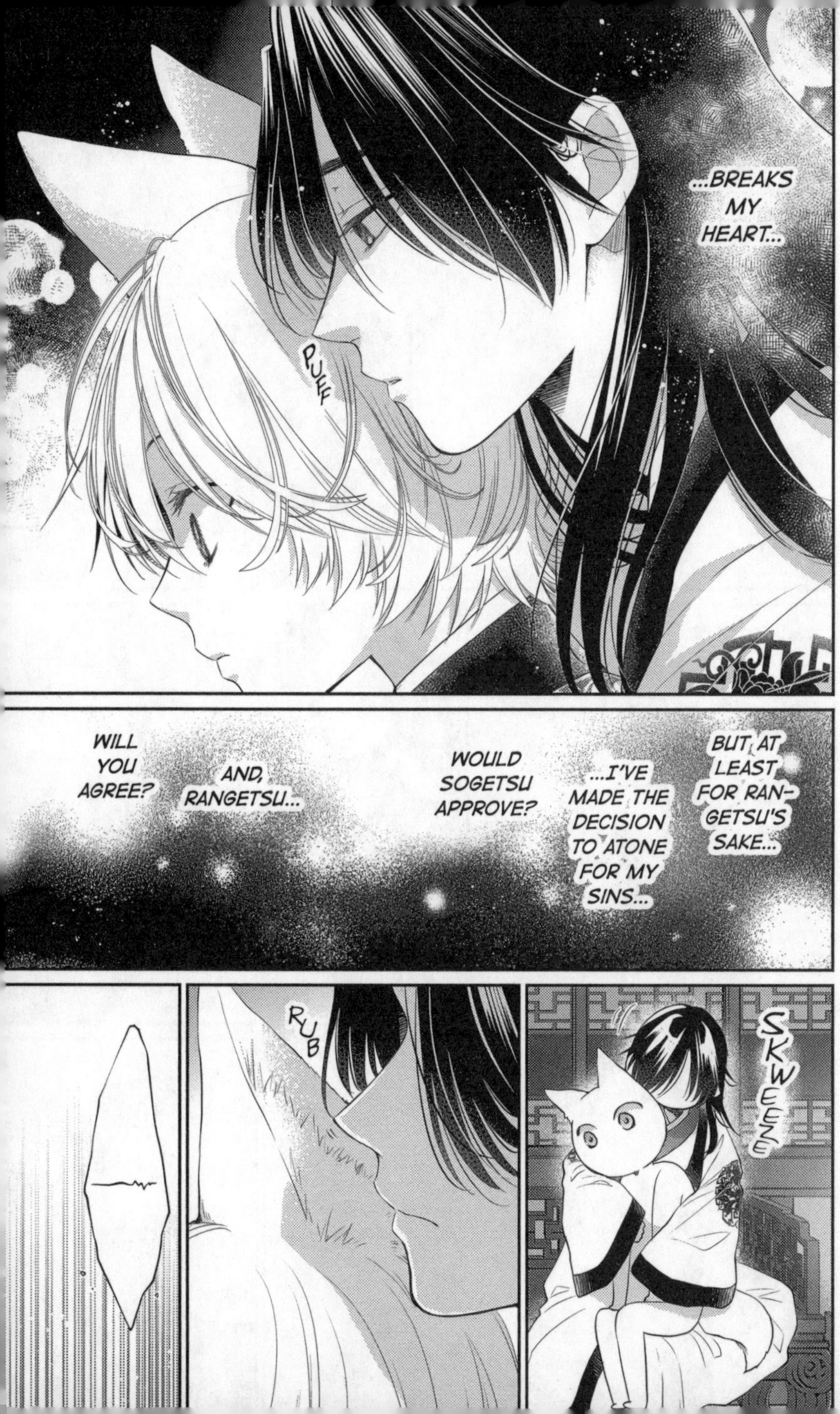
...BREAKS MY HEART...
PUFF
BUT AT LEAST FOR RAN-GETSU'S SAKE...
...I'VE MADE THE DECISION TO ATONE FOR MY SINS...
WOULD SOGETSU APPROVE?
AND, RANGETSU...
WILL YOU AGREE?
SKWEEZE
RUB

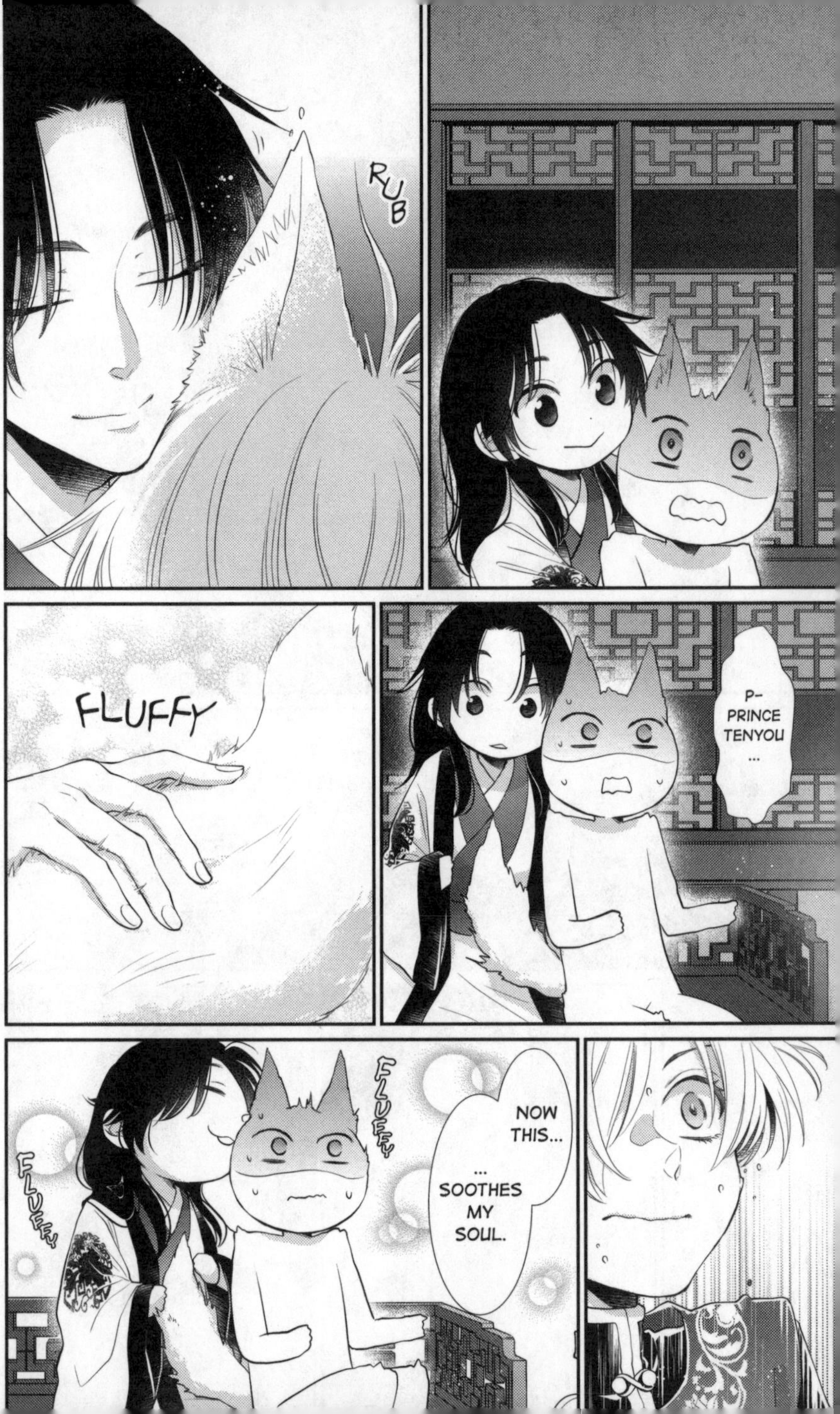
RUB
P-PRINCE TENYOU ...
FLUFFY
NOW THIS...
... SOOTHES MY SOUL.
FLUFFY
FLUFFY

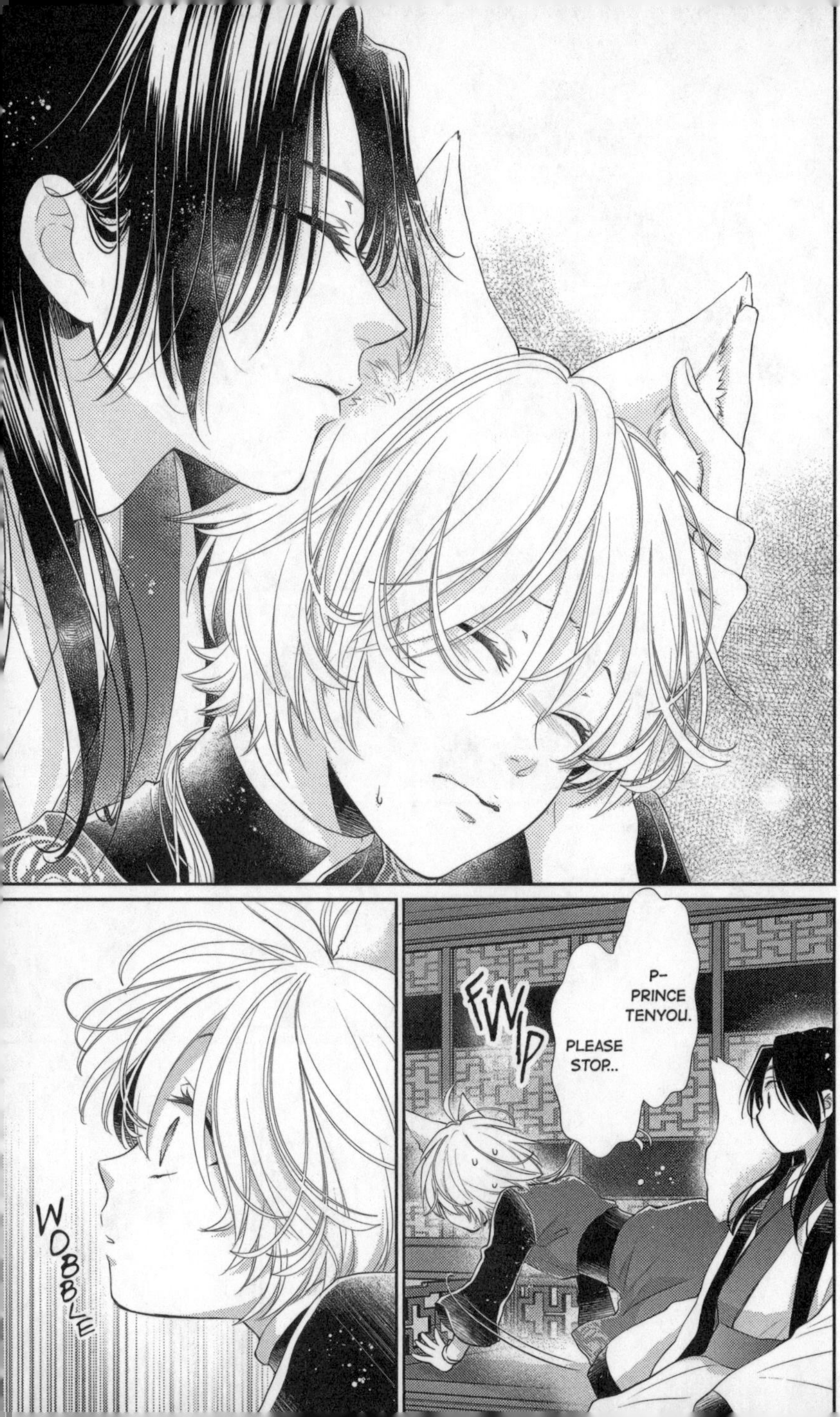
P-
PRINCE
TENYOU.
PLEASE
STOP...
FWIP
WOBBLE

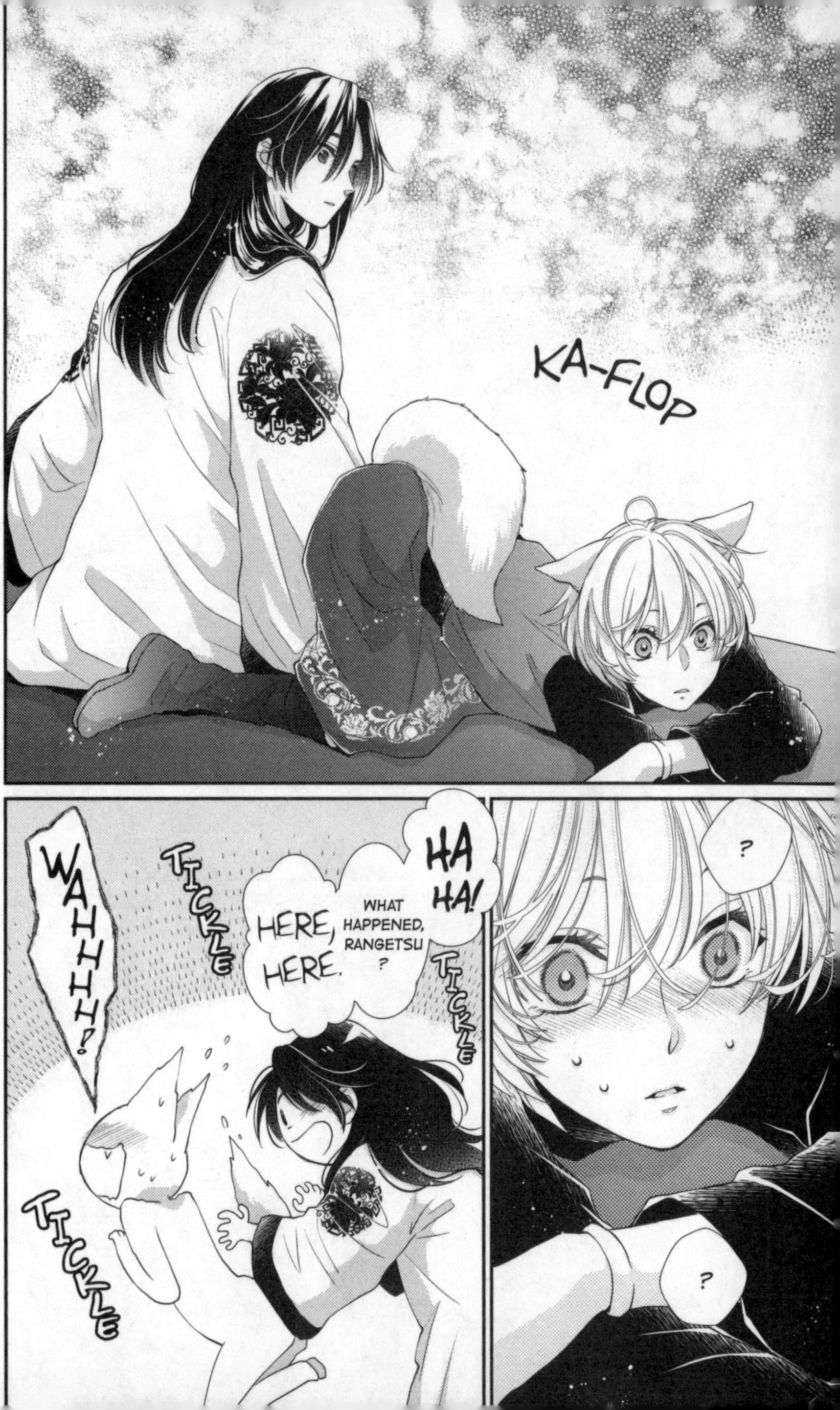
KA-FLOP
?
?
HA HA!
WHAT HAPPENED, RANGETSU?
HERE, HERE.
TICKLE
TICKLE
WAHHHH!
TICKLE

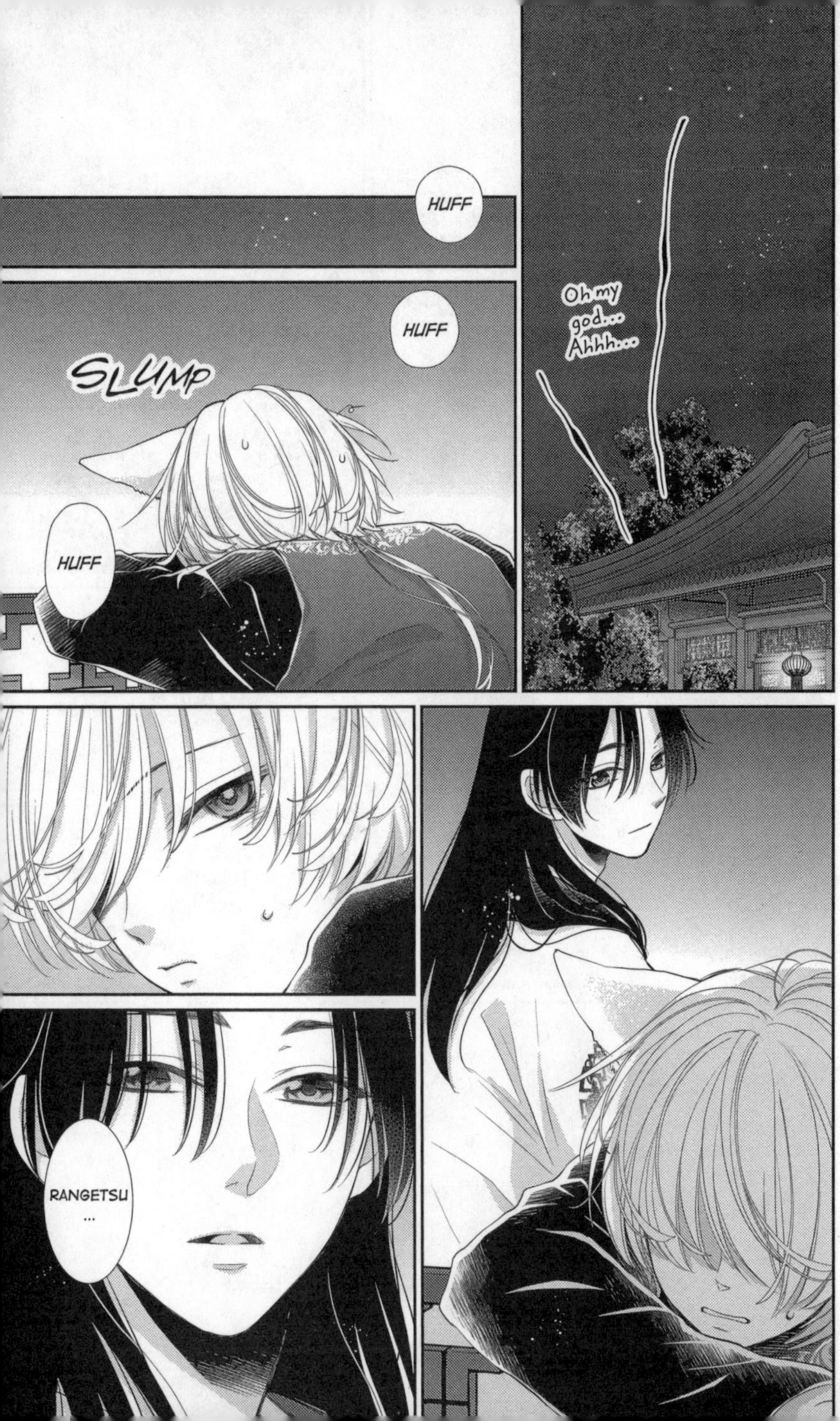

Oh my god... Ahhh...
HUFF
HUFF
SLUMP
HUFF
RANGETSU ...

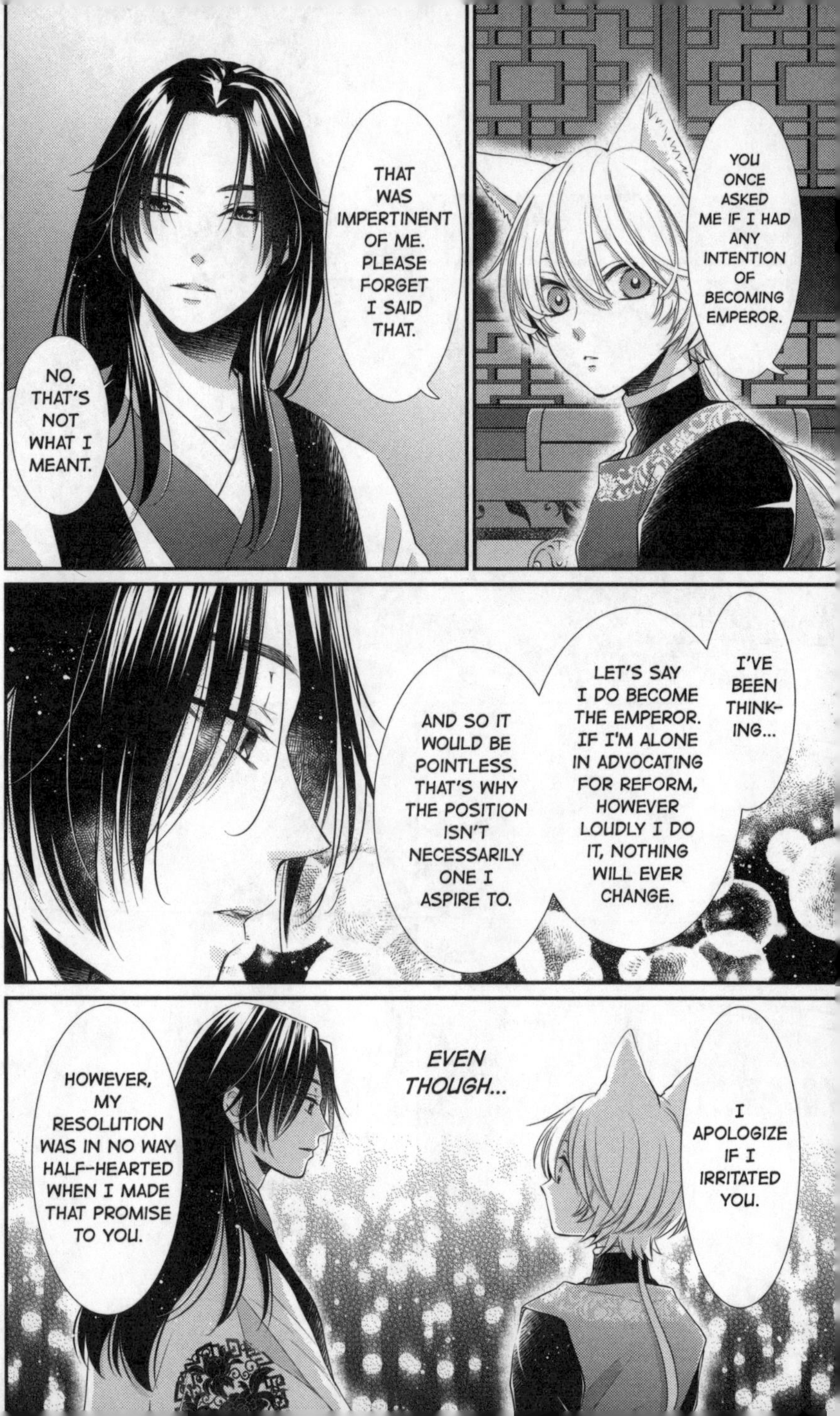
YOU ONCE ASKED ME IF I HAD ANY INTENTION OF BECOMING EMPEROR.
THAT WAS IMPERTINENT OF ME. PLEASE FORGET I SAID THAT.
NO, THAT'S NOT WHAT I MEANT.
I'VE BEEN THINKING...
LET'S SAY I DO BECOME THE EMPEROR. IF I'M ALONE IN ADVOCATING FOR REFORM, HOWEVER LOUDLY I DO IT, NOTHING WILL EVER CHANGE.
AND SO IT WOULD BE POINTLESS. THAT'S WHY THE POSITION ISN'T NECESSARILY ONE I ASPIRE TO.
I APOLOGIZE IF I IRRITATED YOU.
EVEN THOUGH...
HOWEVER, MY RESOLUTION WAS IN NO WAY HALF-HEARTED WHEN I MADE THAT PROMISE TO YOU.

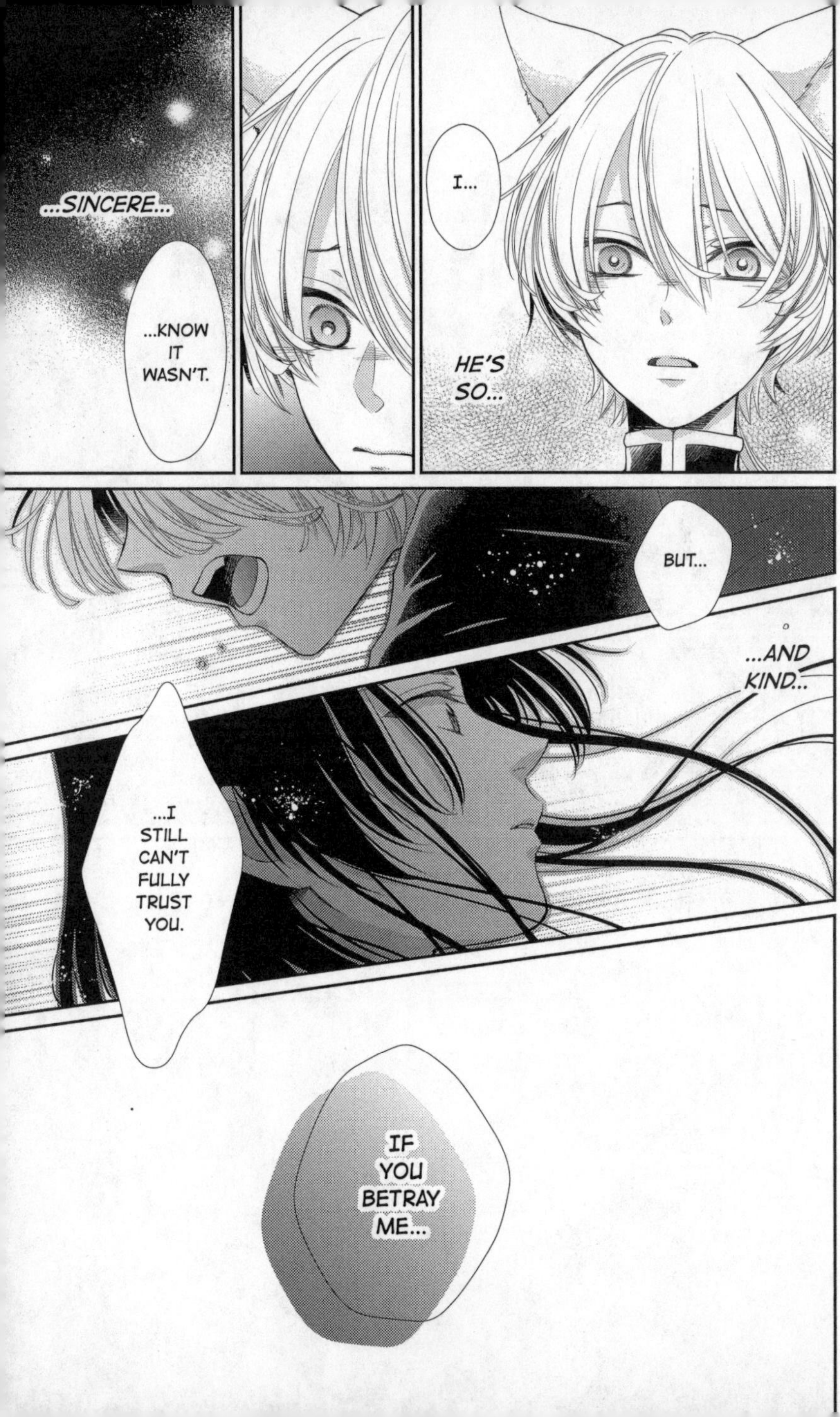
I...
HE'S SO...
...SINCERE...
...KNOW IT WASN'T.
BUT...
...AND KIND...
...I STILL CAN'T FULLY TRUST YOU.
IF YOU BETRAY ME...

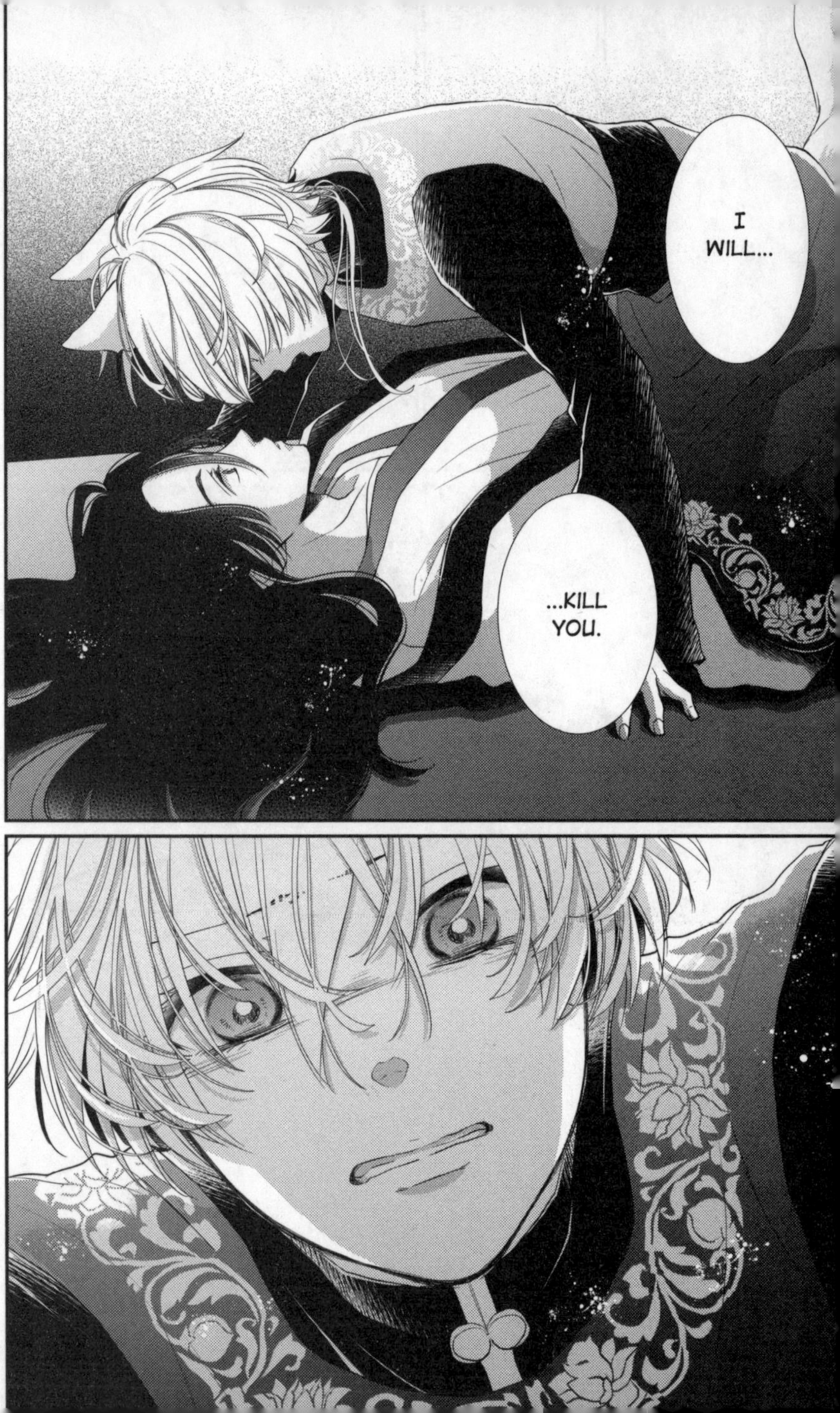
I WILL...
...KILL YOU.

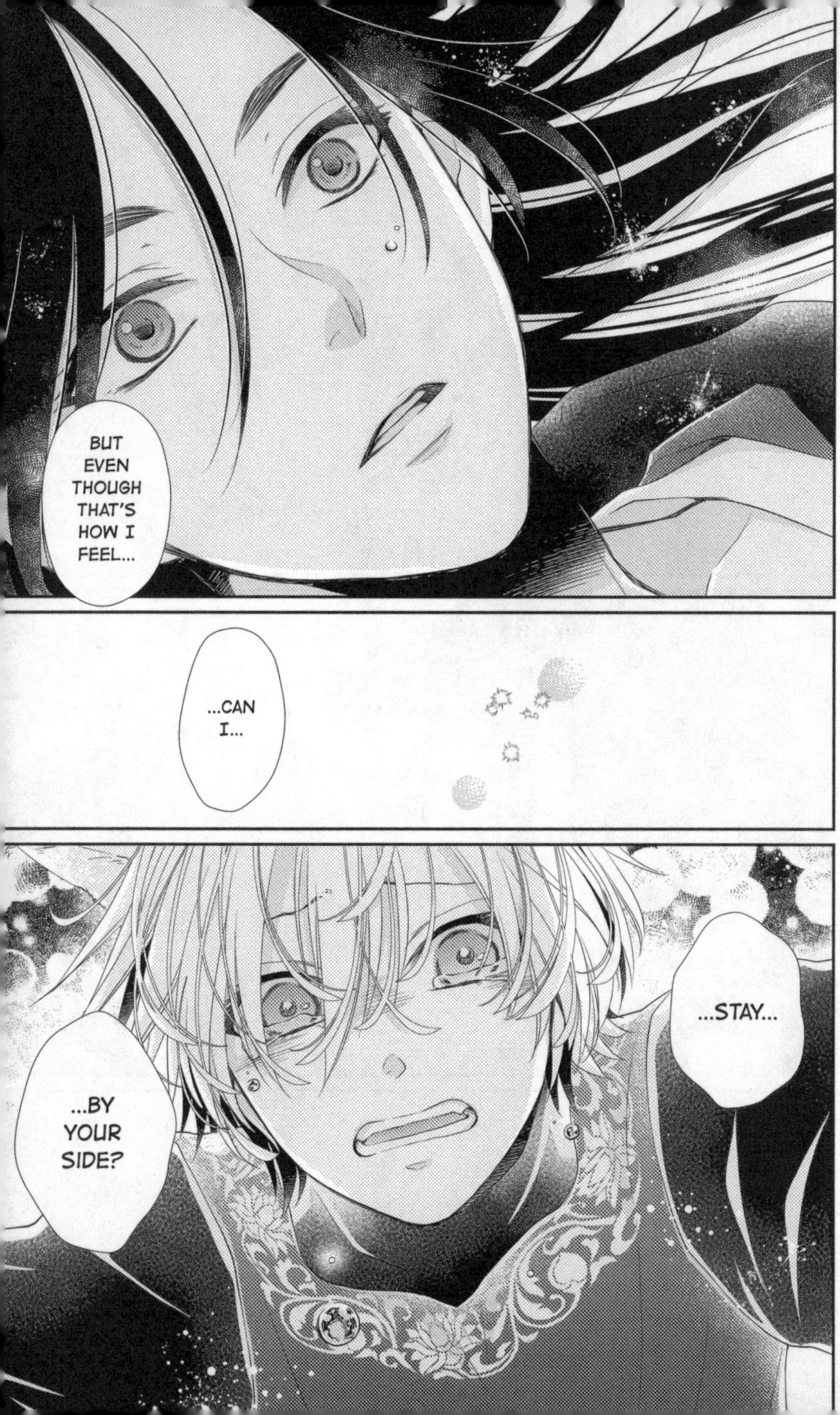
BUT EVEN THOUGH THAT'S HOW I FEEL...
...CAN I...
...STAY...
...BY YOUR SIDE?

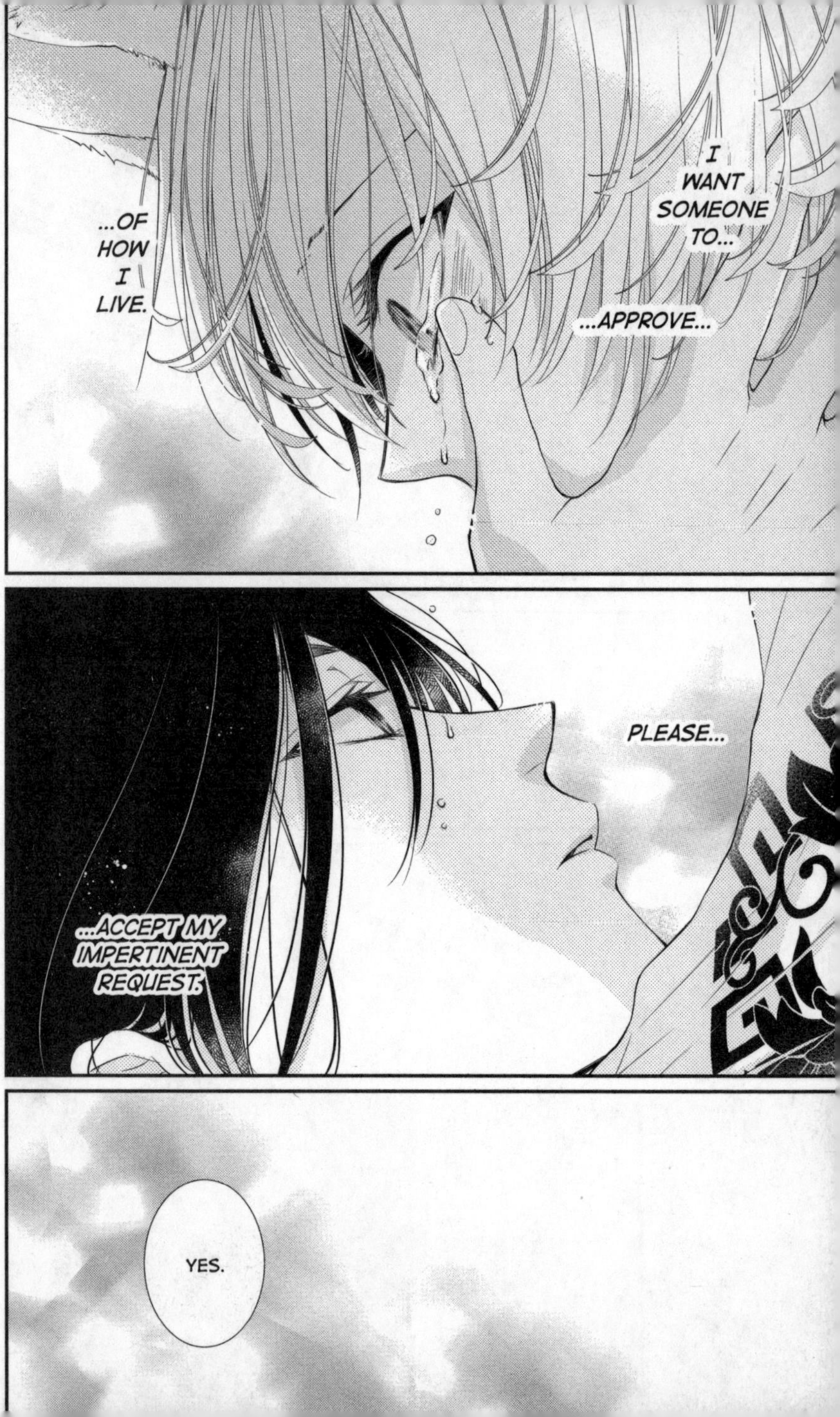
I WANT SOMEONE TO...
...APPROVE...
...OF HOW I LIVE.
PLEASE...
...ACCEPT MY IMPERTINENT REQUEST.
YES.

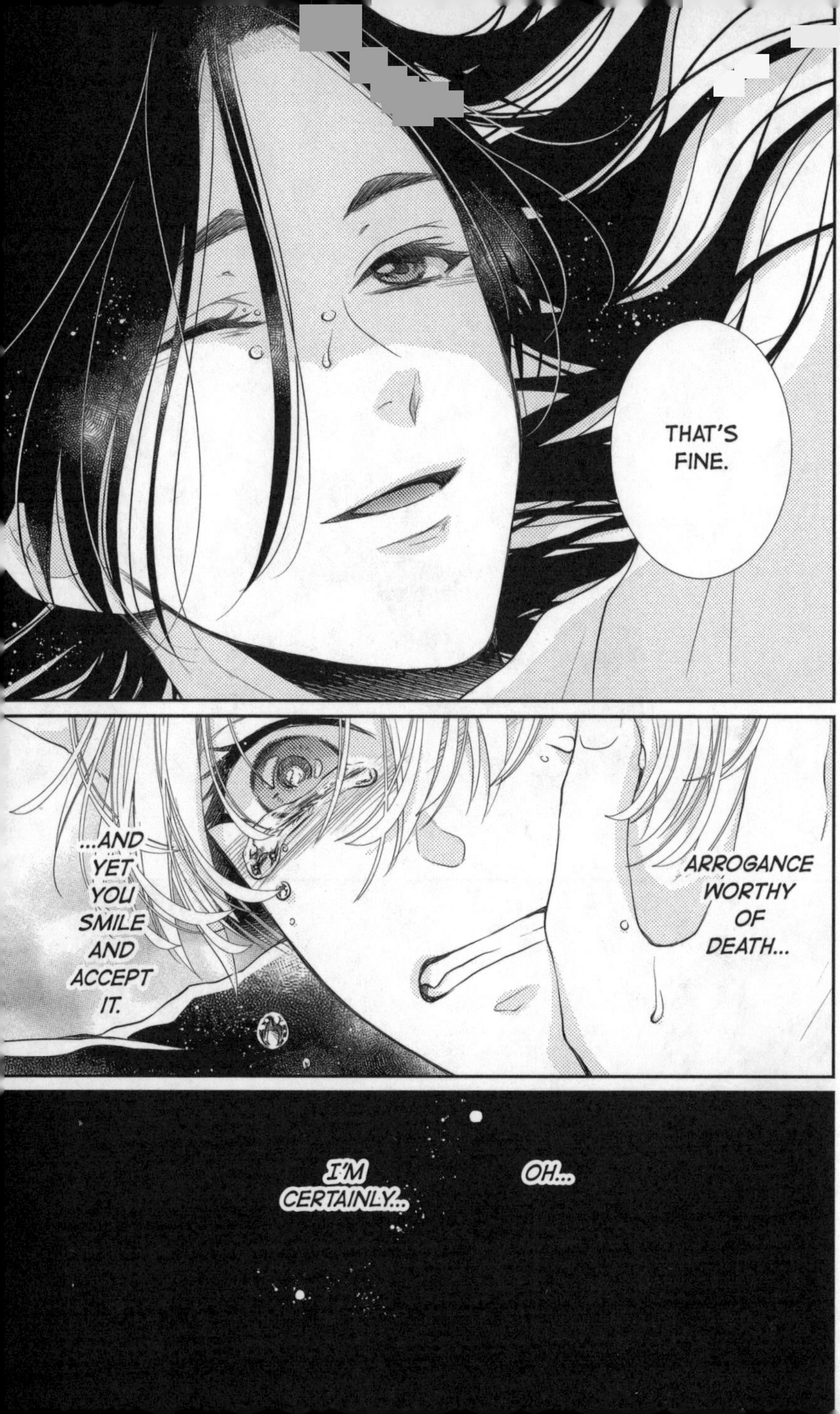
THAT'S FINE.
ARROGANCE WORTHY OF DEATH...
...AND YET YOU SMILE AND ACCEPT IT.
OH...
I'M CERTAINLY...

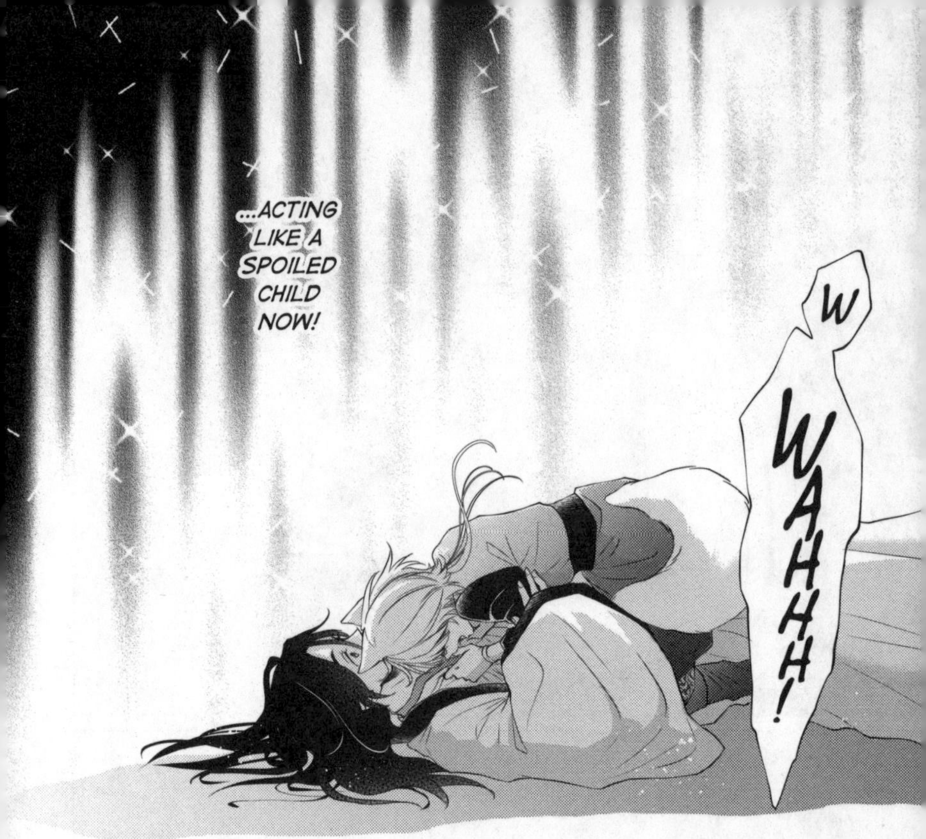
W WAHHHH!
...ACTING LIKE A SPOILED CHILD NOW!
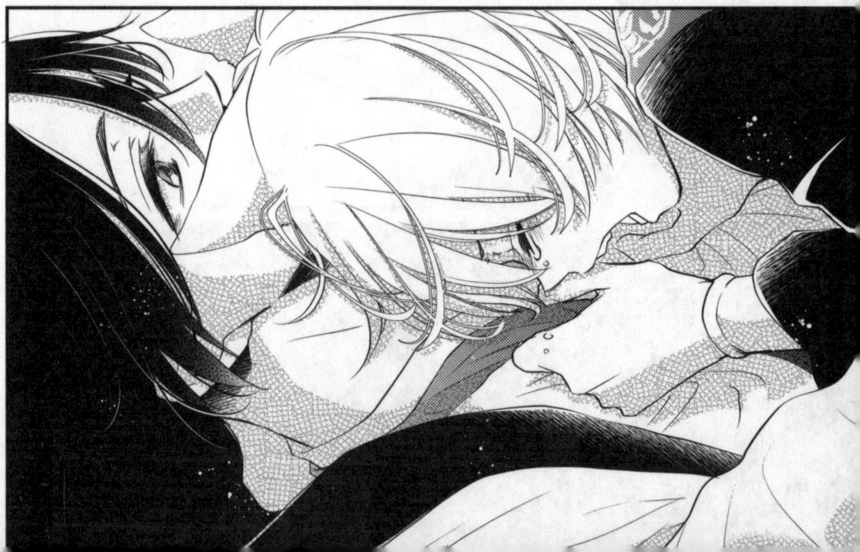

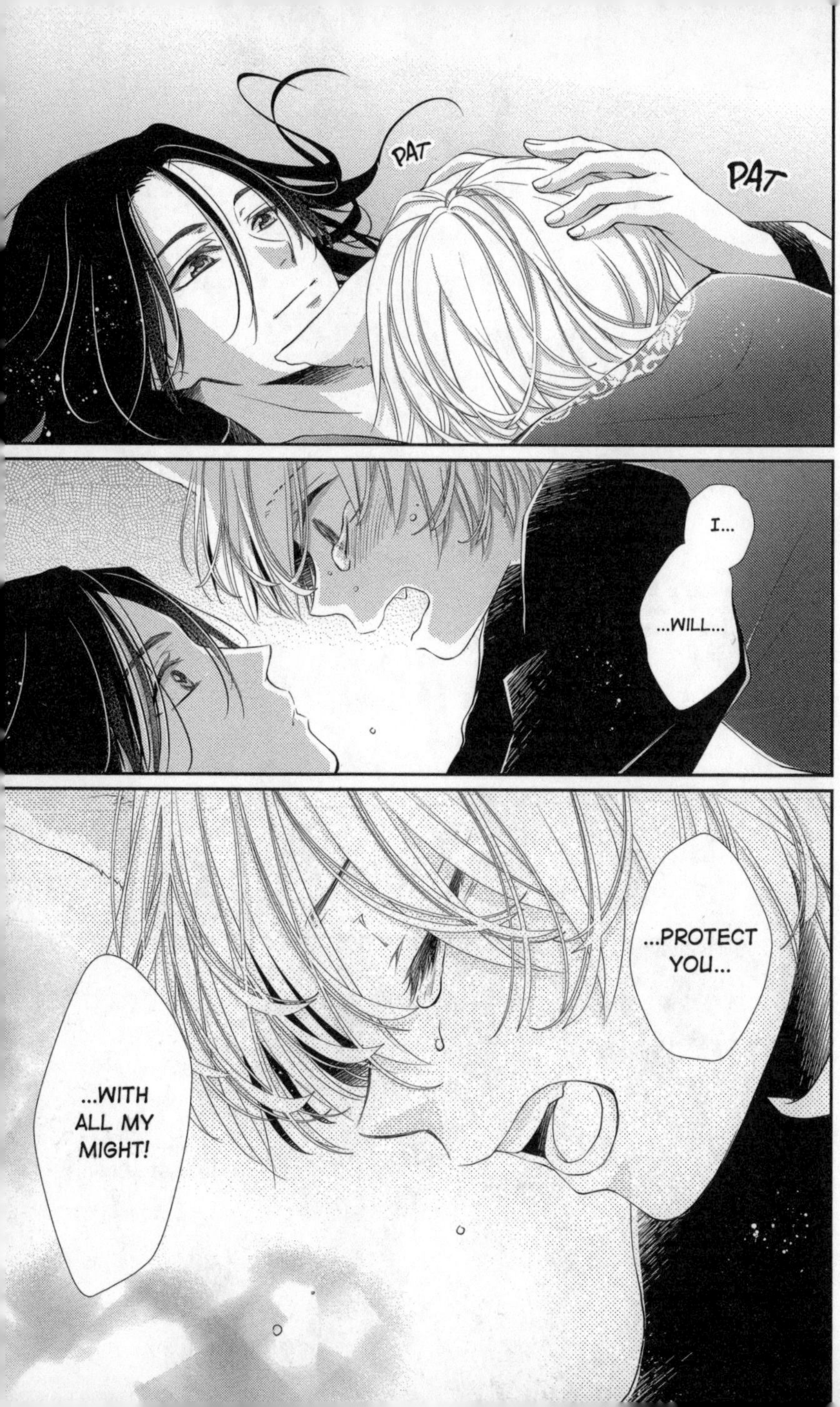
PAT
PAT
I...
...WILL...
...PROTECT YOU...
...WITH ALL MY MIGHT!

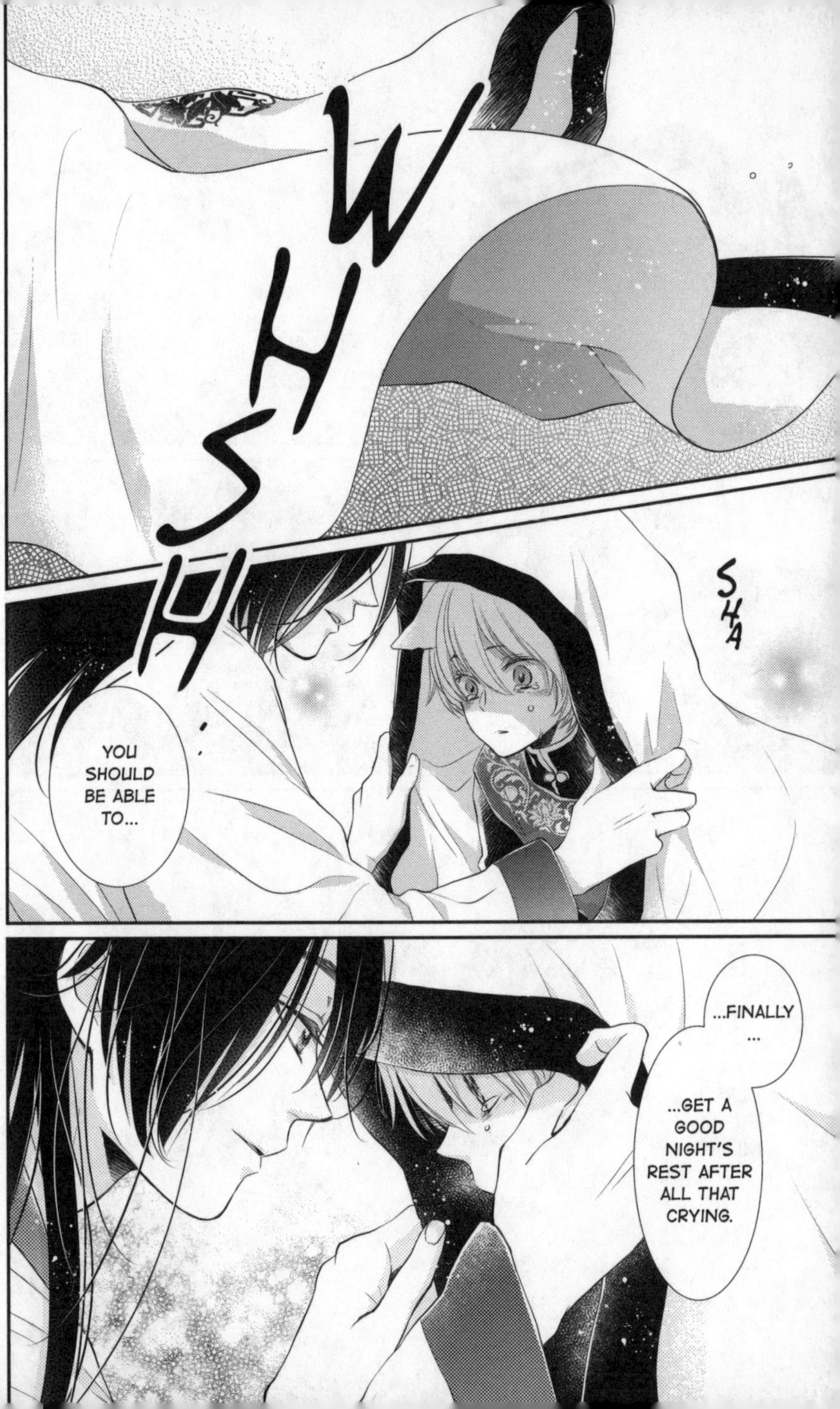
SHA
YOU SHOULD BE ABLE TO...
...FINALLY ...
...GET A GOOD NIGHT'S REST AFTER ALL THAT CRYING.

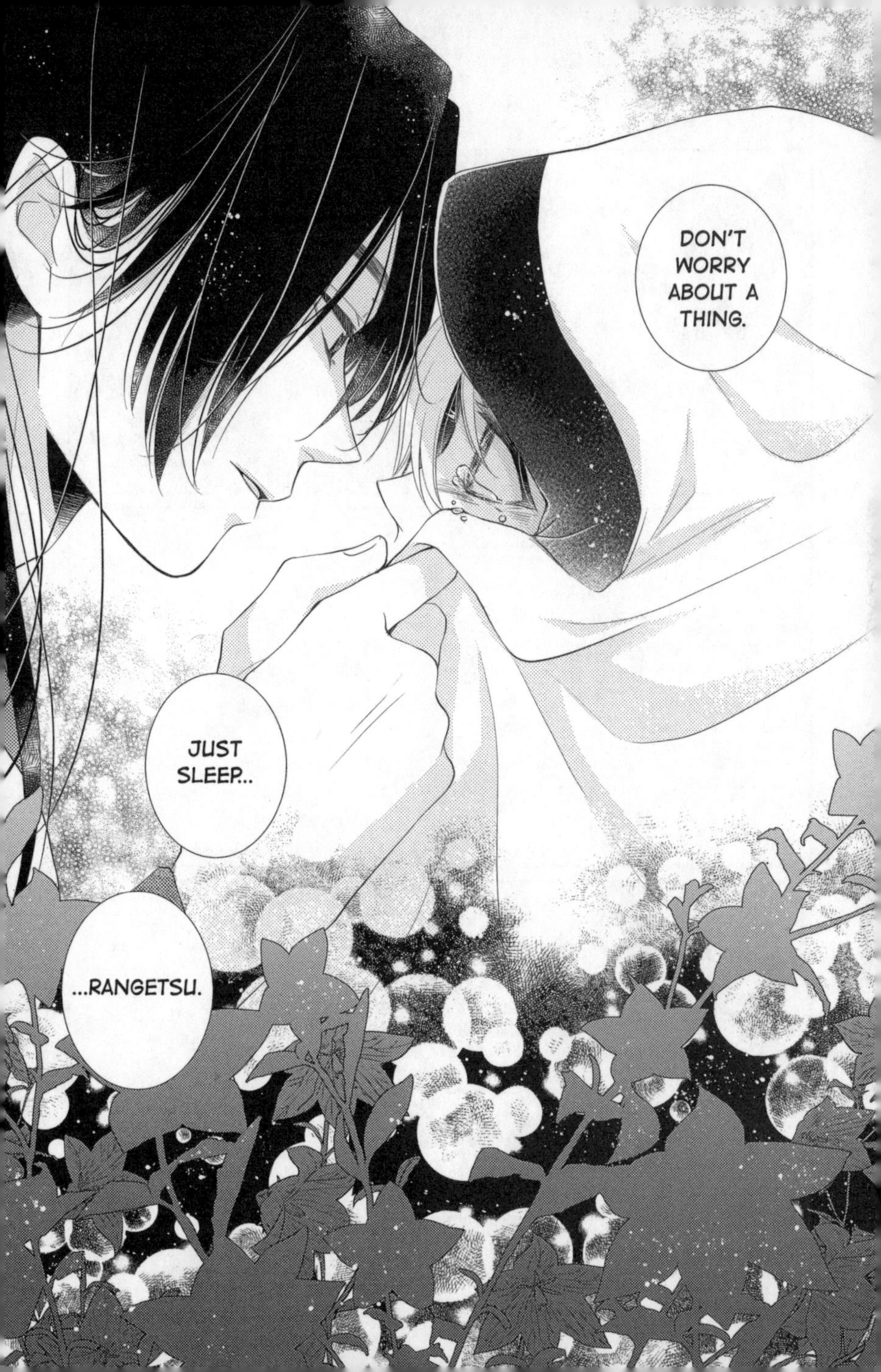
DON'T WORRY ABOUT A THING.
JUST SLEEP...
...RANGETSU.

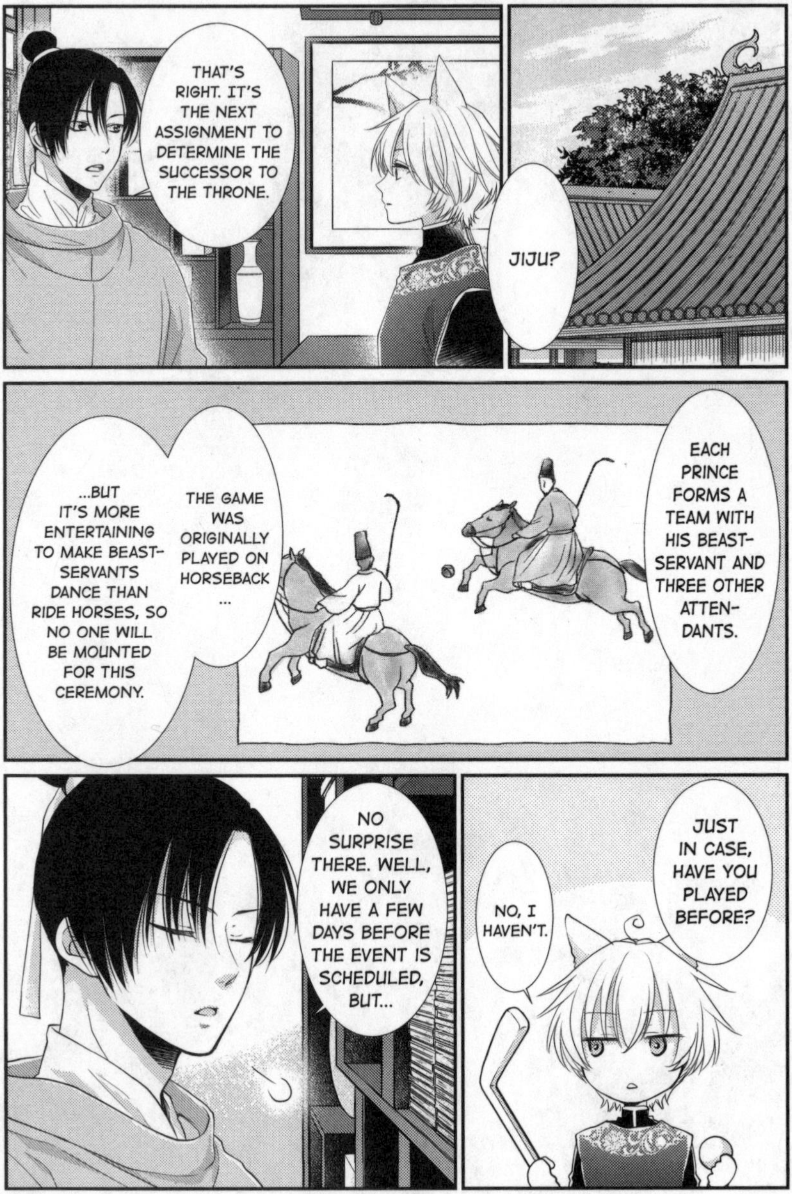
JIJU?
THAT'S RIGHT. IT'S THE NEXT ASSIGNMENT TO DETERMINE THE SUCCESSOR TO THE THRONE.
EACH PRINCE FORMS A TEAM WITH HIS BEAST-SERVANT AND THREE OTHER ATTEN-DANTS.
THE GAME WAS ORIGINALLY PLAYED ON HORSEBACK ...
...BUT IT'S MORE ENTERTAINING TO MAKE BEAST-SERVANTS DANCE THAN RIDE HORSES, SO NO ONE WILL BE MOUNTED FOR THIS CEREMONY.
JUST IN CASE, HAVE YOU PLAYED BEFORE?
NO, I HAVEN'T.
NO SURPRISE THERE. WELL, WE ONLY HAVE A FEW DAYS BEFORE THE EVENT IS SCHEDULED, BUT...

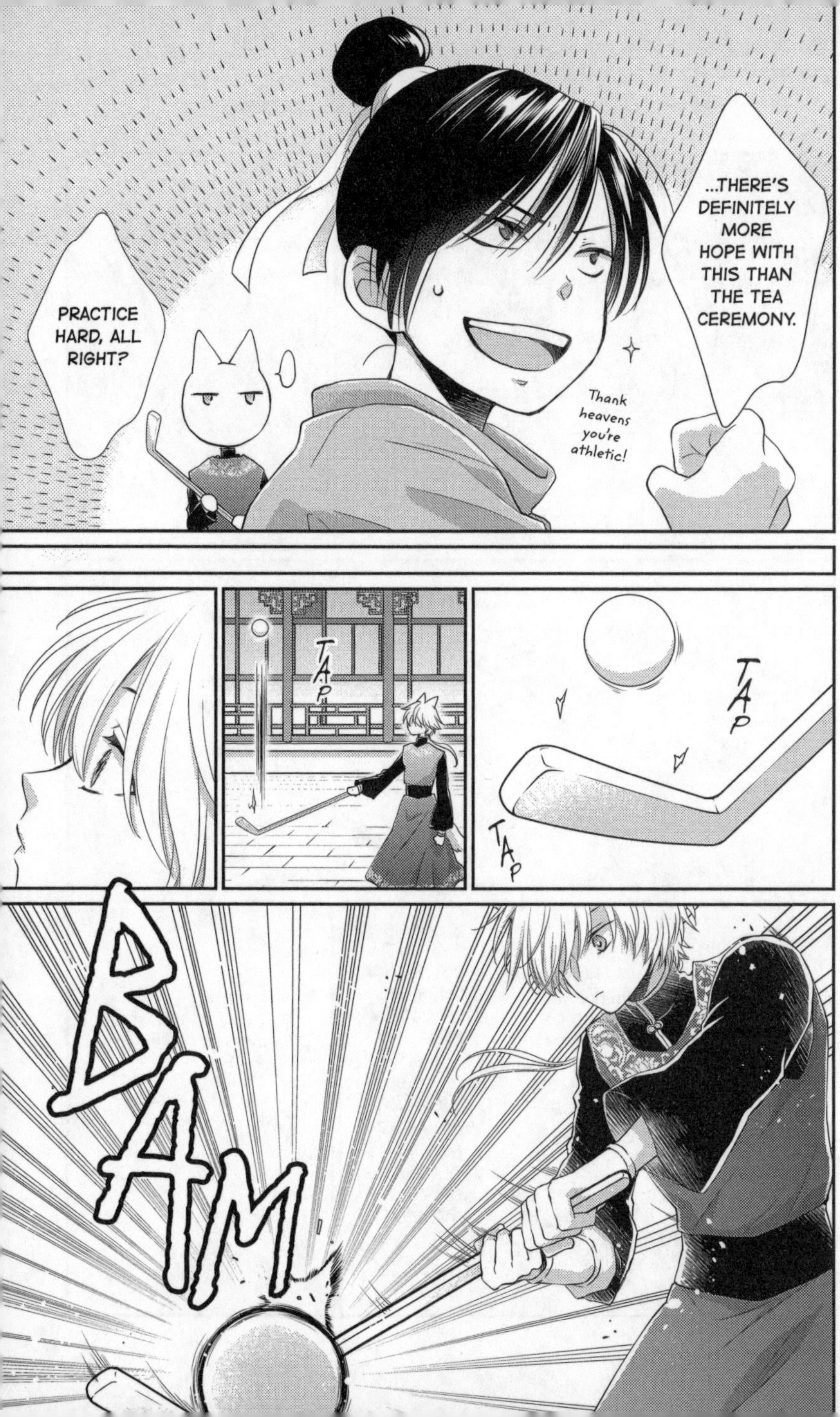
...THERE'S DEFINITELY MORE HOPE WITH THIS THAN THE TEA CEREMONY.
Thank heavens you're athletic!
PRACTICE HARD, ALL RIGHT?
TAP
TAP
TAP
BAM

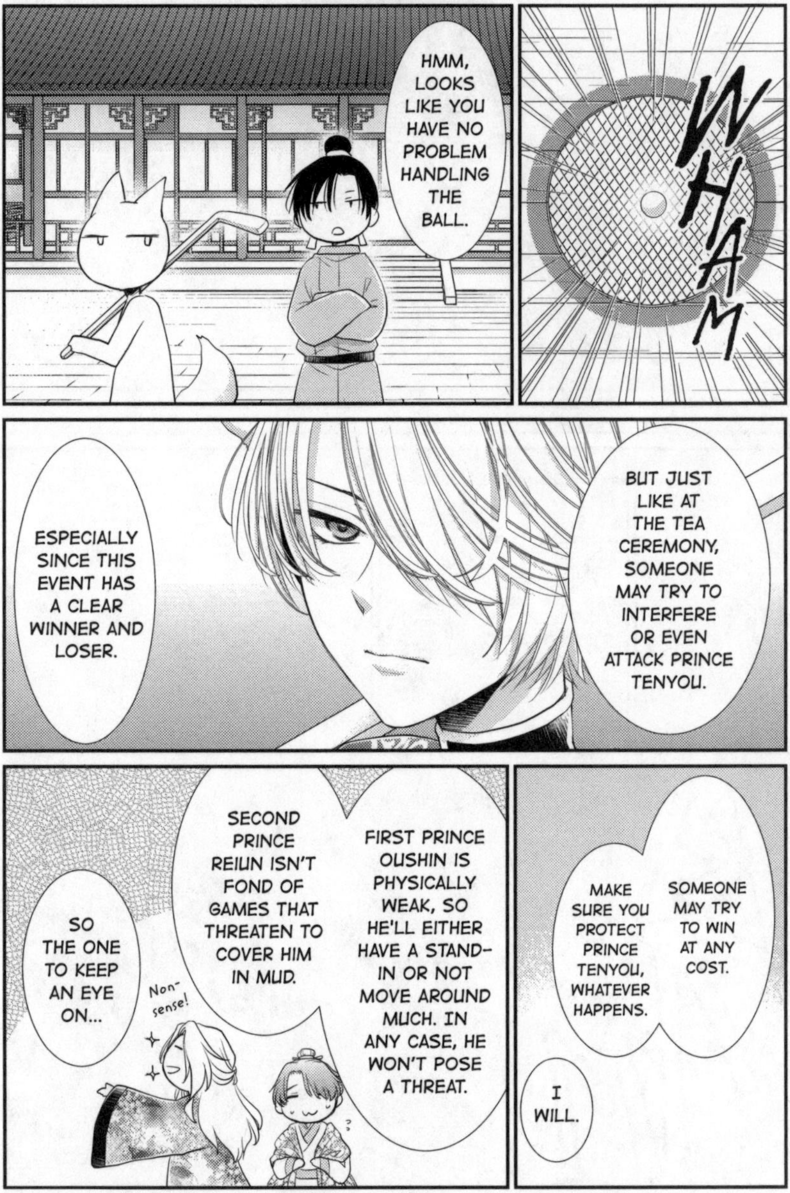
WHAM
HMM, LOOKS LIKE YOU HAVE NO PROBLEM HANDLING THE BALL.
BUT JUST LIKE AT THE TEA CEREMONY, SOMEONE MAY TRY TO INTERFERE OR EVEN ATTACK PRINCE TENYOU.
ESPECIALLY SINCE THIS EVENT HAS A CLEAR WINNER AND LOSER.
SOMEONE MAY TRY TO WIN AT ANY COST.
MAKE SURE YOU PROTECT PRINCE TENYOU, WHATEVER HAPPENS.
I WILL.
FIRST PRINCE OUSHIN IS PHYSICALLY WEAK, SO HE'LL EITHER HAVE A STAND-IN OR NOT MOVE AROUND MUCH. IN ANY CASE, HE WON'T POSE A THREAT.
SECOND PRINCE REIUN ISN'T FOND OF GAMES THAT THREATEN TO COVER HIM IN MUD.
SO THE ONE TO KEEP AN EYE ON...
Non-sense!

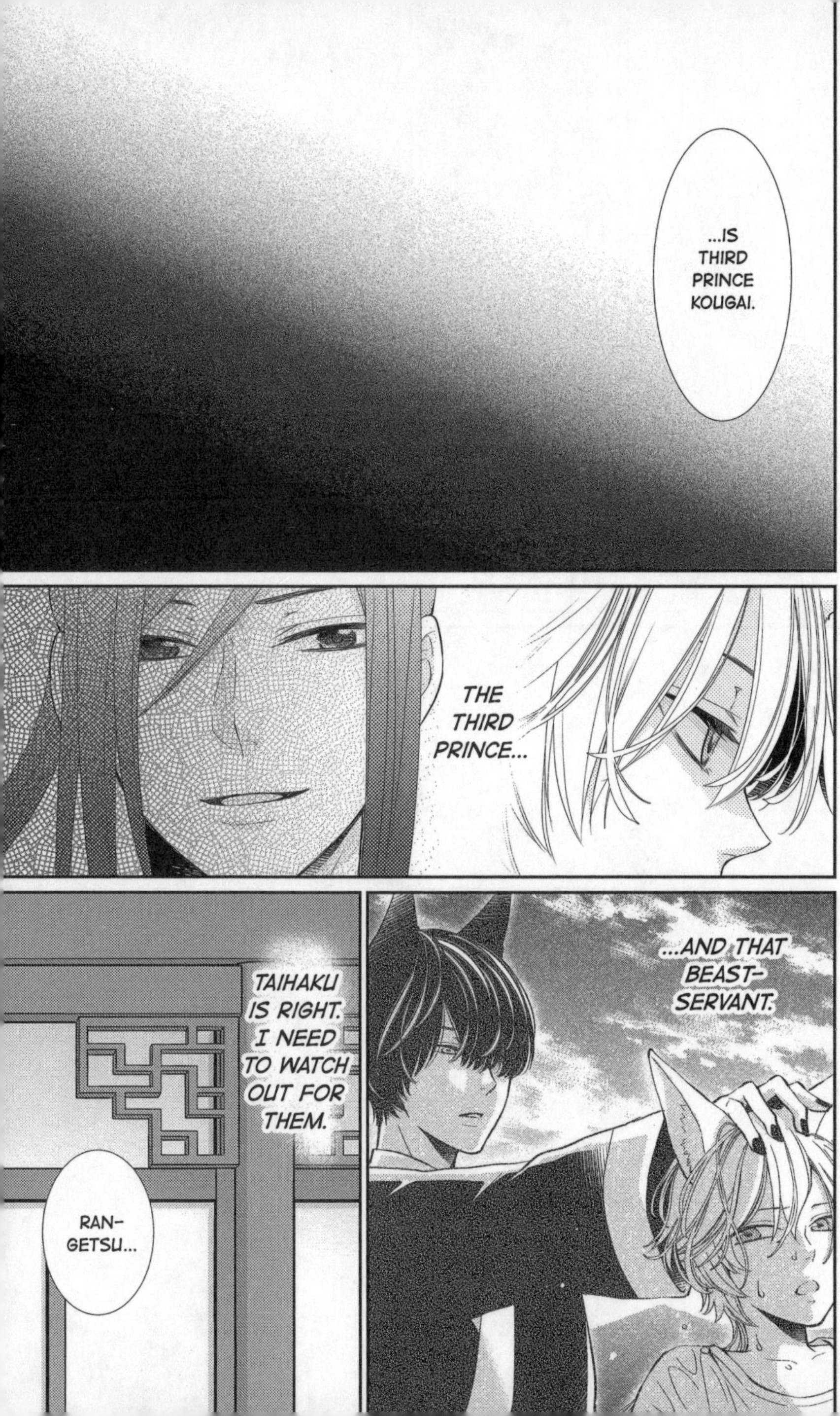
...IS THIRD PRINCE KOUGAI.
THE THIRD PRINCE...
...AND THAT BEAST-SERVANT.
TAIHAKU IS RIGHT. I NEED TO WATCH OUT FOR THEM.
RAN-GETSU...

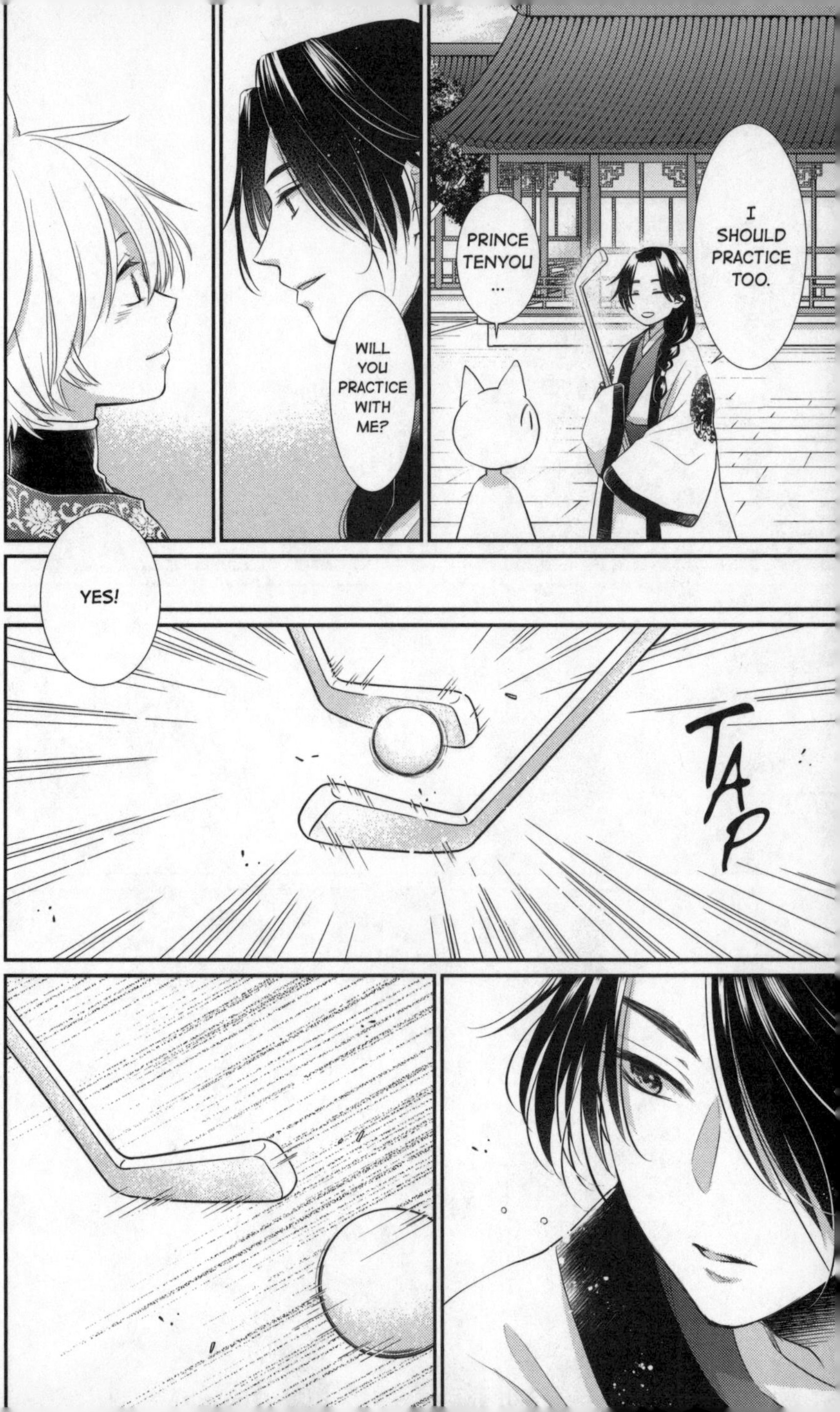
I SHOULD PRACTICE TOO.
PRINCE TENYOU ...
WILL YOU PRACTICE WITH ME?
YES!
TAP

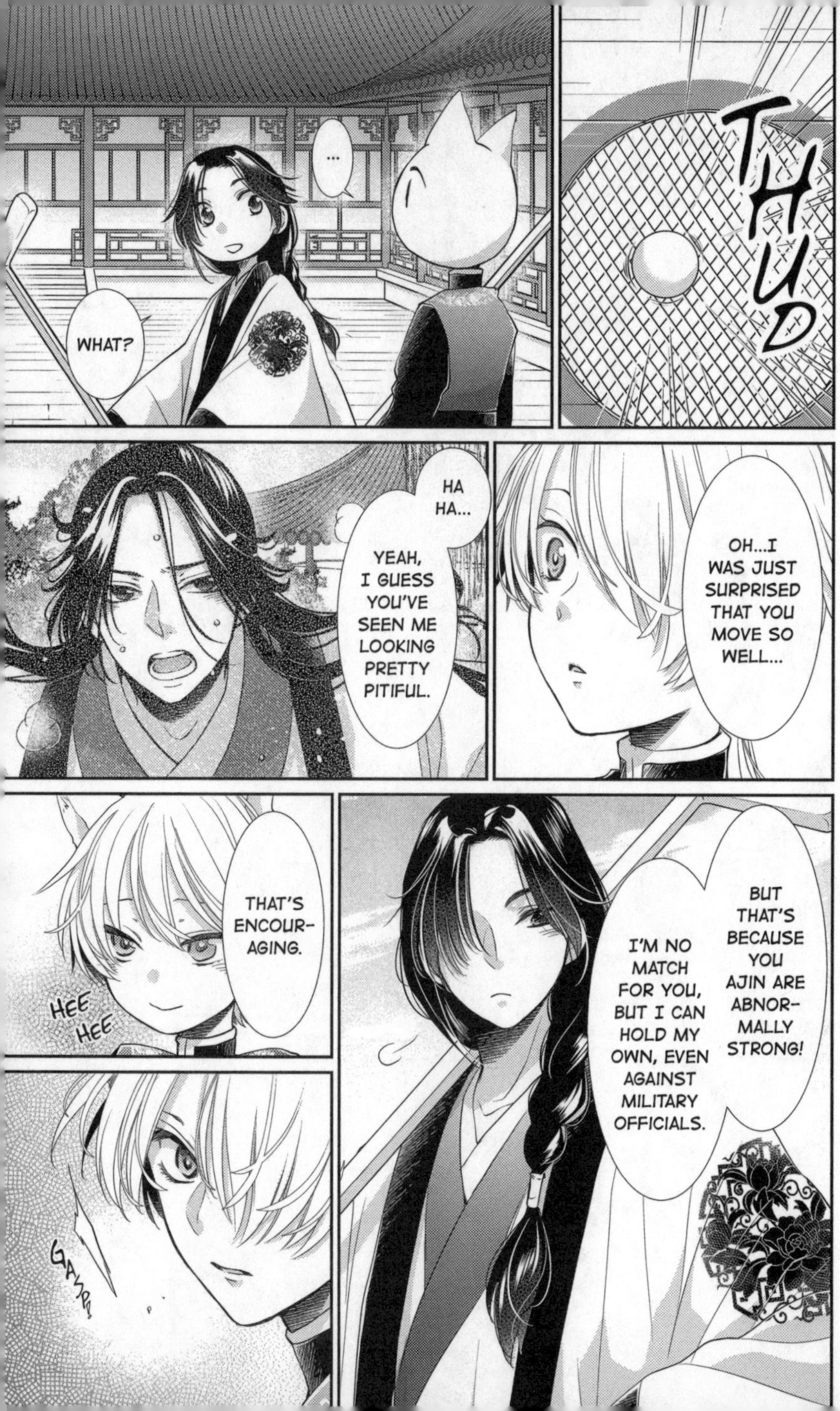
THUD
...
WHAT?
OH...I WAS JUST SURPRISED THAT YOU MOVE SO WELL...
HA HA...
YEAH, I GUESS YOU'VE SEEN ME LOOKING PRETTY PITIFUL.
BUT THAT'S BECAUSE YOU AJIN ARE ABNORMALLY STRONG!
I'M NO MATCH FOR YOU, BUT I CAN HOLD MY OWN, EVEN AGAINST MILITARY OFFICIALS.
THAT'S ENCOURAGING.
HEE HEE
GASP

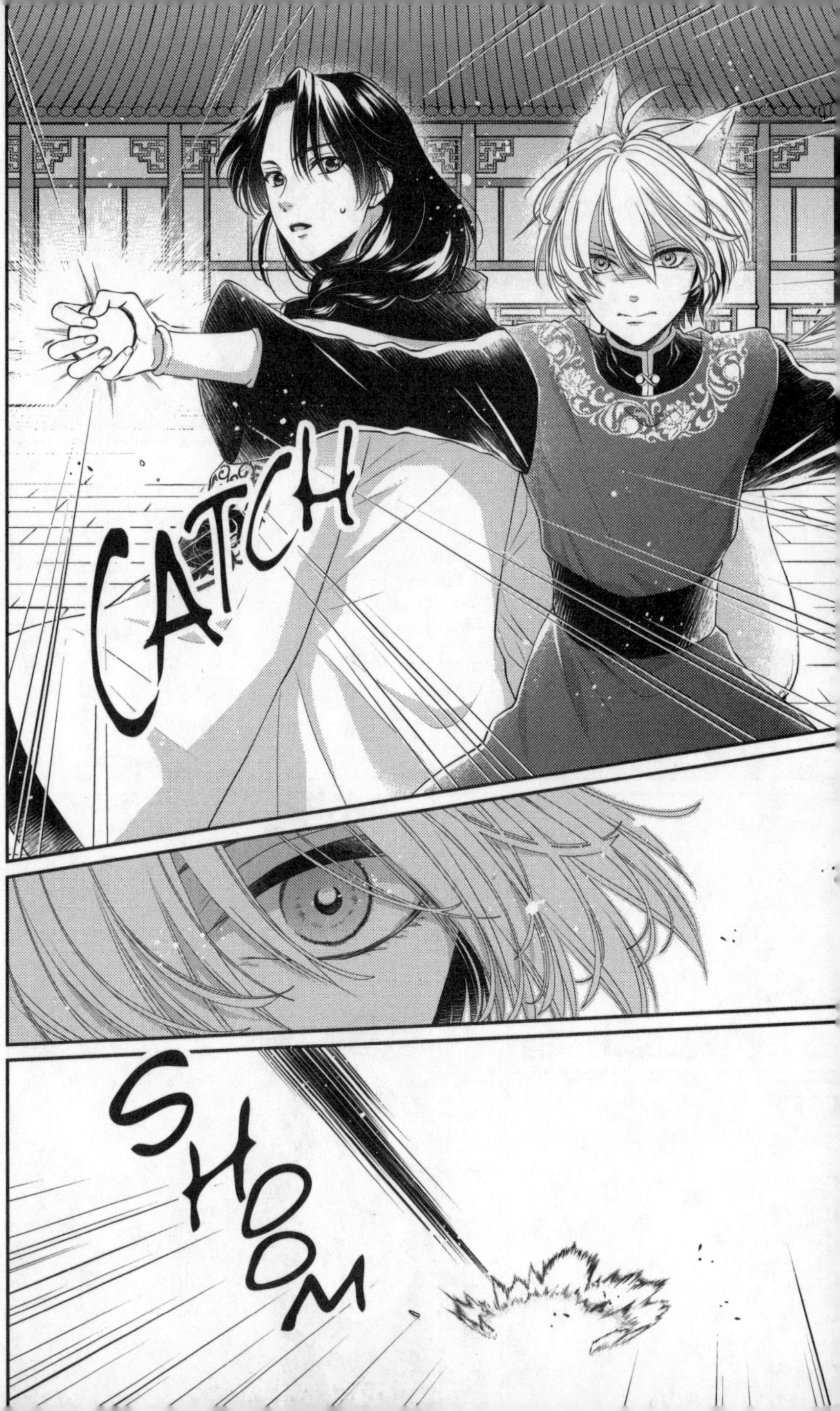
CATCH
SHOOM

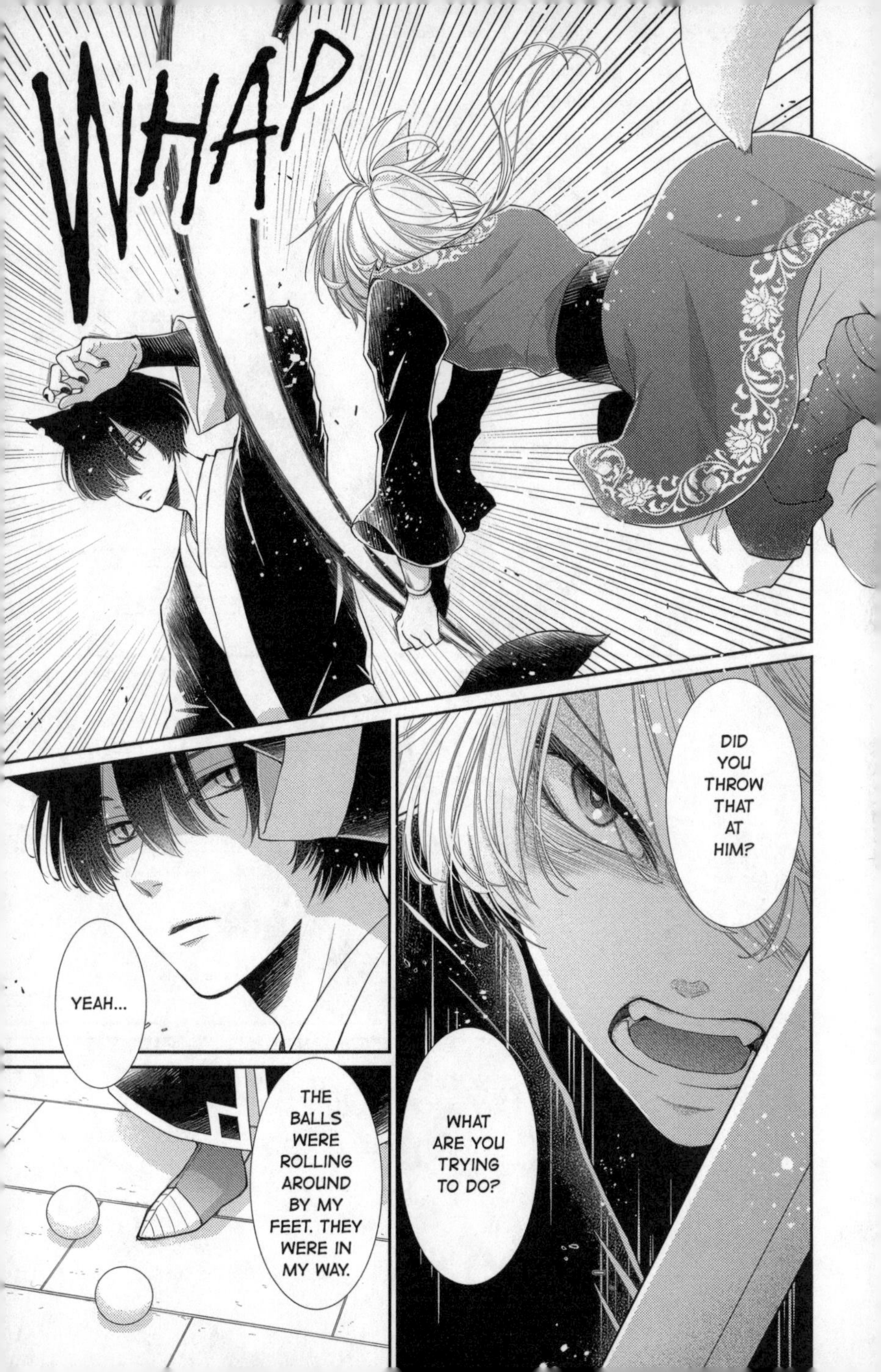
WHAP
DID YOU THROW THAT AT HIM?
WHAT ARE YOU TRYING TO DO?
YEAH...
THE BALLS WERE ROLLING AROUND BY MY FEET. THEY WERE IN MY WAY.

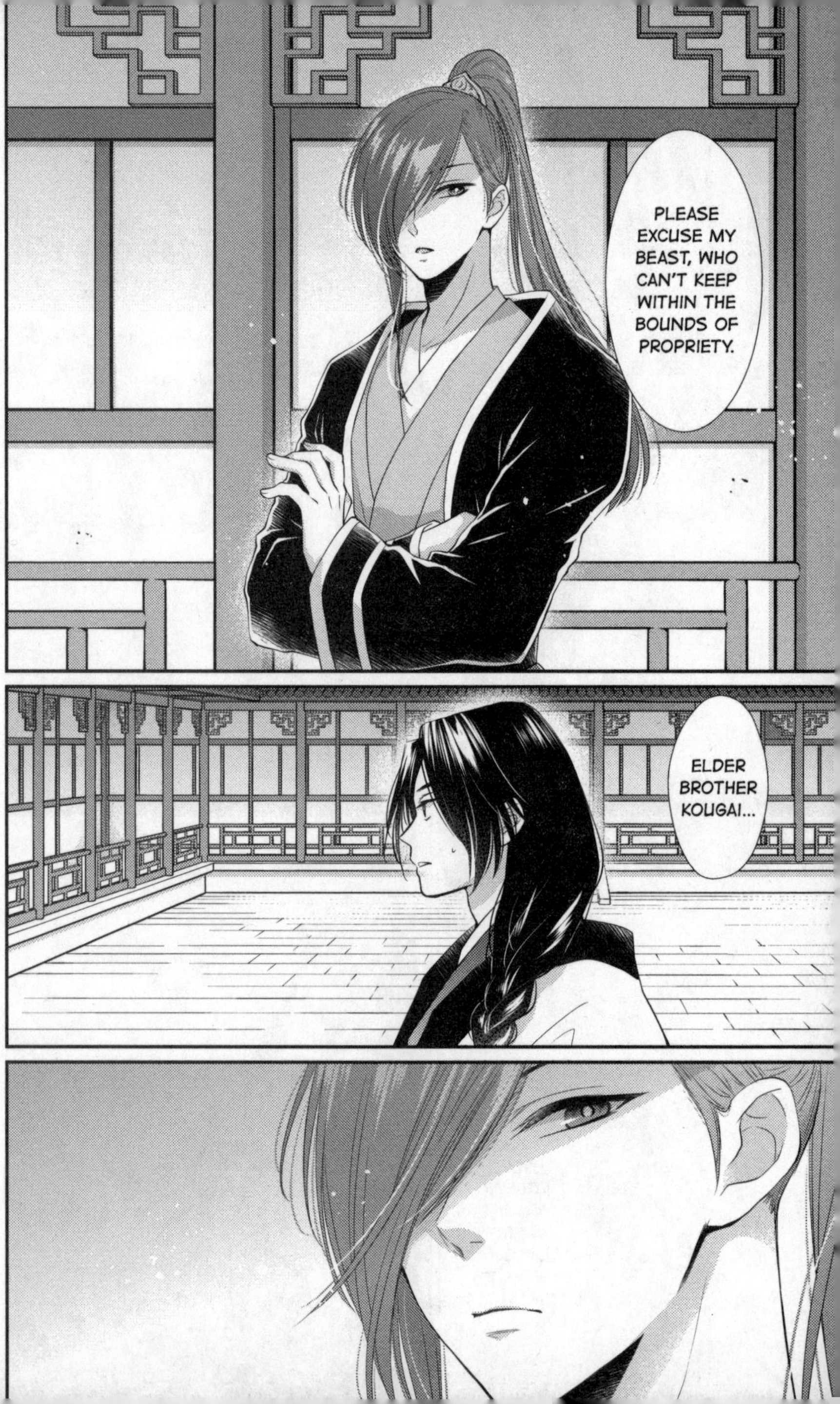
PLEASE EXCUSE MY BEAST, WHO CAN'T KEEP WITHIN THE BOUNDS OF PROPRIETY.
ELDER BROTHER KOUGAI...

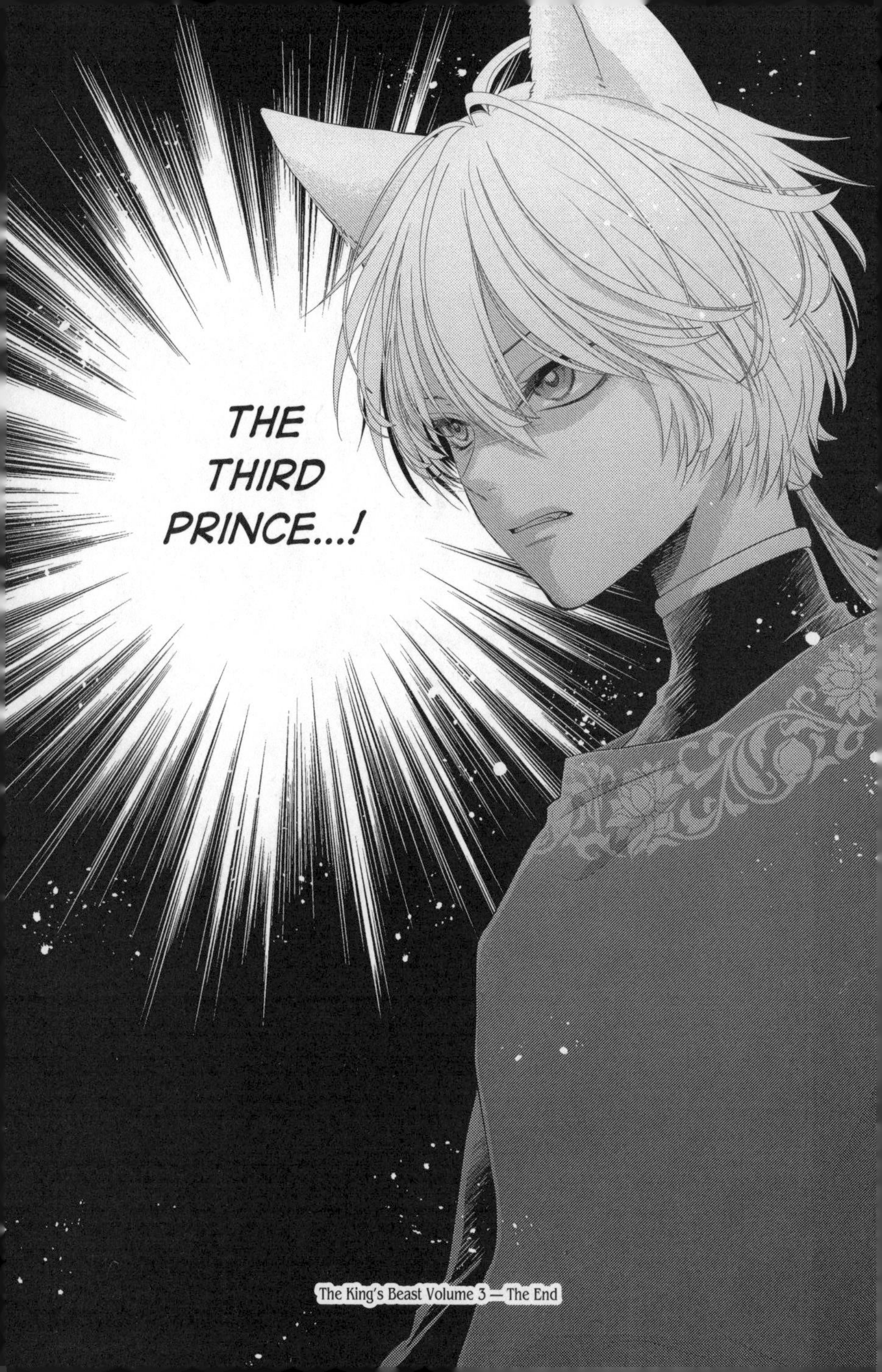
THE THIRD PRINCE...!
The King's Beast Volume 3 — The End

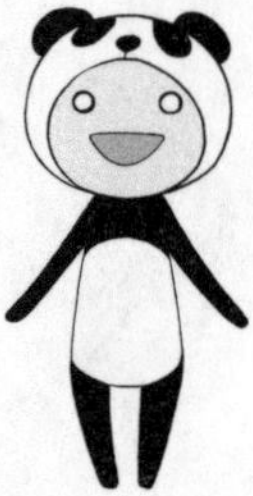

I love Chinese food.

—Rei Toma

麗

Rei Toma has been drawing since childhood, and she created her first complete manga for a graduation project in design school. When she drew the short story manga "Help Me, Dentist," it attracted a publisher's attention and she made her debut right away. After she found success as a manga artist, acclaim in other art fields started to follow as she did illustrations for novels and video game character designs. She is also the creator of *Dawn of the Arcana* and *The Water Dragon's Bride,* both available in English from VIZ Media.

THE KING'S Beast 3

SHOJO BEAT EDITION

STORY AND ART BY **Rei Toma**

ENGLISH TRANSLATION & ADAPTATION **JN Productions**
TOUCH-UP ART & LETTERING **Monaliza De Asis**
DESIGN **Joy Zhang**
EDITOR **Pancha Diaz**

OU NO KEMONO Vol. 3
by Rei TOMA
© 2019 Rei TOMA
All rights reserved.
Original Japanese edition published by SHOGAKUKAN.
English translation rights in the United States of America,
Canada, the United Kingdom, Ireland, Australia and New
Zealand arranged with SHOGAKUKAN.

Original Cover Design: Hibiki CHIKADA (fireworks. vc)

Printed in the U.S.A.

Published by VIZ Media, LLC
P.O. Box 77010
San Francisco, CA 94107

10 9 8 7 6 5 4 3 2
First printing, August 2021
Second printing, August 2021

viz.com   shojobeat.com

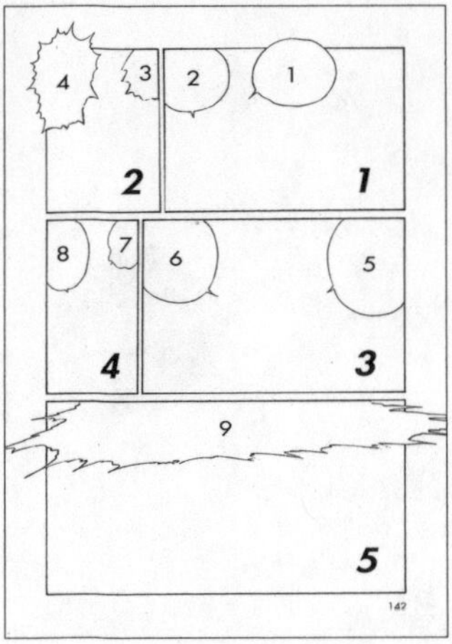

THIS IS THE LAST PAGE.

THE KING'S BEAST has been printed in the original Japanese format to preserve the orientation of the artwork.

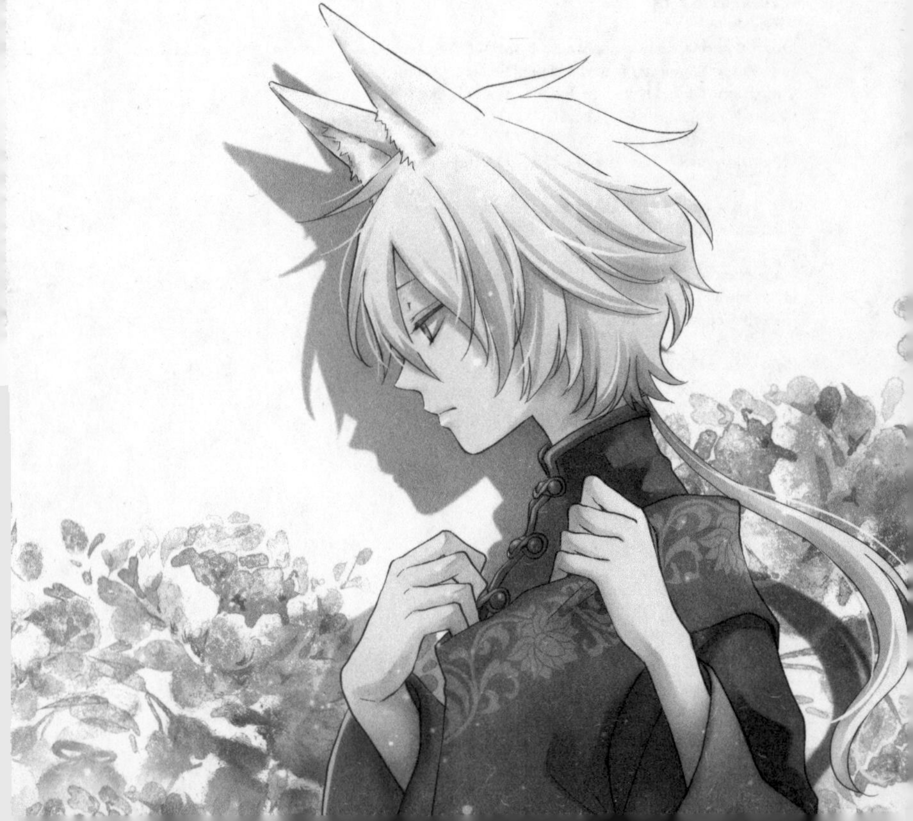